CAPE COD KITCHEN TREASURES

CHOICE FAMILY GROCERIES 1908
Telephone Headquarters and Pay Station.
Jarves Street, SANDWICH, MASS.

Here is a greeting from old Cape Cod
Home of the sacred fish,
Where the waves croon softly, day and night,
Where the skies are blue and the sands are white
And there's joy for your every wish!

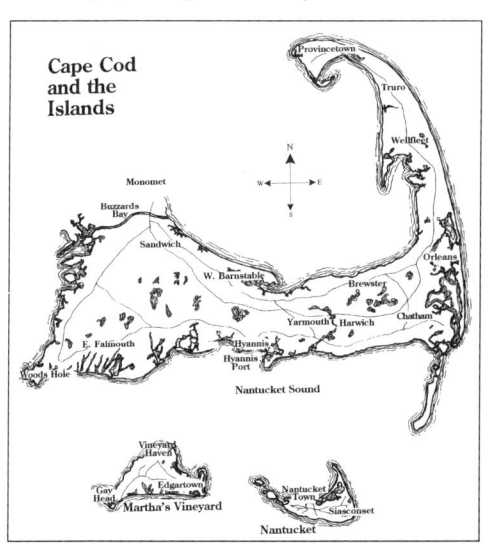

Cooking in 1925 in the Green Briar Jam Kitchen.

Today the Jam Kitchen is a working museum where visitors may view the old fashioned cooking process in the turn of the century kitchen at the Thornton W. Burgess Society's Green Briar Nature Center.

CAPE COD
KITCHEN TREASURES
COOK BOOK

Over 600
Favorite Recipes
Submitted with love
by
Members, Friends, and Supporters
of
The Thornton W. Burgess Society
in honor of the
100th Anniversary
of the
Green Briar Nature Center
Jam Kitchen

Rosemary ~ Herb of Remembrance

A special thanks to all our friends and members for sharing their tried and true favorite recipes to make this wonderful collection of delectable delights.

THE TOWN OF SANDWICH AND ITS NAME

The name Sandwich was clearly applied to this settlement in 1637, but none of the original settlers were from Sandwich, Kent, England. We expect that the name was suggested by Mr. John Humphrey, the Assistant Governor of Massachusetts Bay Colony for Saugus, who approved the transfer of people here and who had lived in Sandwich, Kent. There are physical similarities in the two towns, in wide marshes, shallow harbor and a Dutch trading history.

Copyright 2003 by Thornton W. Burgess Society, Inc.
6 Discovery Hill Road
East Sandwich, Massachusetts 02537

ISBN 0-9621171-2-9
Library of Congress catalog card number

Printed in U.S.A.
Rogers Print & Design
Kathleen Branigan - Graphic Artist
Plymouth, Massachusetts

Covers courtesy of Kathryn Kleekamp
P.O. Box 1300 • Sandwich, MA 02563
www.sandwichart.com

For information and additional books
Call 508-888-6870

TABLE OF CONTENTS

FOREWORD, John Carafoli 7

APPETIZERS & SNACKS 9

DRINKS & CORDIALS 21

BREADS, MUFFINS, & BRUNCH 27

CRANBERRY RECIPES 59

DESSERTS 81

    Cakes and Pies 83

    Cookies, Bars and Squares 103

    Puddings and Desserts 125

    Confections 137

JAMS, JELLIES, & PRESERVES 147

MEATS & POULTRY 167

PASTA & RICE 187

QUICK & EASY 201

SEAFOOD 225

SOUPS, STEWS, & CHOWDERS 253

SALADS 273

VEGETABLES 285

INDEX 301

ACKNOWLEDGMENTS

COOKBOOK COMMITTEE MEMBERS

Nancy Titcomb, Chairperson

Pat Bryant	Jeanne Johnson
Bettina Dinsmore	Judy Koenig
Chris Evans	Judi Lesiak
Georgia Flagg	Pat Maguire
Mae Foster	Ann McDonnell
Debbie Hauck	Mary Williams
Karel Huber	Jennie Zanthuos

SPECIAL CONTRIBUTORS

Maria Bishop, Editor
Kathryn Kleekamp, Cover Artist

HISTORICAL FACTS

Bethany Routledge
Russell Lovell
Judy Koenig
Nancy Hladik

PHOTOGRAPHS

John Cullity
Town of Sandwich Archives
Ellen Holway

DECORATIVE ART

Jim McDonnell
Shirley Cross
1908 Business Directory of Sandwich, Bourne, and Falmouth
Thornton W. Burgess Society archives

TYPISTS

Chris Foisy
Andrea Harrington
Judy Heller
& All the Committee members

FOREWORD

As I looked through the recipes in this book, I realized how much one can discern about a culture and its history from a recipe, as well as gain insight into the people who created and documented them. Granted there is a certain format to writing a recipe, but if you look closely at the ingredients and the ways in which instructions are worded, they can provide a fascinating glimpse into the past.

The act of writing down a recipe, then passing it along from generation to generation, keeps traditions alive. Many of the recipes in this book have been handed down from family members, representing those families' history and traditions. In my experience it is important to document these recipes, since I have found that people who lack a sense of family heritage often find themselves adrift in life. If one has not inherited traditions, it is important to create one's own. One important and thoroughly satisfying way to do this is through food.

These recipes typically use local ingredients, providing a further link to the region. Various types of fish, including oysters, sea clams, and mussels, as well as blueberries, cranberries, and raspberries, all appear locally in mid- to late- summer and fall. Many ingredients are culled from local resources such as Crow Farm, one of the few working farms remaining on Cape Cod, the Green Briar Jam Kitchen, and the Dexter Grist Mill. All of these places are located in the historical town of Sandwich.

I was fortunate to grow up in the small Italian American community of Sagamore Village where traditions were an important part of life. The Italian immigrants who settled in Sagamore and Sandwich in the late 1800's brought with them a strong heritage, including traditions and customs from the old country, many revolving around food.

Food was a big part of my upbringing, and over the years I have discovered the many purposes it serves. Food can comfort, heal, soothe and celebrate. It nourishes people physically, emotionally, and spiritually. It can reawaken a friendship. It can bring people together, and transform a mood.

Food is powerful in a myriad of personal, cultural, and spiritual ways. And, of course, what a delight for the senses it provides.

The recipes in this book strongly attest to all those benefits: read, cook, share, savor, and enjoy!

John F. Carafoli

[John Carafoli is a renowned Cook, Food Stylist, and author of a featured column on food in the Cape Cod Times *newspaper.]*

THE DAN'L WEBSTER INN

The oldest portion of the building was built in 1729 by Rev. Benjamin Fessenden as his parsonage near The Old Meetinghouse at the corner of River St. This became the Fessenden Tavern, a Patriot center in the Revolution. It was enlarged as the Central House in the Glass Factory period, and included a room reserved for Daniel Webster, a nationally known senator, orator, and statesman. The large addition shown here was built in 1915 by a new owner to include a dining room, kitchen, and guest room. This became the Daniel Webster Inn, which burned in 1971. The present Dan'l Webster Inn was built on the site in 1973.

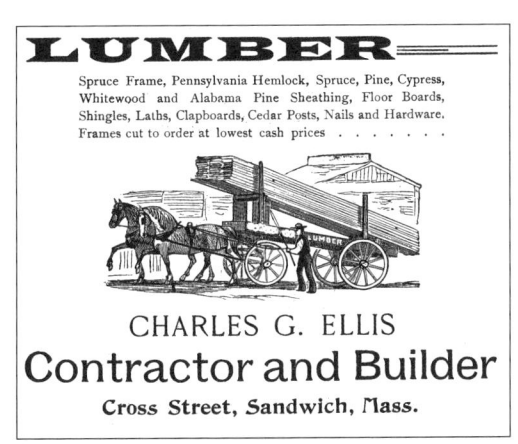

LUMBER

Spruce Frame, Pennsylvania Hemlock, Spruce, Pine, Cypress, Whitewood and Alabama Pine Sheathing, Floor Boards, Shingles, Laths, Clapboards, Cedar Posts, Nails and Hardware. Frames cut to order at lowest cash prices . . . .

CHARLES G. ELLIS
Contractor and Builder
Cross Street, Sandwich, Mass.

Advertisement in the 1905 Bourne, Falmouth, & Sandwich Business Directory.

CENSUS OF MASSACHUSETTS.
1905.
Total, 3,003,680.

Name of Cities are printed in CAPITALS.

Barnstable Co.

Barnstable	4,336
Bourne	1,786
Brewster	739
Chatham	1,634
Dennis	1,998
Eastham	519
Falmouth	3,241
Harwich	2,291
Mashpee	317
Orleans	1,052
Provincetown	4,362
Sandwich	1,433
Truro	743
Wellfleet	958
Yarmouth	1,422
Total	26,831

Berkshire Co.

Adams	12,486
Alford	275
Becket	890
Cheshire	1,281
Clarksburg	1,200
Dalton	3,122
Egremont	721
Florida	424
Great Barrington	6,152
Hancock	434
Hinsdale	1,452
Lanesborough	845
Lee	3,972
Lenox	3,058
Monterey	444
Mount Washington	87
New Ashford	100
New Marlborough	1,209
NORTH ADAMS	22,150
Otis	534
Peru	268
PITTSFIELD	25,001
Richmond	601
Sandisfield	657
Savoy	549
Sheffield	1,782
Stockbridge	2,022
Tyringham	314
Washington	339
West Stockbridge	1,023
Williamstown	4,425
Windsor	513
Total	98,330

Bristol Co.

Acushnet	1,284
Attleborough	12,702
Berkley	931
Dartmouth	3,793
Dighton	2,070
Easton	4,909
Fairhaven	4,235
FALL RIVER	105,762
Freetown	1,470
Mansfield	4,245
NEW BEDFORD	74,362
North Attleborough	7,878
Norton	2,079
Raynham	1,662
Rehoboth	1,991
Seekonk	1,917
Somerset	2,294
Swansea	1,839
TAUNTON	30,967
Westport	2,867
Total	269,257

Dukes Co.

Chilmark	322
Cottage City	1,138
Edgartown	1,175
Gay Head	178
Gosnold	161
Tisbury	1,120
West Tidsbury	457
Total	4,551

The first cookbook by an American author, "American Cookery" was written by Amelia Simmons in 1796. The early American cookbook was usually divided into three parts, with sections on cookery, medicine, and general household hints.

HOT CRAB DIP

This recipe was served numerous times by a woman in our investment group. When she moved away, I asked her for the recipe because we all wanted to continue having it each time we met. Serve with crackers or raw vegetables. This recipe can be halved.

Ingredients:

1 lb. crabmeat
Two 8-oz. packages cream cheese, softened
8 oz. sour cream
4 heaping Tbs. mayonnaise
1/2 tsp. lemon juice
1 tsp. dry mustard
1/4 tsp. garlic salt
2-3 tsp. Worcestershire sauce
One 8-oz. package of grated white cheddar cheese (save some to put on top)

Steps:
- Mix ingredients together well, and bake uncovered for 30-40 minutes at 350°F.
  Serves 8

Nancy Standring
Ann McDonnell

GINNY'S ANTIPASTO SQUARES

Ingredients:

2 pkgs. of Pillsbury crescent-roll dough
1/4 lb. boiled ham, thinly sliced
1/4 lb. Genoa salami, thinly sliced
1/2 lb. Provolone cheese
1 jar roasted peppers
1 egg
1/4 cup Parmesan cheese

Steps:
- Cover the bottom of a 9x13-inch baking dish with one package of crescent-roll dough.
- Layer ham, salami, Provolone, and peppers over the dough. Cover the top layer with the other pkg. of dough.
- Mix together egg and Parmesan and pour over the top layer of dough. Bake at 350°F for 30 minutes.
- Remove from the oven and cool slightly before cutting into squares. Use a sharp knife and cut into small pieces so they can be served as finger food.
  Serves 6-10

Clare Morash

CREAMY SHRIMP IN PASTRY CUPS

Ingredients:

1/2 lb. cooked shrimp, diced (or 1 can of tiny shrimp, drained)
1 cup mayonnaise
4 oz. shredded Swiss cheese
1/3 cup chopped scallions
1 Tbs. lemon juice
1 1/2 tsp. fresh dill, chopped
dash of cayenne pepper
3 pkgs. phyllo cups

Steps:
- Combine first seven ingredients well and refrigerate; this makes it easier to fill the phyllo cups.
- Spoon mixture into phyllo cups, and bake on a cookie sheet for 8-10 minutes at 450°F.
Serves 8

Pat Arkinson

SPINACH AND ARTICHOKE DIP

Ingredients:

One 14-oz. can artichoke hearts, drained and chopped
One 10-oz. pkg. frozen chopped spinach, thawed and drained
1 cup mayonnaise
1 cup grated Parmesan cheese
2 1/2 cups shredded Monterey Jack cheese

Steps:
- Preheat oven to 350°F.
- Lightly grease a 1-quart baking dish.
- In a medium bowl, mix together artichoke hearts, spinach, mayonnaise, Parmesan cheese and two cups of the Monterey Jack cheese.
- Transfer the cheese mixture to the prepared baking dish, and sprinkle with remaining 1/2 cup Monterey Jack.
- Bake until cheese is melted, about 15 minutes.
Serves 10

Christine Maguire

> "You don't get ulcers from what you eat, you get them from what's eating you."
>
> -Vicki Baum, writer

BACON AND WATER-CHESTNUT ROLL-UPS

These are easy and delicious!

Ingredients:
1 large can water chestnuts
1/2 cup soy sauce
3/4 to 1 cup sugar
1 lb. lean bacon

Steps:
- Drain chestnuts and cover with soy sauce. Let chestnuts sit for three or more hours.
- Put sugar into a plastic bag; add "marinated" chestnuts to the sugar in the bag. Shake to cover well.
- Cut bacon slices in halves or thirds, and wrap them around the sugared chestnuts; secure with toothpick.
- Place bacon-wrapped chestnuts on a baking sheet and broil or bake until crisp.
- Transfer to a paper towel to drain. Serve hot.
Serves 8

Barbara Driscoll

GARDEN SALSA

This is a great way to use small leftover vegetables from recipes. Excellent as an appetizer on toasted French bread (toast both sides first), or as a side to meat/poultry.

Ingredients:
tomatoes
peppers (green, red, yellow, orange)- any one or a combination
onion (scallions can also be used)
celery
cucumbers
herbs of choice
salt and pepper to taste

Steps:
- Chop and combine all ingredients together. Let sit overnight for the flavors to meld.
Serves a crowd

Barbara Driscoll

BLEU-CHEESE SPREAD

Ingredients:

1/2 cup walnut pieces
1/2 cup bleu cheese
1/4 cup cream cheese
1 tsp. cognac
1 tsp. minced walnut for garnish

Steps:
- Process the walnuts in a food processor until they are finely chopped, using short pulses to avoid over-processing.
- Add the bleu cheese and cream cheese, and process until they are thoroughly combined. Add the cognac, process until well mixed.
- Transfer the mixture to one large or two small ramekins. Sprinkle with the minced walnuts and serve.
Serves 8-10

Ann Mc Donnell

GARY'S HOT CLAM DIP

Ingredients:

3 cans minced clams
2 Tbs. onion, chopped
16 oz. cream cheese, at room temperature
3 Tbs. parsley, chopped
2 Tbs. Worcestershire sauce
salt and pepper to taste
12 dashes Tabasco sauce
1 large round sourdough bread
1 French-bread baguette

Steps:
- Drain clams, reserving 1/2 cup of liquid.
- With electric mixer (not food processor), mix together all remaining ingredients except bread.
- Slice top off of sourdough bread round and hollow it out. Fill the bread round with dip and replace the top. Wrap tightly in foil.
- Bake the dip-filled bread round at 350°F for 30 minutes.
Serves 8 to 10

Ann Mc Donnell

BAKED BRIE

This recipe was passed on to me by a friend who has her own catering business. I have sometimes added a generous portion of pepper jelly, cranberry relish or apricot preserves to the spices. Works great!

Ingredients:

1 wedge of Brie (about 12 oz.) or
1 whole small round Brie
1 sheet of puff pastry, frozen
coarse black pepper
garlic salt
Granny Smith apples
Triscuit crackers (original flavor)

Steps:
- Thaw the pastry sheet, and preheat the oven to 350°F.
- When thawed, place the Brie cheese in the middle of the pastry sheet. Generously sprinkle seasonings on the Brie, and wrap it in the pastry sheet, pinching it closed.
- Bake the pastry-wrapped Brie for approximately one hour, or until pastry is golden brown.
- Remove from oven and let sit for 15 minutes.
- Serve with apple wedges and Triscuits.
  Serves 8 to 10

Jack Mondin

SUMMER DIP

Great for summer, when you have lots of garden peppers — and guests.

Ingredients:

1 small onion, chopped
2 garlic cloves, minced
1/4 cup olive oil
6 red peppers, roasted, seeded and peeled
1/4 cup nuts, finely chopped
1/3 cup basil, chopped
2 Tbs. skim milk
pita bread

Steps:
- Saute onion and garlic in oil until translucent.
- Place onion and garlic in food processor and puree for a few seconds.
- Blend remaining ingredients in well, and season the mixture to taste with salt and pepper.
- Serve with warm or crispy pita bread.
  Serves 8

Charlene Sinko-Evans

PISTACHIO-STUFFED MUSHROOMS

Ingredients:

20 medium mushrooms
3 Tbs. minced onion
1/2 cup butter, divided
1/4 cup shelled pistachios, finely chopped

2 Tbs. chopped parsley
1/4 tsp. salt
1/3 cup dry bread crumbs

Steps:
- Remove the stems from the mushrooms and sauté the stems with the onion in 1/4 cup butter until tender.
- Add all remaining ingredients except mushroom caps and mix well.
- Spoon mixture into mushroom caps.
- Place filled mushroom caps on baking sheets. Drizzle remaining butter (1/4 cup) over the caps.
- Bake at 350°F for five minutes.
Makes 20 mushroom caps

Norma Coleman

HUMMUS

This always tastes better the next day, after the flavors have mixed together. Serve with cut up pitas or crackers.

Ingredients:

1 large can chickpeas
2 Tbs. tahini (sesame paste)
5 cloves of garlic, crushed
1 Tbs. minced parsley

dash of salt
1 Tbs. olive oil
juice of two lemons
pita bread or crackers

Steps:
- Drain chickpeas and crush with a mallet in a bowl.
- Add crushed garlic and salt.
- Mix in tahini, lemon juice, and parsley. Mixture should be thick.
- Add olive oil.
Serves 12

> "Hospitality is making your guests feel at home, even though you wish they were."
>
> -Unknown

SALMON DIP

Serve with crackers or on small slices of bread. Chopped pimento or sweet pickle can be added for color and flavor.

Ingredients:

16 oz. cream cheese
One 6.5-oz. can smoked salmon or regular salmon
3 Tbs. minced onion
1 tsp. garlic powder
1/4 cup mayonnaise or sour cream
2 tsp. Worcestershire (optional)

Steps:
- Whip cream cheese until smooth.
- Add rest of ingredients and blend well.
- Let stand overnight.
  Serves 8

Pat Bryant

TURKEY-PECAN MEATBALLS HOR D'OEUVRES

Ingredients:

1 beaten egg
1/4 cup fine dry bread crumbs
1/4 tsp. salt
1/3 cup sour cream
1 Tbs. snipped chives
12 oz. ground turkey
1 cup finely chopped pecans
One 18-oz. jar apricot preserves
1/3 cup chili sauce
dash of Tabasco (optional)

Steps:
- Preheat oven to 350°F.
- Combine egg, crumbs, salt, sour cream and chives. Mix well.
- Add turkey and nuts. Mix well.
- Form turkey mixture into 3/4-inch balls and place them in a shallow baking pan.
- Bake turkey balls for 15 minutes, then drain on paper towels.
- To make the sauce, process apricot preserves in food processor or blender until smooth. Place the preserves in a large saucepan.
- Add chili sauce to preserves and bring mixture to a boil. Add a dash of Tabasco sauce if you like.
- Add the turkey balls to the sauce and heat through.
- Serve with toothpicks.
  Makes 30 hors d'oeuvres

Norma Coleman

PINEAPPLE-CHEESE BALL

You can make one large ball or two smaller balls with this recipe. It stores well in the refrigerator, but can also be frozen for later use.

Ingredients:
Two 8-oz. pkgs. of cream cheese
2 Tbs. onion, finely chopped
One 8-oz. can of crushed pineapple, drained
One 10-oz. pkg. of walnuts, finely chopped
2 Tbs. green pepper, finely chopped
Garlic salt and celery salt to taste, or 1/2 tsp. seasoned salt

Steps:
- Mix above ingredients together except walnuts.
- Add 1/4 of the nuts into the mixture and mix up well.
- Roll mixture into a ball.
- Line a bowl with Saran wrap, and put the cheese ball into the bowl. Store in the refrigerator until firm.
- Roll in the remainder of the chopped nuts and serve or refrigerate. Serves 12

Jennie Zantuhos

FESTIVE ROASTED-PEPPER DIP

Ingredients:
1 jar roasted red peppers, drained
1 cup Kraft mayonnaise
1 can chopped green chilies, drained
1 Tbs. lemon juice
1 cup sour cream
1/2 tsp. garlic powder

Steps:
- Mix ingredients until well blended and refrigerate. Serves 8

Ann Mc Donnell

CURRIED SCALLOP CAKES

This recipe makes moist, plump little cakes. Prepare ahead, and simply reheat just before guests arrive.

Ingredients:

3 1/2 cups panko (Japanese bread-crumbs-can be found locally at Stop and Shop)	3/4 tsp. salt
	3 eggs
	1/2 tsp. pepper
1 1/2 lb. fresh scallops, cut into 1/4 inch pieces	3 chopped green onions
	1 1/2 Tbs. dry mustard
1 1/2 Tbs. curry powder	vegetable oil
3/4 cup mayonnaise	

Steps:
- Mix 1 1/2 cups of panko with remaining ingredients except vegetable oil. Cover mixture and refrigerate one hour or more.
- Place remaining 2 cups of panko on a large plate. Form the scallop mixture into balls, using 1 heaping tablespoon of the mixture for each ball.
- Coat each ball in panko crumbs, flattening them slightly.
- Heat some vegetable oil in a skillet.
- Saute the cakes until golden and cooked through.
- Transfer to paper towels to drain.
  Makes 40 scallop cakes

Norma Coleman

TORTILLA ROLL-UPS

Ingredients:

1 small can black olives, chopped	1 pkg. Hidden Valley Ranch Salad Dressing mix, dry
One 4-oz. can diced green chilies	
One 4-oz. jar diced pimento	2 green onions, chopped
Two 8-oz. pkgs. cream cheese, softened	Four 12-inch flour tortillas

Steps:
- Drain olives, chilies and pimento, and pat them dry. Place together in a bowl.
- Add remaining ingredients to the bowl except tortillas.
- Spread the cheese mixture on the tortillas.
- Roll the tortillas, and chill for at least two hours.
- Cut rolls into 1-inch pieces, discarding the ends.
  Makes three dozen

Pat Maguire

HOT SEAFOOD-CHEESE HORS D'OEUVRES

This recipe was submitted by both Anne Quagge and Barbara Driscoll. Barbara Driscoll calls them "Crabbies", and uses 1/2 tsp. seasoned salt in hers. She says she has also made these without the crabmeat (served as a cheese hors d'oeuvre). These appetizers can be frozen for later use, then thawed and broiled when you're ready.

Ingredients:

6 English muffins, split in half
1 jar processed cheese spread
1 stick butter, softened
1/2 tsp. garlic powder
1 1/2 tsp. mayonnaise
1 small can of shrimp, crabmeat or minced clams (or equivalent amount of fresh, cooked seafood)

Steps:
- Mix the butter and cheese until well blended.
- Add garlic powder, mayonnaise and seafood to the mixture. Blend well.
- Spread the mixture on the muffin halves. Cut into wedges if desired.
- Broil the muffins until lightly browned.
  Makes 12 pieces

Submitted by both Anne Quagge and Barbara Driscoll

"PUPPY CHOW" (CHEERIOS PARTY MIX)

Red and green M&Ms are festive for the Christmas holidays, or use your imagination for a special occasion.

Ingredients:

One 12-oz. pkg. chocolate chips
1 cup peanut butter
6 cups Cheerios cereal
2 cups powdered sugar
Peanuts, M&Ms, raisins

Steps:
- Melt the chocolate chips and peanut butter in the microwave or on the stove.
- Stir in the Cheerios until coated with chocolate mixture.
- Place powdered sugar in a heavy plastic bag (one that won't break). Put the Cheerios mix into the bag and shake until the Cheerios are well coated with sugar.
- Add peanuts, M & Ms, raisins or whatever you like.
  Serves 10

Tari and Tamra Novinska

Axel Roos ca. 1905 at his farm on Spring Hill Road now at the corner of Roos Road. Mr. Roos was a Swedish immigrant who settled in East Sandwich to manage cranberry bogs.

Photo courtesy of Jean George, granddaughter of Axel Roos

S. I. MORSE
Hack, Livery and Boarding Stable

ALSO DEALER IN

Hay, Grain, Groceries, Lime and Cement

===COAL===

HARDWARE, KITCHEN UTENSILS, FARMING IMPLEMENTS, SEEDS, Etc.

Jarves Street, Sandwich, Mass.

DRINKS & CORDIALS

21

Sandwich Free Public Library

Main Street. Founded 1891. Number volumes, 3,100.
Librarian, Annie A. Rogers.
Library open Wednesdays and Saturdays from 2.30 to 5.30 and 7 to 9 p.m.

The first public library in Sandwich was located in the Town Hall

18   CASSELL'S CHILDREN'S ALBUM.

How many Tables are there?

1

How many Houses are there?

1   2

How many Horses are there?

1   2   3

How many Cots are there?

1   2   3   4

How many Chairs are there?

1   2   3   4   5

CAPE CODDER

Ingredients:
Ice
1 shot vodka
6 oz. cranberry juice

Steps:
- Fill a large glass with ice.
- Pour vodka over the ice.
- Add cranberry juice to glass.
- Serve immediately.
  Serves 1

Judi Lesiak

COFFEE LIQUEUR

Ingredients:

3 cups sugar	1 qt. vodka
3 cups water	1 Tbs. vanilla extract
3 1/2 Tbs. instant-coffee granules	

Steps:
- Combine sugar, water, and coffee granules in a heavy saucepan. Bring to a boil; cover, reduce heat, and simmer 10 minutes. Remove from the heat and cool.
- Stir in the vodka and vanilla; pour into bottles, and cover with plastic wrap.
- Punch holes in the plastic wrap, and store in a cool, dark place for 4 weeks.
- For later use, store in airtight containers.
  Makes 6 1/2 cups

Ann McDonnell

> **Food without hospitality is medicine.**
> **Tamil Proverb**

CRANBERRY SCOOP (non-alcoholic)

Ingredients:

1 cup cranberry-juice cocktail
8 fresh or frozen strawberries
1/2 banana, sliced
1/2 cup vanilla frozen yogurt.

Steps:
- In a blender, mix all ingredients until smooth.
  Makes 4 servings

Sheryl Przybylski-Ashley

HAZELNUT LIQUEUR

Ingredients:

1/2 lb. hazelnuts, finely chopped
1 1/2 cups vodka
1/3 cups sugar
3 Tbs. water
1 tsp. vanilla extract

Steps:
- In a glass bottle or jar, steep the chopped hazelnuts in vodka for about two weeks. Store the bottle in a cool, dark place, gently shaking it every day.
- After two weeks, pour the contents of the bottle through a strainer or sieve, pressing hard on the nuts to release all of their flavor.
- Follow this with two strainings through a slightly dampened cheesecloth or large coffee filter. (Loosely cover the contents with plastic wrap, since this process may take several hours.)
- In a very small saucepan, combine the sugar and water and bring them to a boil over moderate-high heat. Simmer, uncovered, for five minutes.
- Let the liquid cool to room temperature, then stir in the vanilla. This is your sugar syrup.
- Funnel the hazelnut vodka into a glass bottle, then funnel in the sugar syrup. Cover tightly, then shake to blend the two liquids.
- Let your liqueur mature at room temperature (or slightly cooler) for at least three weeks.

Ann McDonnell

> "I have always maintained that there is nothing wrong with nursery food now that we are grown up and can have a glass of wine with it."
>
> -Unknown

ORANGE LIQUEUR

Ingredients:
3 med. oranges
3 cups brandy
1 cup honey

Steps:
- Peel the oranges, leaving the inner white skin on the fruit. Cut the orange rind into 2x1/4-inch strips. Reserve the orange pulp for other uses.
- Combine the brandy and orange rind in a jar. Cover tightly, and let stand at room temperature for three weeks.
- Remove the orange rind, and stir in the honey. Let stand for three days.
- Strain off the clear portion, and store in airtight containers. (Reserve the cloudy portion for cooking.)
  Make three cups

Ann McDonnell

ROSY CRANBERRY CIDER (non-alcoholic)

Serve hot.

Ingredients:

2 oranges
2 qts. cranberry juice
Four 3-inch cinnamon sticks

Two 2-inch pieces fresh ginger, peeled and sliced lengthwise
Sugar to taste

Steps:
- With a vegetable peeler or a sharp knife, remove four 3-inch-long strips of peel from the orange, and set aside.
- Juice the orange, and strain out the pulp.
- In a medium stockpot, combine the orange juice, reserved orange peel, cranberry juice, cinnamon sticks, and ginger. Taste, adding sugar if desired.
- Heat over medium-high heat until simmering.
- Reduce heat to low, then simmer for 20 minutes.
- Strain, and discard solids.
  Serves 6 to 8

Christina Evans

RASPBERRY SYRUP

This recipe came from the Swedish cookbook used by my grandmother, Louise Peterson. Fruit syrups serve many purposes in a Swedish home. Diluted with cold water they are a favorite children's drink, especially in the summer. (A Swedish mother finds these fruit drinks invaluable for children's parties and picnics.) Fruit syrups are also used by Swedish cooks for making cold fruit soups, fruit-syrup cream and sauces to go with sweet puddings and creams.

Ingredients:
7 pints raspberries
3 cups cold water
Sugar

Steps:
- Pick and rinse fruit, crushing it and putting it in a preserving pan together with the cold water. Let it come to the boil quickly, stirring, then simmer for 15 minutes.
- Leave the contents of the saucepan to run through a jelly bag or fine cloth, until next day.
- Weigh the juice, then add the sugar, allowing 1 1/2 cups to each lb. of juice.
- When sugar has dissolved, boil briskly for about 10 minutes, skimming carefully all the time.
- Bottle the syrup when cold.

Christina Evans

SPARKLING FRUIT SMOOTHIE (non-alcoholic)

Ingredients:
1 cup plain or fruit-flavored yogurt*
1 1/2 to 2 cups fresh fruit, chopped
2/3 cup ice-cold champagne, sparkling water or ginger ale

Steps:
- Combine the yogurt and fruit in a blender and process on high until smooth.
- Pour blended fruit-yogurt mixture into glasses, filling each one only a quarter full.
- Top the glass off with your choice of sparkling liquid, and stir gently to combine.
- Serve immediately.
  Serves 2
  Note: For a thicker drink use frozen yogurt.

Mary Williams

Old Mill, Sandwich, Mass.

Sandwich's original old grist mill was built around 1638 and rebuilt in 1654. The hill served the town for over two hundred years. During the latter half of the 19th century new methods of grinding corn replaced the water-driven grist mills. Flour and other staples became available to the area by railroad.

GRIST MILLS IN SANDWICH

1. Dexter Grist Mill 1638 Sandwich Village
2. Nye Grist Mill 1669 Old County Road East Sandwich
3. Herring River Mill 1695 Bournedale
4. Back River Grist Mill Monument Beach
5. Spring Hill Grist Mill 1742
6. Sagamore Grist Mill at Willow Crossing Dam 1770
7. Barlow Grist Mill 1771 Pocasset
8. Red Brook Grist Mill built before 1831 Cataumet
9. Upper Shawme Pond 1811 Sandwich Village

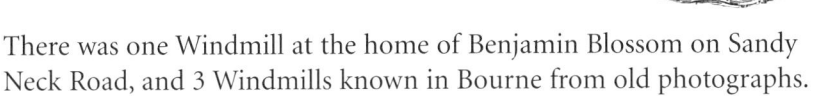

There was one Windmill at the home of Benjamin Blossom on Sandy Neck Road, and 3 Windmills known in Bourne from old photographs.

BREADS, MUFFINS & BRUNCH

North Harwich Railroad Station

Dough Nuts.

cups of Sugar, and 6 cups of Flour sifted together, 1 pint of Milk and a piece of Butter the size of two eggs, warmed together, and Spice to the taste; add half a cup of good Yeast. Mix all this into a stiff dough and set it to rise 4 or 5 hours. Roll it thin, cut it into any shape you please, and fry it in hot lard.   Mrs. Locke.

Dough Nuts.

1 lb of Butter, 1½ lbs of Sugar, 6 eggs, 1 qt of milk, 1 Turnpike or a Teacup of Emptins, Flour enough to make a not very stiff dough Spice to your taste either Cinnamon or Orange peel.
  Maria L. Titus.

Page from a nineteenth century hand-written book of recipes.

28

OATMEAL SCONES

This is an old family Scottish recipe, best served with butter and jam or marmalade.

Ingredients:

4 cups oatmeal
1 1/2 to 2 cups flour
1/4 cup brown sugar
1 tsp. salt
1 tsp. baking soda
4 large Tbs. shortening - may need 5
1 1/2 cups cold water (enough for handling)

Steps:

- Preheat oven to 400°F.
- Combine dry ingredients.
- Add enough shortening to have a crumbly dough.
- Divide dough in half and roll it out about 3/4-inch thick on a floured board. (The thickness depends on how thin you like your scones.)
- Place dough on a cookie sheet and bake until golden brown.
- Cool and cut into squares.

Serves 6

Barbara Walsh

MOTHER'S BANANA BREAD

This is an old recipe from my husband's mother, Mary Hendricksen. I find it is moister if you use very ripe bananas; I will often use four. You can peel and freeze overripe bananas in Ziploc bags until you're ready to make this delicious bread.

Ingredients:

3 bananas, mashed
3/4 cup sugar
2 Tbs. shortening, melted or liquid vegetable oil
1 egg
2 cups flour
1 tsp. baking soda
1 tsp. baking powder
1/2 tsp. salt
1/2 cup chopped nuts, optional

Steps:

- Preheat oven to 350°F.
- Cream sugar and shortening. Beat in egg. Add bananas and mix well.
- In a separate bowl, sift together dry ingredients and add all at once to banana mixture. Stir by hand just until well combined.
- Stir in nuts, if desired.
- Grease the bottom and halfway up the sides of a 9x5x3 inch loaf pan. Pour in batter and bake for about 45 minutes or until toothpick inserted in middle of loaf comes out clean. Do not overbake!

Serves 8

Diane Martin

YOGURT CORN BREAD

Serve immediately. It's best piping hot!

Ingredients:

3/4 cup cornmeal
1 cup flour
1/3 cup sugar
1/2 tsp. baking soda
2 1/2 tsp. baking powder

1 cup plain yogurt
1/4 cup milk
1 egg, well beaten
2 Tbs. melted butter

Steps:
- Preheat oven to 425°F. Butter an 8 inch-square baking pan.
- Sift together all dry ingredients.
- Combine the beaten egg separately with the remaining ingredients.
- Mix dry and wet ingredients just until well moistened, and spoon the resulting batter into the greased pan.
- Bake mixture 20 minutes or until golden brown and puffed on top. Serves 6

Monique Szechenyi

IRISH BREAKFAST SODA BREAD

Very tasty!

Ingredients:

shortening for greasing pans
1 tsp. baking soda
1/2 tsp. ground cinnamon
1 scant tsp. salt
3 tsp. baking powder

4 cups flour
1 cup raisins or currants
1 1/2 cups buttermilk
1 large egg

Steps:
- Grease two 8 inch round cake pans.
- Preheat oven to 375°F.
- In a large bowl, sift together all dry ingredients.
- Add the raisins or currants.
- In a separate bowl, beat the buttermilk and egg. Stir the buttermilk mixture into the dry ingredients until you have a smooth batter.
- Flour a board heavily, and knead the batter on the board until it is smooth.
- Cut the dough into two parts and form them into flat rounds. Place each

round in one of the greased pans, pressing it right up to the edges of the pan.
- With a knife, make a deep 1/2-inch "x" to divide each round into wedges. (Do not cut all the way through.)
- Bake loaves for 35 minutes or until lightly browned on top. Cool on rack, and wrap while slightly warm.
Serves 8-10

Regina Murphy Silvia

EGGNOG TEA BREAD

Easy, tastes terrific and everyone loves it.

Ingredients:

One 16-oz. pkg. pound-cake mix
2 large eggs
1/2 tsp. ground nutmeg
3/4 cup eggnog
1 Tbs. eggnog
1 cup confectioners' sugar

Steps:
- Preheat oven to 350°F.
- Combine first four ingredients in a bowl and beat with an electric mixer at medium speed for three minutes.
- Pour batter into four greased 6x3x2 inch loaf pans.
- Bake for 30 minutes.
- Remove from pans and cool on wire racks.
- Combine sugar and 1 Tbs. eggnog and stir well. Drizzle over bread.
Makes 4 loaves

Norma Coleman

GARLIC BUBBLE LOAF

Ingredients:

1/4 cup butter or margarine, melted
1 Tbs. dried parsley flakes
1 tsp. garlic powder
1/4 tsp. garlic salt
1 loaf (1 lb.) frozen white bread dough, thawed

Steps:
- In a bowl, combine the butter, parsley, garlic powder and garlic salt.
- Cut the frozen dough into 1" pieces, and dip them into the butter mixture.
- Layer pieces in a greased 9x5x3 inch loaf pan. Cover and let rise until doubled, about 1 hour.
Bake dough at 350° F for 30 minutes, or until golden brown.
Serves 8

Pat Maguire

ZUCCHINI BREAD

We love this. It's delicious! It makes two loaves, and we freeze one.

Ingredients:

3 eggs
1 cup vegetable oil
2 cups grated zucchini (do in blender)
3 tsp. vanilla

3 cups flour
2 cups sugar
1 tsp. soda
1/4 tsp. cinnamon
1 cup chopped nuts

Steps:

- Preheat oven to 350°F.
- Mix all ingredients together.
- Pour batter into two loaf pans.
- Bake for 1 hour.
  Makes 2 loaves

Nancy Hallaren

FAVORITE CORNBREAD

Ingredients:

1 cup sugar
1/4 cup cornmeal
1 3/4 cups flour
2 1/4 tsp. baking powder
1/2 tsp. baking soda
1/4 tsp. allspice

1/2 tsp. salt
1 egg, beaten
1/2 cup milk
1/2 cup light cream
1/4 cup plus 1 Tbs. butter or margarine, melted

Steps:

- In a bowl, mix sugar and cornmeal.
- Sift in flour, soda, baking powder, allspice and salt; mix well.
- Add egg, milk, cream and melted butter. Stir-don't beat, just until blended.
- Pour into an 8x8-inch greased and floured pan.
- Bake at 400°F for 30 minutes or until done.
  Serves 8

Jennie Zantuhos

BANANA BREAD

My very favorite banana bread.

Ingredients:

3 bananas, mashed
dash salt
1 tsp. baking soda
1 cup sugar
2 Tbs. shortening
1 egg
1 1/4 cups flour
1/2 cup finely chopped walnuts

Steps:

- Preheat oven to 350°F.
- Mix bananas with a dash of salt and the baking soda until foamy.
- Add remaining ingredients.
- Bake in greased loaf pan for 50-60 minutes.
  Serves 8

Jennie Zantuhos

REFRIGERATOR DINNER ROLLS

Ingredients:

2 cups hot water
1/2 cup sugar
1 Tbs. salt
2 Tbs. shortening
2 Tbs. yeast
1/4 cup warm water (115-125°F)
1 tsp. sugar
2 eggs
8 cups flour

Steps:

- In a bread bowl, combine the hot water, 1/2 cup sugar, salt, and shortening.
- In a liquid-measuring cup combine yeast, warm water and 1 tsp. sugar.
- When the yeast mixture has proofed, stir it into the shortening mixture.
- Beat in the eggs, and then beat in the flour, two cups at a time. The dough should be soft enough to handle, but not stiff enough to knead.
- Brush the top of the dough with melted butter, cover and refrigerate. (The dough may be kept for as long as a week in the refrigerator and used as needed.)
- Remove the dough from the refrigerator 2 1/2 hours before you wish to serve the rolls. Knead it on a floured surface and shape as desired.
- Preheat oven to 425°F.
- Brush the top of the rolls with melted butter and set to rise for 1 1/2 hours.
- Bake the rolls for 15-20 minutes.
  Serves 6

Pam Mittendorff

ALL-BRAN BREAD

Ingredients:

2 cups milk
1 cup Crisco or oil
2 cups All Bran
2 pkgs. dry yeast
2 cups water, lukewarm
2 Tbs. salt
1 cup sugar
about 12 cups flour

Steps:
- Scald the milk. Add Crisco and All Bran, and stir to melt the Crisco.
- Dissolve the yeast in 2 cups warm water. When the milk mixture is cool, stir in the yeast mixture. Add salt and sugar, then flour, 2 cups at a time.
- When dough is stiff, knead it. Set it to rise until doubled, then knead again.
- Divide and shape into four loaves. Let dough rise again until about doubled.
- Bake at 300°F for about 55 minutes.
  Makes 4 loaves

Pam Mittendorff

PUMPKIN 'N' SPICE TEA BREAD

Ingredients:

2 cups sugar
1 cup vegetable oil
3 eggs, lightly beaten
1 can (16 ozs.) pumpkin
3 cups sifted all-purpose flour
1 tsp. baking soda
3/4 tsp. baking powder
1 tsp. ground cinnamon
1/2 tsp. ground nutmeg
1/2 tsp. ground cloves
3/4 tsp. salt
confectioners' sugar

Steps:
- Blend sugar and oil well with an electric mixer.
- Beat in eggs, one at a time, and continue beating until light. Add pumpkin and blend.
- Sift flour, baking soda, baking powder, cinnamon, nutmeg, cloves and salt into the creamed mixture. Beat at low speed until blended.
- Pour batter into four greased 6x3x2-inch loaf pans or two greased 9x5x3-inch loaf pans.
- Bake in a moderate oven (350°F) for one hour, or until lightly browned.
- When done, leave the bread in the pans for 15 minutes on a wire rack. Remove from pans and cool completely on wire rack.
- Sprinkle with confectioners' sugar before serving.
  Serves 16-20

Chris Evans

BRAIDED BUTTERMILK BREAD

Ingredients:

4 1/2 cups flour, approximately
2 pkgs. dry yeast
1 cup buttermilk
3/4 cup water
2 Tbs. shortening
2 Tbs. sugar

1 Tbs. salt
warm water
poppy seeds, optional
sesame seeds, optional
butter

Steps:

- In a large mixing bowl, stir together two cups flour and yeast.
- In a saucepan, combine buttermilk, water, shortening, sugar, and salt, and place over low heat until warm (120-130°F). If the buttermilk curdles, don't be concerned.
- Add the liquid to flour-and-yeast mixture, and beat with an electric mixer for 30 seconds at low speed.
- Scrape the sides of the bowl. At high speed, beat for 3 minutes.
- Stop the mixer and stir in the balance of the flour, a half a cup at a time—first with a spoon and then by hand, until a soft dough is formed.
- Turn the dough onto a heavily floured work surface and knead for eight minutes (six minutes with a dough hook) until dough is smooth and elastic.
- Form into a ball, cover with a tent of wax paper or towel and let rest for 20 minutes.
- Punch down the dough and knead for 30 seconds to press out the bubbles.
- Divide the dough into six equal parts, rolling each into a 14-inch-long rope. Lay three ropes side-by-side and weave them into a thick braid. Pinch the ends together and turn under slightly. Repeat with next piece.
- Place braids on a buttered baking sheet. Place a length of wax paper over them and put them in a warm spot (80-85°F) to rise until doubled in size, about 45 minutes. After the dough has risen for 25 minutes, brush the dough with warm water and leave for 20 more minutes.
- Preheat the oven to 400°F.
- If you wish, brush loaves again with warm water and sprinkle with sesame or poppy seeds or both. Bake in the oven for 30 minutes. Shift the loaves around for even baking, and bake for another 15 minutes, or until the loaves are golden brown.
- Test a loaf by tapping the bottom crust with a forefinger. A hard hollow sound means the bread is baked. If not, return it to the oven for 10 minutes.
- Remove loaves from oven, and brush with water immediately. Place on a wire rack to cool.
  Makes two 1-lb. loaves

Chris Evans

GRANDMA'S OATMEAL BREAD

This recipe is from The Silo Cooking School in New Milford, CT

Ingredients:

2 pkgs. active dry yeast
1/2 cup warm water
1 1/4 cups boiling water
1 cup quick-cooking rolled oats
1/2 cup light molasses
1/3 cup shortening
1 Tbs. salt
6 to 6 1/4 cups sifted flour
2 beaten eggs
4 Tbs. rolled oats
1 egg white
1 Tbs. water

Steps:
- Soften dry yeast in warm water.
- Combine boiling water, rolled oats, molasses, shortening and salt. Cool to lukewarm.
- Stir in 2 cups sifted flour, and beat well. Add eggs and the yeast; beat well.
- Add enough remaining flour to make a soft dough. Turn out onto a lightly floured surface; cover and let rest 10 minutes, then knead till smooth. Place in a lightly greased bowl, turning dough once to grease top. Cover; let rise until doubled (about 1 1/2 hours).
- Punch down dough.
- Coat two well-greased 8 1/2 x 4 1/2 x 2 1/2-inch loaf pans with 2 Tbs. rolled oats each. Divide dough in half. Shape into loaves and place in pans. Cover, and let double (45-60 minutes). Brush with a mixture of egg white and water; sprinkle lightly with rolled oats.
- Bake loaves at 375°F for 40 minutes. Cover with foil after baking for 15 minutes, if tops are getting too brown.
  Makes two loaves

Chris Evans

FOOLPROOF CHALLAH BREAD

Ingredients:

7 to 7 1/2 cups flour
2 pkgs. active dry yeast
2 cups water
1/4 cup sugar
1/4 cup margarine
2 tsp. salt
3 eggs
1 egg yolk
1 Tbs. water
poppy or sesame seeds

Steps:
- In a large mixing bowl, combine 3 cups of flour and the yeast.
- In a saucepan, heat together the 2 cups of water, sugar, margarine and salt

just until warm, stirring constantly until the margarine almost melts.
- Add the liquid mixture to the dry mixture in the bowl; add the eggs. Beat at the low speed of an electric mixer for 30 seconds, scraping the sides of the bowl constantly. Beat for three minutes at high speed.
- By hand, stir in enough remaining flour to make soft dough. Turn out onto lightly floured surface and knead about 8 minutes, or until smooth and elastic.
- Place in lightly greased bowl, turning once to grease surface. Cover and let rise in warm place about 45 minutes or until double in size.
- Punch down and divide dough into three portions. Divide each portion into three pieces. Cover and let rest 10 minutes.
- Roll each piece into a 16-inch rope. Using three ropes for each loaf, braid and score ends, making three loaves. Place on greased baking sheets.
- Cover and let rise again about 35 minutes or until almost double. Brush loaves with a mixture of egg yolk and 1 Tbs. water. Sprinkle with poppy or sesame seed, if desired.
- Bake at 375°F for 25-30 minutes, or until light brown.
Makes three loaves.

Chris Evans

ZUP FE (SWISS BRAIDED CHRISTMAS BREAD)

Ingredients:

1 1/2 cups milk
3 Tbs. sugar
1 Tbs. salt
1/2 stick butter (4 Tbs.)
2 pkgs. yeast

1/2 cup hot water
2 eggs, beaten
7 cups flour
3 Tbs. butter, melted
1 egg yolk, beaten with 1 Tbs. water

Steps:
- Heat milk to a near boil, and remove from heat. Add sugar, salt and butter, cool.
- Sprinkle yeast over the hot water in a large bowl, and stir until dissolved.
- Stir the milk mixture into the yeast mixture. Add the eggs and 3 1/2 cups flour; beat with a spoon for two minutes until smooth. Work in the remaining flour and knead for 10 minutes.
- Place the dough in a greased bowl, and turn dough over to grease. Cover and let rise.
- Return dough to the floured board and divide it in half. Divide each half into thirds.
- Roll each piece into 15-inch-long strips. Place the strips on greased cookie sheets and braid. Brush the braided dough with melted butter, cover with a towel and let it rise.
- Brush each loaf with an egg-and-water wash.
- Preheat the oven to 400°F. Bake loaf for 40 minutes.
  Makes 1 loaf

Chris Evans

COTTAGE TEAHOUSE WHITE BREAD

Ingredients:

2 cups milk
1/2 cup sugar
1/4 cup (1/2 stick) butter, room temperature
2 tsp. salt

1 pkg. dry yeast
1/2 cup warm water (105-115°F)
6 1/2 to 7 cups bread flour
melted butter

Steps:
- Scald the milk in a heavy medium-size saucepan. Remove milk from heat and stir in 1/4 cup sugar, 1/4 cup butter and salt. Cool to lukewarm.
- Sprinkle the remaining 1/4 cup sugar and yeast over warm water in a large bowl; let dissolve, then stir to blend. Let the yeast stand until foamy and proofed, about 15 minutes.

- Stir the milk mixture into the yeast. Add enough flour, 1 cup at a time, to form a soft dough. Turn out the dough onto a floured surface, and knead it until smooth and elastic, about 10 minutes.
- Grease a large bowl. Place the dough in the bowl, turning it to coat the entire surface. Cover the bowl with a towel and let dough rise in a warm draft-free area until doubled in volume, about 1 1/2 hours.
- Grease two 9x5-inch loaf pans or eight 4 1/2 x 2 1/2-inch loaf pans. Punch dough down. Turn out onto a lightly floured surface and knead for two minutes. Shape dough into loaves and fit into pans. Cover and let rise in warm draft-free area until almost doubled in volume, about 45 minutes.
- Preheat oven to 350°F. Bake until loaves are golden brown and bottoms sound hollow when tapped, about 30 minutes.
- Brush tops with melted butter and serve warm.
  Makes two large or eight small loaves

Chris Evans

APPLE-ROSEMARY TEA BREAD

Ingredients:

3/4 cup + 1 Tbs. milk
1/2 cup raisins, coarsely chopped
4 Tbs. + 1 tsp. unsalted butter
2 Granny Smith apples, peeled, cored and diced
1/2 cup + 1 Tbs. sugar

1 Tbs. chopped fresh rosemary
1 1/2 cups flour
2 tsp. baking powder
1/4 tsp. salt
1 large egg

Steps:

- Preheat oven to 350°F.
- Butter and flour three 5 1/2 x 2 1/2 x 2-inch loaf pans. Set them aside.
- Heat milk to scalding; remove from heat and add the raisins.
- Stir in four tablespoons of the butter and let the mixture cool.
- In a small sauté pan over medium heat, cook the apples with the one tablespoon of sugar and the one remaining teaspoon of butter until the apples are glazed and somewhat soft (about three minutes). Add the rosemary.
- Separately, combine the flour, the remaining 1/2 cup sugar, baking powder and salt. Whisk the egg into the cooled milk-raisin mixture.
- Add the diced apples to the dry ingredients, but do not combine. Pour the wet mixture over the dry, and mix with a few quick strokes—just until the dry ingredients are moistened. Do not overmix!
- Fill the prepared pans to about 3/4 full. Bake for 30 minutes, or until a toothpick inserted into the middle comes out clean. Let cool.
  Yields 3 small loaves

Mae Foster

DINNER ROLLS

Serve warm!

Ingredients:

3 1/2 tsp. active dry yeast
pinch of sugar
1/3 cup warm water (105-115°F)
1 cup tepid buttermilk (90°F)
1/4 cup sugar or honey
1/2 cup unsalted butter, melted

2 large eggs, lightly beaten
1 tsp. salt
4 1/2 to 5 cups unbleached flour, plus extra as needed
canola oil for greasing

Steps:

- In a bowl, sprinkle the yeast and sugar over the warm water and stir to dissolve. Let stand until foamy, about 10 minutes.
- In a heavy-duty mixer fitted with the paddle attachment, combine the buttermilk, sugar, melted butter, eggs, salt, and 1 cup of the flour. Beat on medium-low speed until creamy, about 2 minutes.
- Add the yeast mixture and 1 cup of the flour, and beat for another minute.
- Beat in the remaining flour, 1/2 cup at a time, until the dough pulls away from the bowl sides.
- Switch attachment to a dough hook. Knead on low speed, adding flour 1 Tbs. at a time if the dough sticks, until a very soft dough forms, about 1 minute. The dough should be softer than typical bread dough, yet smooth and springy.
- Transfer the dough to an oiled deep bowl and turn the dough once to coat it. Cover loosely with plastic wrap and let rise at room temperature until doubled in bulk, about 1 1/2 hours.
- Grease two 8-inch round cake pans. Turn the dough out onto a lightly floured board. Divide the dough in half and roll each half between your palms into a rope 18 inches long. Cut each rope into eighteen 1-inch pieces.
- Shape each 1-inch piece into a ball, and place the balls, sides just touching, in the prepared cake pans. Cover pans loosely with plastic, and let rise at room temperature until puffy, 30-45 minutes.
- Preheat the oven to 375°F. Bake the rolls until light golden brown (18-23 minutes). Let the rolls cool slightly in the pans or transfer to a rack.
Makes 3 dozen rolls

Chris Evans

BLUEBERRY PANCAKES WITH HOT BLUEBERRY SYRUP

Ingredients for Blueberry Pancakes:

1 1/3 cups unsifted flour	1 egg, beaten
1/2 tsp. baking soda	1 cup sour cream
1 tsp. salt	1 cup milk
1 Tbs. sugar	1 cup blueberries
1/4 tsp. nutmeg	

Steps for Blueberry Pancakes:
- Stir the dry ingredients together.
- Combine egg, sour cream and milk. Add wet mixture to dry ingredients, and stir just to combine.
- Add blueberries, stirring just enough to mix.
- Drop by 1/4-cupfuls onto a hot, greased griddle. Cook the pancakes until their top surfaces are covered with bubbles. Flip, then cook the other side.

Ingredients for Hot Blueberry Syrup:
1 cup blueberries
1/4 cup water
1/4 cup sugar

Steps for Hot Blueberry Syrup:
- Combine all ingredients in a saucepan, and bring to a boil. Simmer for two to three minutes.
- Serve over hot blueberry pancakes.
Serves 4

Jennie Zantuhos

> "Optimism is a cheerful frame of mind that enables a tea kettle to sing, though in hot water up to its nose."
>
> -Anonymous

SPINACH PIE FOR A CROWD

This dish can be served warm, or you can chill it and serve it cold.

Ingredients:

3 lbs. fresh spinach or four 10-oz. pkgs. frozen chopped spinach, thawed
salt
1 cup olive oil
2 lg. onions, chopped
2 bunches scallions, including 4 inches of green tops, finely chopped
1/2 cup chopped parsley
1/2 cup chopped fresh dill or 3 Tbs. dried dill
4 eggs
1/2 lb. feta cheese, crumbled
1/2 lb. ricotta or cottage cheese
1/4 cup butter, melted
16 sheets phyllo pastry

Steps:

- If using fresh spinach, remove and discard the coarse stems. Wash leaves well. Sprinkle spinach leaves lightly with salt, and stir to spread salt evenly. Let salted spinach stand for 15 minutes. Rinse off salt, and with your hands squeeze out excess water. Cut up spinach leaves, and place in a colander so that remaining moisture will drip out. (It is important that spinach be dry.)
- If using frozen spinach, do not salt. Just squeeze thawed spinach as dry as possible and place in a colander to drain.
- In the meantime, heat 1/2 cup olive oil and sauté the onions and scallions until soft but not brown.
- To the sautéed onions and scallions, add the spinach, parsley and dill, and cook, stirring, until the spinach has wilted, two or three minutes. Remove from heat. Transfer to a bowl and let cool.
- Preheat the oven to 350°F.
- Beat the eggs lightly, and add them to the cheeses. Stir.
- When the spinach mixture has cooled, pour the egg-cheese mixture into the spinach mixture and blend well.
- Combine the remaining 1/2 cup olive oil with 1/4 cup melted butter and set aside in a bowl.
- Grease a shallow 9x13-inch baking pan.
- Take eight phyllo sheets from the package. Center one sheet in the baking pan, and brush it with the oil-butter mixture from the bowl. Stack the other seven sheets one by one on top of the first, brushing each with the oil-butter mixture as you stack. The sheets should extend up the sides of the pan.
- Pour the spinach-cheese mixture over the finished phyllo stack and spread it out evenly. Fold the overhanging sides and ends of the phyllo sheets over the filling to enclose it, then brush the phyllo with oil-butter mixture.
- Top this with another stack of eight more phyllo sheets, again brushing

each with the oil-butter mixture as you stack it in the pan. Tuck the overhanging edges around the inside of the baking pan when the stack is done, and, using the point of a sharp knife, score the surface into 20 rectangles.
- Bake until golden, about 45 minutes.
- Do not cut through the scored lines until you are ready to serve.
Serves 20

Monique Galipeau

OVEN FRENCH TOAST

Ingredients:

2 eggs, beaten
1 cup milk
dash of salt
1/4 tsp. nutmeg (optional)
8 slices French bread (or any white bread)

Steps:
- Combine eggs, milk, salt, and nutmeg in a shallow bowl.
- Dip the bread slices in the egg mixture, coating both sides.
- Place the dipped slices on a greased baking sheet and broil them 4-5 inches from the heat source for five minutes on each side, or until golden brown.
Serves 4

Judi Lesiak

HANGTOWN-FRY OMELET

Ingredients:

3 eggs
3 Tbs. milk
fried oysters (pre-dipped in flour, beaten egg and breadcrumbs, then fried until lightly browned)
bacon, cooked and crumbled
cheese (one slice of your favorite)

Steps:
- Beat the eggs and the milk together.
- Pour the egg-milk mixture into a hot, two-sided omelette pan or griddle, and cook until partially set.
- Add fried oysters, bacon and cheese.
- Cook until done.
NOTE: These omelettes can also be partially cooked in the oven. Place them in a 400°F oven after adding the oysters, bacon and cheese, then cook until set.
Serves 1+

Judi Lesiak

FRUIT-TOPPED OVEN PANCAKE

As a variation, I quite often add blueberries.

Ingredients for pancake:
1/2 cup flour
2 Tbs. sugar
1/2 cup milk
1 egg

Ingredients for filling:
1 1/4 cups fresh or frozen cranberries
2 apples, diced
1/2 cup chopped walnuts
1/4 cup butter or margarine
1/2 cup brown sugar
1 tsp. cinnamon
1/2 tsp. nutmeg

Steps:
- Preheat the oven to 400°F.
- Combine the flour, sugar, milk, and egg in a medium mixing bowl. Beat well for one minute, using an electric mixer.
- Pour the batter into a greased 9-inch pie plate and bake it in the oven for 20 minutes or until golden.
- Meanwhile, sauté the cranberries, apples, and nuts in the butter, sugar, and spices in a medium skillet, until fruit is tender.
- Remove the baked pancake from the oven and, if the batter has puffed, gently push it down. Spoon the fruit over the pancake.
- Cut into wedges to serve.
Serves 2

Wayne Joyce

SWEDISH PANCAKES

This recipe is from my grandmother, Alida Olson, who emigrated from Sweden when she was 20 years old.

Ingredients:
Butter for frying
2 cups milk
5 eggs
2 cups flour
1 Tbs. sugar
1 tsp. salt
1 tsp. vanilla
1 stick butter, melted

Steps:
- Heat a skillet on medium high and melt butter into it.
- Mix milk and eggs together in a large mixing bowl, then stir in the flour, sugar, salt and vanilla. Add melted butter, and stir until blended.
- Pour enough batter into the hot skillet so that, when rotating the skillet, the batter can form an even layer over the entire bottom.
- Cook until the pancake bottom is light brown, then flip. Cook until the other side is light brown, then flip it onto a dinner plate.
- Spread on the butter and maple syrup (or your favorite topping), then roll the pancake up like a rug.
- Cut, eat, and enjoy!
Serves 6

Dorsey Titcomb

FINNISH "PANNUKAKKU"

This egg recipe is similar to a soufflé. It is great when unexpected company arrives, and I like it for a Sunday-evening light supper, too.

Ingredients:

2 eggs	2 Tbs. sugar
2 cups milk	1/2 tsp. salt
1 cup flour	1/4 cup butter for frying

Steps:
- Mix the eggs and milk lightly with a beater.
- Sift together the flour, sugar and salt, then add the dry mixture to the milk-egg mixture.
- Preheat the oven to 400°F.
- Melt the butter in a heated cast-iron frying pan (I use my mother's black iron "spider," but a 9x9-inch Pyrex baking dish could also be used, just heat it in the oven with the butter in it first). Pour the batter on top of the heated butter, then bake in the oven for 25 minutes or until light brown.
- Serve immediately with butter and maple syrup or with jelly.
Serves 2

Helmi Wiinikainen Viliesis

APPLE-CRAISIN PASTRY BASKETS WITH RUM CREAM

Garnishing these with dried cranberries and cinnamon sticks makes them really attractive.

Ingredients:

6 puff pastry pre-made shells
6-8 medium-sized baking apples
1/4 cup dried cranberries (Craisins) or raisins
1/2 cup apple juice or cranberry juice
1/4 cup packed light brown sugar
1 1/2 tsp. cinnamon
1/4 tsp. nutmeg
3 whole cloves
1/2 cup chopped walnuts
1/2 pint heavy cream
1/4 tsp. rum flavoring

Steps:
- Bake the puff pastry according to the package directions. When baked, remove and save the tops of the pastry puffs, then scoop out the insides and discard the dough, leaving pastry shells. Set the hollow shells aside.
- Core the unpeeled apples and slice them thick.
- Place the apples, Craisins, juice, brown sugar, cinnamon, nutmeg and cloves in a saucepan over medium-high heat. Bring to a boil and reduce heat, stirring occasionally. Cook until the apples are soft but still retain their shape.
- Remove the cloves and add the walnuts.
- Assemble the baskets by filling the puff pastry shells with the apple-nut mixture. Place the pastry tops back on the filled shells.
- Whip the heavy cream with an electric mixer until it forms soft peaks. Fold the rum flavoring into the whipped cream and top the shells with the rum cream.

Serves 6

Marilyn Goldstein

PICANTE-OMELET PIE

Tomato sauce may be substituted for the picante sauce, which adds a bit of flavor to ordinary eggs. Garnish with tomato slices and fresh cilantro or parsley, if desired.

Ingredients:

1/2 cup picante sauce
1 cup (4 oz.) shredded Monterey Jack cheese
1 cup (4 oz.) shredded Cheddar cheese
6 large eggs
1 cup (8 oz.) sour cream

Steps:
- Preheat the oven to 375°F.
- Pour the picante sauce into a greased 10-inch pie plate or quiche dish.
- Sprinkle the picante sauce with the cheeses, then set the pie plate aside.
- Use a whisk to beat the eggs.
- Add sour cream to the eggs and whisk until combined. Pour the mixture over the cheeses in the pie plate.
- Bake for 20-25 minutes, or until a knife inserted near the center comes out clean.
- Let the pie stand for five minutes before cutting it.
Serves 6

Marilyn Goldstein

BAKED FRENCH TOAST

Ingredients:

2/3 cup packed light brown sugar
1/2 cup (1 stick) butter, melted
2 tsp. ground cinnamon
6 large eggs, beaten

1 3/4 cups milk
1 lb. French bread, cut into 1-inch slices
confectioners' sugar

Steps:
- Preheat the oven to 350°F.
- Combine the brown sugar, melted butter and cinnamon. Spread this mixture evenly across the bottom of a greased 15x10x1-inch baking pan, and set aside.
- Combine the eggs and milk in a shallow dish.
- Place the bread slices in the dish, and soak them for five minutes, turning once.
- Place the soaked bread slices over the sugar mixture in the baking pan.
- Bake, uncovered, for 25-30 minutes or until golden brown.
- Serve with the brown-sugar side up, and dust with confectioners' sugar.
Serves 6 to 8

Marilyn Goldstein

> "As for butter versus margarine,
> I trust cows more than chemists."
>
> -Joan Gussow, nutritionist,
> writer and organic-food promoter

COUNTRY BREAKFAST PIE

Ingredients:

1 pkg. bulk Jimmy Dean sausage, any flavor
1 1/2 cups grated Swiss cheese
9-inch pie crust
3 eggs, slightly beaten
1/4 cup green pepper, chopped
1/4 cup red pepper, chopped
2 Tbs. onion, chopped
1 cup light cream

Steps:
- Cook the sausage until browned. Crumble, then drain. Cool slightly.
- Preheat the oven to 375°F.
- Mix the grated cheese and sausage.
- Sprinkle the cheese and sausage into the prepared pie crust.
- Lightly beat the eggs in a bowl. Add the remaining ingredients to the egg mixture, and pour it into the shell, over the sausage and cheese.
- Bake for 40-45 minutes.
- Cool on a rack for 10 minutes.
  Serves 6 to 8

Pat Maguire

ZUCCHINI PANCAKES

This recipe, from Pensey's Spice Catalog, is a tasty way to use up extra zucchini from the garden. These pancakes are good with syrup for brunch, but I also like them with butter served with a fish fillet.

Ingredients:

1 cup flour
2 eggs
1/2 cup milk
1 tsp. baking powder
1/2 to 1 tsp. salt
1 Tbs. vegetable oil
1/2 cup Parmesan cheese, finely grated
1 1/2 cups coarsely shredded or grated zucchini
1/4 tsp. rosemary, crushed
1 tsp. basil
1/2 tsp. garlic powder
1/4 tsp. black pepper
1 to 2 Tbs. margarine or vegetable-oil spray

Steps:
- In a large bowl, lightly beat together the flour, eggs, milk, baking powder, salt and oil until blended. Add the cheese, zucchini, herbs and seasonings. Mix to blend.
- Coat a large non-stick skillet with margarine or vegetable spray and set it over medium heat.

- Drop large spoonfuls of the batter into the skillet, and cook over medium heat until the pancake bottoms are browned (about four minutes). Flip the pancakes and cook a few more minutes.
- Pancakes will rise up a bit and be springy to the touch when done.
Serves 4

Barbara Lucas

BREAKFAST PIZZA

This was a big hit at the Herb-Festival Thank-You Breakfast held at Green Briar.

Ingredients:

1 lb. bulk pork sausage (cooked, drained and crumbled)	1 cup (4 oz.) sharp cheddar cheese, shredded
1 pkg. refrigerated crescent-roll dough (enough to make 8 rolls)	5 eggs
	1/4 cup milk
1 cup frozen loose-pack hash-brown potatoes, thawed	1/2 tsp. salt
	1/8 tsp. pepper
	2 Tbs. grated Parmesan cheese

Steps:
- Preheat the oven to 375°F.
- Separate the crescent-roll dough into eight triangles, and place them on an ungreased 12-inch pizza pan, with the points toward the center. Press the dough over the bottom and up the sides of the pizza pan to form a crust. Seal the perforations.
- Spoon the sausage over the crust. Sprinkle the sausage with the potatoes and top all with the cheddar cheese.
- In a bowl, beat together eggs, milk, salt and pepper, and pour it all onto the crust.
- Sprinkle Parmesan over the top.
- Bake for 25-30 minutes.
Serves 8

Chris Foisy

> *"Part of the secret of success in life is to eat what you like and let the food fight it out inside."*
>
> -Mark Twain

TOAD-IN-THE-HOLE

This recipe—Mary Lou found hers in a farming newspaper called The Lancaster Farming—is easy enough for children to make, with help from Mom and Dad.

Ingredients:

1 lb. pork sausage (small links)
1 cup milk
2 eggs
1 cup flour
black pepper
1/2 tsp. salt
1 Tbs. melted butter

Steps:
- Fry the sausage links until they are lightly browned and all the fat is rendered.
- Place the sausages in a 9-inch-square baking dish.
- Preheat the oven to 400°F.
- To make the batter, place the milk, eggs, flour, pepper, salt and melted butter in a blender, or beat well until smooth.
- Pour the batter over the cooked sausages.
- Bake uncovered for 30 minutes. The batter will become puffed, crisp and golden brown.
Serves 4

Nancy Carvalho and Mary Lou Happ

QUICHE LORRAINE

Ingredients:

2 cups milk
3/4 cup Bisquick baking mix
1 cup grated cheese, Swiss or cheddar
4 eggs
1/2 cup margarine
Toppings: chopped bacon, ham, or veggies

Steps:
- Preheat oven to 350°F.
- Put all ingredients in a blender (except for the toppings). Mix thoroughly.
- Pour the batter into a deep greased pie plate and top with the bacon, ham, etc.
- Bake for 45 minutes.

NOTE: This dish can be frozen and reheated to serve later.
Serves 6 to 8

ORANGE-VANILLA FRENCH TOAST

This recipe can easily be doubled. It's delicious for a holiday brunch, garnished with orange slices. Remember that it needs to soak for several hours, so start it the night before for an easy finish in the morning.

Ingredients:

One 10-oz. loaf French or Italian bread
6 eggs
3/4 cup orange juice
1/2 cup heavy cream
2 Tbs. sugar
4 tsp. pure vanilla extract
1 tsp. grated orange peel (zest)
1/4 tsp. salt
1 Tbs. butter or margarine for frying
Confectioners' sugar

Steps:

- Cut the bread into 3/4-inch slices.
- In a well-greased 15x10-inch jellyroll pan, arrange the bread in a single layer.
- In a large bowl, beat the eggs, orange juice, cream, sugar, vanilla extract, orange zest and salt until well blended. Pour this mixture over the bread, turning the slices to coat them completely.
- Cover and refrigerate this dish until all the liquid is absorbed (six hours or overnight).
- In the morning, either grill or bake the French toast. To grill it, heat the butter until melted in a large skillet or on a flat grill. Add the bread slices in batches, cooking them until they are brown on both sides (turn the bread only once, and add more butter if necessary).
- To bake the French toast, preheat the oven to 450°F. Cover a large baking sheet with foil, and grease the foil with butter or margarine. Place the bread on the foil in a single layer and bake for 13-15 minutes, turning after 10 minutes.
- Sprinkle the toast with confectioners' sugar, if desired.
Serves 6

Pat Maguire

"If you have two loaves of bread, sell one and buy a hyacinth to feed your soul."

-Persian saying

JORDAN MARSH BLUEBERRY MUFFINS

Ingredients:

1/2 cup butter
1 cup sugar
2 eggs
1/2 cup milk
1/2 tsp. salt
2 cups flour
2 tsp. baking powder
1 tsp. vanilla
2 1/2 cups blueberries, fresh (if frozen, use a pint package)
Sugar for muffin tops

Steps:
- Preheat the oven to 375°F.
- On low speed, cream the butter and sugar until fluffy.
- Add the eggs, one at a time, and mix until blended.
- Sift in the dry ingredients and add them, alternately, with the milk.
- Stir in the vanilla.
- Stir in the blueberries by hand.
- Grease the muffin cups and the surface of the pan well.
- Pile the batter high in each muffin cup and sprinkle sugar over the tops.
- Bake the muffins for 25-30 minutes.
- After removing from the oven, cool the muffins in the pan for 30 minutes or more.
  Makes 18 muffins

PUMPKIN MUFFINS

Ingredients:

1 pkg. yellow cake mix
1 pkg. instant butterscotch-pudding mix
4 eggs
1/4 cup water
1/4 cup vegetable oil
1 cup canned pumpkin
2 tsp. pumpkin-pie spice

Steps:
- Preheat the oven to 350°F.
- In a large mixing bowl, combine all ingredients, then beat on low speed for 30 seconds. Continue beating, but on medium speed, for four minutes.
- Pour the batter into greased and floured or paper-lined muffin cups.
- Bake the muffins for 20-25 minutes or until a wooden pick inserted near the center comes out clean. Cool the muffins for 15 minutes before removing them to a wire rack to cool completely.
- Makes 2 dozen muffins

Pat Maguire

ZUCCHINI-OATMEAL MUFFINS

Ingredients:

2 1/2 cups flour
1 1/2 cups sugar
1 cup pecans, chopped
1/2 cup quick-cooking oats, uncooked
1 Tbs. baking powder
1 tsp. salt
1 tsp. cinnamon
4 eggs
One 10-oz. med. zucchini, finely shredded
3/4 cup salad oil
Sugar, for sprinkling on muffin tops

Steps:
- Preheat the oven to 400°F.
- Into a large bowl, measure the first seven ingredients.
- In a separate medium bowl with a fork, beat the eggs slightly.
- Stir the zucchini and oil into the eggs.
- Stir the wet mixture all at once into the dry mixture just until moistened. (Batter will be lumpy.)
- Spoon the batter into greased or paper-lined muffin cups, and sprinkle tops with sugar.
- Bake for 25 minutes or until a toothpick inserted into the middle of a muffin comes out clean.
  Makes 12 muffins

Judy Koenig

LOW-FAT APPLE MUFFINS

Ingredients:

2 1/4 cups oat-bran cereal
1/4 cup brown sugar
1 1/4 tsp. cinnamon
1 Tbs. baking powder
3/4 cup apple juice
1/2 cup skim milk
2 egg whites
2 Tbs. vegetable oil
1 med. apple, chopped
1/4 cup walnuts, chopped
1/4 cup raisins

Steps:
- Preheat oven to 400°F.
- Combine the first four dry ingredients in one bowl and the next four liquid ingredients in another bowl.
- Now combine the wet ingredients with the dry ingredients.
- Add the apple, walnuts and raisins.
- Fill greased muffin cups three-quarters full.
- Bake for 15-17 minutes.
  Makes 18 muffins

Jennie Zantuhos

ORANGE-GINGER MUFFINS

Ingredients:

1 3/4 cups flour
1 1/2 tsp. baking soda
1 1/2 tsp. baking powder
1/2 tsp. salt
1 med. orange
1/2 cup butter or margarine, softened
3/4 cup granulated sugar
1 egg
1/2 cup orange juice
1/4 cup crystallized ginger, finely chopped

Steps:
- Preheat the oven to 375°F.
- Combine the flour, baking soda, baking powder and salt, and set aside.
- Finely grate the zest from the orange rind to make 2 tsp. of zest, and set aside.
- Peel the orange, discarding the rind and white pith, then finely chop the orange, removing the seeds. Set aside.
- With an electric mixer in a large bowl, beat the butter and sugar until light and fluffy.
- Beat in the egg.
- Stir in the chopped orange fruit and the grated orange zest.
- Beat the flour mixture into the bowl, alternating with the orange juice, and ending with flour mixture. Fold in the crystallized ginger.
- Divide the batter among paper-lined muffin cups, filling almost to the top.
- Bake for 18-20 minutes, or until a pick inserted in the center of a muffin comes out clean.
- Remove the muffins from the pan and cool on a wire rack.
  Makes 12 muffins

CRANBERRY-ORANGE MUFFINS

Ingredients:

2 cups flour
3 tsp. baking powder
1 cup sugar
1/2 tsp. salt
3/4 cup orange juice*
2 tsp. orange rind, grated
1/3 cup butter, melted
1 egg
1 cup cranberries, chopped
1/2 cup walnuts, chopped
Sugar, for sprinkling muffin tops

* Use the juice from one orange, adding good-quality packaged juice

Steps:
- Preheat oven to 400°F.
- Stir the first four dry ingredients together in a large mixing bowl.

- Combine the next four ingredients separately until just moistened, then add them to the dry ingredients. Stir in the cranberries and nuts.
- Pour the batter into paper-lined muffin cups and sprinkle the tops lightly with sugar.
- Bake for 20-25 minutes.
  Makes 12 muffins

Judy Koenig

CINNAMON-TOPPED APPLE MUFFINS

Ingredients for Muffins:
1 egg, beaten
3/4 cup milk
1 medium apple, pared and chopped
1/2 cup vegetable oil
1/2 tsp. ground cinnamon

2 cups flour
1/3 cup brown sugar
3 tsp. baking powder
1 tsp. salt
1/3 cup applesauce

Ingredients for Topping:
1/2 tsp. cinnamon
1/4 cup brown sugar
1 Tbs. butter

Steps:
- Preheat the oven to 400°F.
- Combine the egg, milk, apple, and oil, and set aside.
- Separately, add the cinnamon to the flour. Add in the brown sugar, baking powder and salt.
- Combine the flour mixture with the egg mixture, and stir until moistened. The batter will be lumpy.
- Fill 12 lined muffin cups about three-quarters full.
- Dot the top of the muffins with applesauce.
- Prepare the topping by mixing ingredients with a fork to form crumbs.
- Sprinkle the topping on the muffins.
- Bake for 20 minutes.
  Makes 12 muffins

Jennie Zantuhos

BANANA CRUMB MUFFINS

Ingredients for Muffins:

1 1/2 cups flour
1 tsp. baking soda
1 tsp. baking powder
1/2 tsp. salt

3 lg. bananas, mashed
3/4 cup sugar
1 egg, lightly beaten
1/3 cup butter or margarine, melted

Ingredients for Crumb Topping:

1/3 cup packed brown sugar
1 Tbs. flour

1/8 tsp. ground cinnamon
1 Tbs. butter or margarine

Steps:

- Preheat the oven to 375°F.
- In a large bowl, combine the four dry muffin ingredients.
- Separately, combine the bananas, sugar, egg and butter. Mix well.
- Stir the banana mixture into the dry ingredients, just until moistened.
- Fill greased or paper-lined muffin cups three-quarters full.
- Combine the topping ingredients, and sprinkle over the muffin tops.
- Bake for 20-25 minutes, or until muffins test done.
- Cool muffins for 10 minutes before removing them to a wire rack.
  Makes 10 muffins

Pat Maguire

OATMEAL-RAISIN MUFFINS

Serve warm.

Ingredients:

One 8-oz. can crushed pineapple, undrained
1 cup sour cream
1 egg
1/4 cup butter or margarine, melted
1 1/2 cups flour
1 cup old-fashioned oats

1/2 cup sugar
1 Tbs. baking powder
1 tsp. ground cinnamon
1/2 tsp. ground nutmeg
1/2 tsp. salt
1 cup raisins

Steps:

- Preheat oven to 350°F.
- In a small bowl, combine the undrained pineapple, sour cream, egg and butter until blended.
- In a large bowl, combine the remaining dry ingredients, then make a well in the center.

- Pour the pineapple mixture into the well in the dry mixture. Stir until just blended.
- Spoon the batter into greased 2 1/2-inch muffin cups.
- Bake for 30-35 minutes until muffins are lightly browned and a wooden pick inserted in the center of a muffin comes out clean.
  Makes 12 muffins

Jennie Zantuhos

GINGER LEMON SCONES

Ingredients:

3 cups flour
1 Tbs. ground ginger
1 1/8 tsp. baking soda
1 1/8 tsp. cream of tartar
1/4 tsp. salt
12 Tbs. (1 1/2 sticks) cold unsalted butter
3/4 cup buttermilk
1 1/2 tsp. grated lemon peel
1 large egg, beaten
3/4 cup golden raisins
Milk, for brushing tops

Steps:
- Preheat the oven to 425°F.
- Combine the flour, ginger, baking soda, cream of tartar and salt.
- In a food processor or by hand, cut small pieces of butter into the flour mixture.
- Add the buttermilk, grated lemon peel and egg, and process until the mixture is crumb-like.
- Turn the dough onto a floured surface and knead the raisins into it.
- Roll dough into an 8-inch circle and cut it into eight pie-shaped pieces.
- Transfer the wedges to a cookie sheet, and brush their tops with milk.
- Bake for 12 to 15 minutes.
  Serves 8

Mary Williams

SOUR-CREAM MAPLE-PECAN MUFFINS

This is an "adult" muffin, not too sweet, say the Carrs, who own the Old Colony Motel in East Sandwich. They say this recipe is requested by many of their regular patrons who have tasted them at their Continental breakfast.

Ingredients:

1 3/4 cups all purpose flour
2 tsp baking powder
1 tsp baking soda
1/2 tsp salt
1/2 cup unsalted butter at room temperature

3/4 cup maple syrup
1 cup sour cream
1 egg
1/2 cup chopped pecans

Steps:

- Grease or line muffin tins and preheat oven to 400°F.
- In a small bowl, stir and toss together flour, baking powder, baking soda and salt. Set aside.
- In a medium bowl, beat the butter until smooth, then slowly add the maple syrup beating constantly.
- Beat in the sour cream and egg. Stir in the pecans.
- Add the combined dry ingredients and stir just until blended.
- Spoon into prepared tins filling each cup about 2/3 full.
- Bake for 15-18 minutes. You can place a pecan half on top of each muffin before baking if you wish.
  Makes 14-16 regular muffins

Peter and Jamie Carr

CRANBERRY RECIPES

Picking cranberries by hand in carefully defined rows.

Cranberries do not grow on trees and bushes, but on low-lying vines that cover drained and level areas like a thick carpet. The trailing vines have many upright branches, and the fruit grows on these branches.

59

American Cranberry

Few North Americans are as partial to the cranberry as we Cape Codders. This humble little red berry—known as "ibimi" to Cape Cod's native Wampanoag tribe for over 10,000 years—is one of only three fruits native to the Cape. Upon their arrival, so legend has it, the Pilgrims found the tart fruit growing wild, and decided to call it a "crane-berry," because its blossom resembles a crane's neck and head.

The healthful qualities of the cranberry were not lost on those who colonized the area. As time progressed, New England sea captains began providing their crews with cranberries to prevent scurvy.

The first recorded cranberry cultivation here was in 1816 in Dennis on Cape Cod. Today, there are 47 square miles of bog land in North America devoted entirely to cranberry cultivation, and Massachusetts represents 30% of U.S. cranberry production. The Cape Cod Cranberry Growers Association estimates that bogs currently in production occupy 14,400 acres on the Cape and Islands, with an additional 48,000 acres of upland and wetland used as support lands.

So perhaps it is needless to say that Cape Cod cooks have more than a few great cranberry recipes. Some of those recipes were revealed at the annual Thornton W. Burgess Society's Cape Cod Cranberry Day in September 2002, when locals participated in a Cranberry Bake-off at Green Briar Jam Kitchen. All of the recipes submitted for this event are marked with an asterisk, and we've noted the winners for you, too.

> Did you know that cranberries are really good for you? They have loads of Vitamin C, as well as Vitamin A, iodine and many mineral salts. Studies at the University of Massachusetts at Dartmouth show that cranberries contain a variety of potent antioxidants that protect the heart, as well as unique compounds that may inhibit the growth of tumor cells responsible for certain forms of cancer. So get the bounce back in your life, and eat cranberries!

PUMPKIN-CRANBERRY SPICE BARS WITH CREAM-CHEESE FROSTING

Ingredients for Bars:

4 eggs
2 cups sugar
1 16-oz. can solid-pack pumpkin
1 cup vegetable oil
2 cups flour
2 tsp. baking powder
2 tsp. ground cinnamon
1 tsp. baking soda
1/2 tsp. salt
1/2 tsp. ginger
1/4 tsp. ground cloves
1/2 cup dried cranberries
Cream-cheese frosting (recipe follows)

Steps for Bars:
- Preheat the oven to 350°F.
- In a mixing bowl, beat eggs, sugar, pumpkin and oil until blended.
- Separately, combine flour, baking powder, cinnamon, baking soda, salt, ginger and cloves.
- Add the dry mixture to the pumpkin mixture, just to combine.
- Stir in the cranberries.
- Pour the batter into a greased 15x10-inch pan and bake for 25-30 minutes.
- Cool the pan completely on a wire rack.
- Frost, when cool, with cream-cheese frosting. Cut into bars.
  Makes 1 1/2 dozen bars

Ingredients for frosting:

1/4 cup margarine, softened
3 oz. cream cheese, at room temperature
1 tsp. vanilla
1 1/2 cups confectioner's sugar, sifted

Steps for frosting:
- Beat all ingredients together.

Bettina Dinsmore

Each holiday season, Americans consume 10.8 billion cranberries—which amounts to nearly two berries each for every man, woman, and child on earth!

PUMPKIN-CRANBERRY BREAD

Ingredients:

3 cups flour
1 Tbs. + 2 tsp. pumpkin-pie spice
2 tsp. baking soda
1 1/2 tsp. salt
3 cups granulated sugar
1 15-oz. can Libby's pumpkin-pie filling

4 large eggs
1 cup vegetable oil
1/2 cup orange juice or water
1 cup cranberries (fresh, frozen or sweetened dried)

Steps:
- Preheat the oven to 350°F.
- Grease and flour two 9x5-inch loaf pans or five 5x3-inch mini loaf pans.
- Combine the flour, pumpkin-pie spice, baking soda and salt in a large bowl.
- Separately, combine the sugar, pumpkin-pie filling, eggs, vegetable oil and orange juice in a large mixing bowl, and beat until just blended.
- Add the pumpkin mixture to the dry mixture, and stir together until moistened.
- Fold in the cranberries, and spoon the batter into pans.
- Bake for 60-65 minutes for the 9x5-inch pans or for 50-55 minutes for the mini 5x3-inch pans.
- Test for doneness with a wooden pick.
  Serves at least 10 or 12

Bettina Dinsmore

ELEANOR BATES' CRANBERRY TORTE(*)

Serve with whipped cream or ice cream.

Ingredients:

2 cups fresh cranberries
1/2 cup nuts, chopped
1 1/2 cup sugar
2 eggs

1/2 tsp. salt
1 cup flour
1/2 cup margarine or butter
1 tsp. almond extract

Steps:
- Preheat the oven to 325°F.
- Butter a 10-inch pie pan.
- Mix together the cranberries, nuts and 1/2 cup of the sugar, then spread into the pan.

- Mix the eggs with the remaining 1 cup sugar, salt and flour, and beat together well.
- Melt margarine and add it to the batter.
- Add the almond extract and mix well.
- Pour the batter over the cranberry mixture in the pie pan.
- Bake for 40 to 45 minutes.

Mary Williams

(*) *This was the First Place winner (Cake Category) in the Thornton W. Burgess Society Cranberry Bake-off 2002, held at Green Briar Jam Kitchen.*

CAPE COD CRANBERRY VELVET PIE

Ingredients:

One 8-oz pkg. cream cheese, softened
1 cup whipping cream
1/4 cup sugar
1/2 tsp. vanilla extract

One 16-oz can whole-berry cranberry sauce
One 6-oz. Keebler shortbread Ready Crust (chocolate is also great)

Steps:
- In a large mixing bowl, beat the cream cheese until fluffy.
- In a small mixing bowl, beat the whipping cream, sugar and vanilla until soft peaks form.
- Gradually add this mixture to the beaten cream cheese, beating the whole mixture until it is smooth and creamy.
- Set aside a few whole cranberries from the cranberry sauce to use as garnish, then fold the cranberry sauce into the cream-cheese mixture.
- Spoon into the pie crust and freeze the pie for four hours or until firm.
- Remove the pie from the freezer 15 minutes before serving, and garnish with the reserved berries.
Serves 8

Bettina Dinsmore and Chris Evans

Until the 1870s, cranberries were picked by hand. It was the custom for everyone to join in the harvest. Schools were closed for two weeks. Students and teachers would help with the work and join in the fun. Each age group had its own job.

FRESH-CRANBERRY SAUCE

This sauce is good warm or cold, and can go in any number of directions. Add a bit of fresh thyme and black pepper for a savory version. Or for a dessert sauce, add other fruits, such as pears, or walnuts for crunch. Experiment, and enjoy!

Ingredients:

2 Tbs. orange juice, freshly squeezed	1 1/2 cups sugar
2 tsp. cornstarch	1/2 tsp. cinnamon
2 cups fresh cranberries	1/4 tsp. nutmeg, freshly grated
1/2 cup water	2 tsp. orange zest

Steps:
- In a small bowl, mix together the orange juice and cornstarch to form a slurry, and set aside.
- In a saucepan add the cranberries, water, sugar, spices and orange zest, and bring to a boil. Simmer for about five minutes, or until the cranberries are tender, then return the mixture to a boil.
- Add the orange-juice-and-cornstarch slurry.
- Stir well while simmering for another three minutes or so.

Ann McDonnell

TRADITIONAL TEN-MINUTE CRANBERRY SAUCE

Ingredients:

1 1/2 to 2 cups sugar	4 cups cranberries
2 cups water	

Steps:
- Boil the sugar and water for five minutes.
- Add the cranberries, and boil without stirring until all skins are popped open (approximately five minutes). Remove the sauce from the stove when the popping stops.
- Allow the sauce to cool undisturbed.

Judi Lesiak

> **In the history of Massachusetts it is noted that, in 1667, the early colonists sent 10 barrels of "crane berries" as a gift to their sovereign, Charles II of England.**

CRANBERRY JEZEBEL SAUCE

Pour this sauce over cream cheese, and serve with crackers for a wonderful appetizer.

Ingredients:

1 cup water
1/2 cup sugar
1/2 cup brown sugar, firmly packed

One 12-oz. bag (1 1/2 cups) cranberries, fresh or frozen
3 Tbs. prepared horseradish
1 Tbs. Dijon mustard

Steps:

- Combine water, sugar and brown sugar in a medium saucepan. Stir well and bring to a boil over medium heat.
- Add the cranberries and return to a boil. Cook the sauce for 10 minutes, stirring occasionally.
- Spoon the sauce into a bowl, and let it cool to room temperature.
- Stir in the horseradish and mustard.
- Cover and chill.
  Yields 2 1/2 cups.

Judi Lesiak

CRANBERRY SALSA CHICKEN

Serve over rice or couscous.

Ingredients:

4 boneless skinless chicken-breast halves
1 Tbs. olive or canola oil
One 16-oz. jar chunky salsa
1 cup cranberries, dried

1/4 cup water
1 Tbs. honey
2 garlic cloves, minced
3/4 tsp. ground cinnamon
1/2 tsp. ground cumin

Steps:

- In a large skillet, saute the chicken breasts in oil until brown on both sides.
- In a small bowl, combine the remaining ingredients. Mix well and pour over the chicken.
- Lower the heat under the chicken, and cook over medium-low heat for 10-15 minutes, until the chicken is done.
  Serves 4

Judi Lesiak

CRANBERRY-GLAZED PORK ROAST

Ingredients:

1 tsp. salt
1/2 tsp. pepper
1 boneless rolled pork loin roast (3 lbs.)
1 cup jellied cranberry sauce
1/2 cup orange juice
1/4 cup packed brown sugar

Steps:
- Preheat the oven to 350°F.
- Combine the salt and pepper, and rub over the roast.
- Place the roast, fat side up, on a rack in a greased roasting pan and cook uncovered in the oven for 1 1/2 hours.
- Meanwhile, combine the cranberry sauce, orange juice and brown sugar in a saucepan. Cook over medium heat until the cranberry sauce melts.
- Brush 1/4 of the resulting cranberry glaze over the cooking roast.
- Thirty minutes later, brush another 1/4 of the glaze over the roast. Return the roast to the oven for 15 minutes, or until a meat thermometer inserted into it reads 160-170°F.
- Let the roast stand for 10 minutes before slicing.
- Warm the remaining glaze and serve it with the roast.
Serves 6 to 8

Pat Maguire

ROSEANN'S CRANBERRY NUT PIE

This pie is delicious! Serve warm with ice cream.

Ingredients:

2 cups cranberries, fresh
1/2 cup walnuts, chopped
1 cup sugar
1/4 cup butter, melted
2 eggs
1 cup flour
1/2 cup butter, softened

Steps:
- Preheat oven to 325°F.
- Put the whole, washed cranberries in the bottom of a deep 9-inch pie plate.
- Add the walnuts and 1/2 cup of the sugar, and pour the melted butter overtop.
- In a large bowl, beat the eggs with a hand mixer.
- Add the flour and the softened butter to the eggs, and mix thoroughly. Pour this mixture over the cranberries.
- Bake the pie for 50-60 minutes, until the top is medium brown.

Marsha Supranovicz

CHOCOLATE CRANBERRY MOUSSE PIE

Ingredients:

- 8 oz. white chocolate, chopped
- 2 cups heavy cream
- 8 oz. semi-sweet chocolate chips
- 1 prepared pie crust
- 1 tsp. grated orange zest
- 1 cup cranberry sauce

Steps:
- Microwave the white chocolate and 1/4 cup cream on high for 1 minute. Stir until smooth. Refrigerate for 30 minutes.
- Microwave the chocolate chips and 1/4 cup cream on high for 1 minute. Stir until smooth. Spread on the bottom of the pie crust and refrigerate for 30 minutes.
- Beat remaining 1/2 cup of cream until stiff. Fold 1 cup of the cooled white chocolate into the whipped cream. Add the orange zest to the mixture.
- Spoon one third of the white-chocolate/orange/cream mixture into the pie. Spoon half the cranberry sauce on top of it. Repeat.
- Pull a knife through the cranberry to swirl it and add the whipped cream mixture on top.
- Refrigerate for six hours.

Norma Coleman

CRAN-APPLE PIE

Top with ice cream, maple syrup or Cool Whip.

Ingredients:

- 2 or 3 large apples, peeled and sliced
- 3/4 cup fresh cranberries
- Cinnamon (enough for sprinkling)
- 1 Tbs. lemon juice
- 1 stick butter, melted
- 1 egg
- 1 cup flour
- 1 cup sugar

Steps:
- Preheat the oven to 350°F.
- Mix the apple slices and cranberries, and arrange them in a pie plate.
- Sprinkle the fruit with the cinnamon and lemon juice.
- Mix the remaining four ingredients together to form crumbs, and place the crumbs evenly over the fruit.
- Bake for one hour until crispy brown.

Nancy Hallaren

CRANBERRY-BLUEBERRY PIE

Ingredients:

2 cups fresh cranberries
2 cups blueberries
1 1/2 cup sugar
1/3 cup flour
1/8 tsp. salt
Pastry for a two-crust pie
2 Tbs. butter

Steps:

- Preheat the oven to 425°F.
- Put the cranberries through a food chopper. Combine them with the blueberries, sugar, flour and salt.
- Place the fruit mixture in a pastry-lined 9-inch pie plate. Dot the top of the fruit with butter.
- Place and adjust the top crust, fluting the edges to seal.
- Bake in hot oven for 45-50 minutes, or until the crust is golden brown.

Wynne Joyce

MY MOTHER'S CRANBERRY PIE

My mother made this pie for Thanksgiving and Christmas. We all looked forward to it-almost as much as the turkey and the presents!

Ingredients:

3 cups fresh cranberries
1 cup water
3/4 cup raisins
1 1/4 cup sugar
2 Tbs. cornstarch
Pastry for a two-crust pie
(8- or 9-inch)

Steps:

- Preheat the oven to 400°F.
- In a saucepan, combine the cranberries, water and raisins. Bring to a boil and reduce heat. Cover and simmer for 5 minutes.
- Mix sugar and cornstarch and stir into the cranberry mixture. Cook and stir until the mixture is thick and bubbly. Continue stirring for 2 more minutes, then remove from heat, cool slightly, and pour into pie shell.
- For top crust, cut the rolled dough into strips and make a lattice top, leaving spaces between the strips so that the pie filling shows through.
- Bake for 35 minutes, or until browned.

Louise Piazzi

CRANBERRY-RAISIN PIE

Serve with whipped cream, whipped topping or ice cream.

Ingredients:

2 cups cranberries
1 cup sugar
1 1/2 cup raisins
Pinch of salt
1/2 cup water
2 Tbs. flour
Pastry for a 9-inch pie with lattice top

Steps:
- Preheat oven to 450°F.
- Cook the first six ingredients until thick. Stir constantly.
- Pour the fruit mixture into the pie shell and top the pie with strips of pastry in a lattice style.
- Bake in the oven for 15 minutes, then reduce the heat to 350°F and bake for 15 minutes longer.
  Serves 6-8

Denise Ripley

CRANBERRY MUFFINS(*)

Ingredients:

2 cups flour
3 tsp. baking powder
1 cup sugar
1/2 tsp salt
3/4 cup orange juice
2 tsp. grated orange zest
1/3 cup melted butter (or vegetable oil)
1 egg
1 cup cranberries, fresh, chopped
1/2 cup walnuts, chopped
Sugar for sprinkling

Steps:
- Preheat oven to 400°F.
- Sift dry ingredients together in a large mixing bowl
- Combine the orange juice, orange zest, butter or oil and egg, then mix these into the dry ingredients just until moistened.
- Stir in the cranberries and nuts.
- Grease one dozen muffin tins or line them with paper, and spoon the batter in.
- Bake for 20 to 25 minutes.
- Sprinkle sugar on the tops of the muffins.
  Makes one dozen

Judy Koenig

* This was the Grand Prize Winning recipe for the Thornton W. Burgess Society Cranberry Bake-off 2002, held at Green Briar Jam Kitchen.

CRANBERRY-ORANGE MINI SCONES

Ingredients:

1/2 cup cranberries, dried
1 cup water
1 1/2 cups all-purpose flour
1/2 tsp. salt
2 Tbs. sugar

1 Tbs. baking powder
6 Tbs. unsalted butter, cold
1 Tbs. orange zest
3/4 cup heavy cream

Steps:
- Place the cranberries in a saucepan with the water. Bring to a boil and remove from the heat. Allow the cranberries to soak in the hot water until they soften, about 10 minutes. Drain and reserve the soaked cranberries.
- Preheat the oven to 375°F.
- Mix the flour, salt, sugar and baking powder together in a medium-size bowl.
- Cut the butter into the flour mixture until it resembles coarse cornmeal.
- Mix the orange zest and the soaked cranberries into the pastry.
- Add the cream, and continue to mix lightly until the dough forms a ball (use more cream if needed).
- Place the dough on a lightly floured board and roll it out to a half-inch thickness.
- Using a round cookie cutter (about 1 1/2 inches in diameter), press out circles. You could also cut the dough into 1 1/2-inch squares, if you prefer.
- Place the scones on an ungreased cookie sheet about an inch apart.
- Bake the scones for 15 minutes, or until golden brown.
  Serves 18

Mary Williams

CRANBERRY COFFEE CAKE(*)

Ingredients:

1 cup butter
1/4 cup sugar
2 eggs
1 tsp. vanilla
1 cup sour cream
2 cups flour
1/2 tsp. baking soda
1 1/2 tsp. baking powder
2/3 lg. can whole-berry cranberry sauce
1 cup nuts, chopped
1 tsp. cinnamon

Ingredients for an orange glaze:

1 cup confectioners' sugar
2 Tbs. orange juice

Steps:

- Preheat the oven to 350°F.
- In a large bowl, cream together the butter and sugar.
- Add the eggs, vanilla and sour cream, and mix well.
- In another bowl, mix together the flour, baking soda and baking powder. Blend the wet and dry ingredients, but don't overbeat.
- Spoon half the batter into a greased and floured Bundt pan or 8-inch tube pan.
- In a bowl, mix together the cranberry sauce, cinnamon and nuts. Spread this cranberry mixture over the batter in the pan.
- Spoon the remaining batter over the cranberry mixture.
- Bake for 55 minutes.
- While the cake is baking, make the glaze.
- Cool the cake before glazing.

Lorraine Gabellini

A similar recipe was also submitted by Jennie Zantuhos, Bettina Dinsmore, Marie O'Connor and Pat Maguire, all of whom called for an almond glaze (1 tsp. almond extract and 2 Tbs. warm water instead of the orange juice). Claire Burns also submitted a similar recipe, but without the glaze.

CRANBERRY CRUMB CAKE

Serve with whipped topping or ice cream. This cake can be prepared early in the day if that's more convenient for you. Just heat it slightly in the oven before serving.

Ingredients:

1 cup all-purpose flour
1/2 cup + 1/3 cup sugar
2 tsp. baking powder
1/2 tsp. salt
1 egg, lightly beaten
1/2 cup milk

1 Tbs. orange or cranberry juice
1 Tbs. canola oil
1/4 tsp. almond extract
2 cups cranberries, fresh or frozen, chopped
1/2 cup nuts, chopped

Ingredients for crumb topping:

1/3 cup all-purpose flour
1/4 cup sugar
3 Tbs. cold margarine/butter

Steps:

- Preheat oven to 375°F.
- In a bowl, combine the flour, the 1/2 cup sugar, baking powder and salt.
- Separately, combine the egg, milk, juice, oil and almond extract. Stir the wet mixture into the dry ingredients.
- Spoon the resulting batter into an 8-inch-square pan coated with nonstick cooking spray.
- Combine the cranberries, the remaining 1/3 cup sugar and the nuts, and spread this over the batter.
- For the crumb topping, combine the flour and sugar. Cut in the butter or margarine until the mixture appears crumbly. Sprinkle on top of cake.
- Bake for 35-45 minutes, or until the edges of the cake begin to pull away from the sides of the pan.
Serves 6-9

Judi Lesiak

How can you tell a good cranberry from a bad one? Only the good ones will bounce.

Freezing whole cranberries is a good idea because it can be hard to find them in many areas after the holidays. Fortunately, whole fresh cranberries are easily frozen for future use. To prepare berries for freezing, remove the stems, but do not wash. Pour the berries into a plastic freezer container or freezer bag, and place them in the freezer. When you're ready to cook with them, you can either use the cranberries frozen or defrosted. Cranberries are easier to chop if frozen. Just remember to wash them first!

PISTACHIO AND CRANBERRY BISCOTTI

Ingredients:

2 1/4 cups unsifted all-purpose flour
1 cup sugar
1/2 tsp. baking powder
1/2 tsp. salt
6 Tbs. cold butter, cut into small pieces
2 large eggs
1 tsp. vanilla extract
1 cup pistachios, shelled and unsalted (or sliced almonds)
2 Tbs. cranberries, dried

Steps:
- In a large bowl, combine flour, sugar, baking powder and salt.
- With a pastry blender or two knives, cut the butter into the flour mixture until it resembles coarse crumbs.
- Mix the eggs in, one at a time, until they are well blended and a stiff dough begins to form.
- Add the vanilla extract.
- Stir in the pistachios and dried cranberries, being careful not to overmix.
- On a greased baking sheet, divide the dough in half. Shape each half into a 12x2-inch log. Cover the dough logs with plastic wrap and refrigerate them for at least 30 minutes.
- Preheat the oven to 375°F.
- Remove the plastic wrap from the logs and bake them for 20 to 25 minutes, or until the edges start to brown. Cool the logs on a baking sheet for 10 minutes.
- Reduce the oven temperature to 325°F.
- Transfer the logs to a cutting board and cut them crosswise, diagonally, into 1/2-inch-thick slices. On the same baking sheet, place the slices, cut sides down, in a single layer.
- Bake the slices for 20 to 25 minutes, turning once, until they are golden brown on both sides.
- Cool completely on a wire rack.
  Makes 40 biscotti

Mary Williams

CRANBERRY-RHUBARB BREAD(*)

Ingredients:

1 1/2 cups packed brown sugar
2/3 cup canola oil
3 eggs
1 tsp. vanilla
2 1/2 cups flour
1 tsp. baking soda
1 tsp. salt
1 cup buttermilk
2 cups rhubarb, finely diced
1 cup cranberries, dried or 1 1/2 cups cranberries, fresh and finely chopped
1 cup walnuts, chopped

Steps:
- Preheat the oven to 325°F.
- In a large bowl, cream together the brown sugar, oil, eggs and vanilla. Mix well.
- In a medium bowl, combine the flour, baking soda and salt. Add this dry mixture to the wet ingredients, alternating with the buttermilk. Mix until all is combined (do not overmix).
- Fold in the rhubarb, cranberries and walnuts.
- Pour the batter evenly into two greased loaf pans.
- Sprinkle sugar evenly over top of the batter and lightly spray the top with cooking spray.
- Bake for 60 minutes.
  Makes two loaves

Sherry C. Rougeau

* This recipe won First Place (Bread Category) in the Thornton W. Burgess Society Cranberry Bake-off 2002, held at Green Briar Jam Kitchen.

CAPE-COD CHEWS

Ingredients:

14 graham crackers, crushed
1 can condensed milk
One 12-oz. pkg. Nestle white chocolate or chocolate morsels
1 cup cranberries, sweetened dried

Steps:
- Preheat oven to 350°F.
- To the crushed graham crackers, add the other ingredients and mix well.
- Place the mixture in a well-greased, 9x13-inch pan and bake for 20 minutes.
- When cooled, cut the chews into squares. They may be difficult to cut, so shape into squares if necessary. Cape Cod Chews also freeze well.
  Makes 2 dozen

Mary Cosgrove

CRANBERRY-RASPBERRY COMPOTE

This recipe can be prepared two days ahead. Keep refrigerated.

Ingredients:

One 12-oz. pkg. frozen, unsweetened raspberries, thawed
1 cup fresh cranberries
3/4 cup golden brown sugar, packed
1 Tbs. fresh lemon juice
2 tsp. grated lemon peel
1/2 tsp ground cinnamon
1/4 tsp ground nutmeg
1 Tbs. vanilla extract

Steps:
- Combine all ingredients except vanilla in a heavy medium saucepan, and simmer over medium heat until the cranberries burst and the mixture thickens, stirring occasionally (about 10 minutes).
- Remove from heat and cool slightly.
- Stir in the vanilla, and cool to room temperature.
- Cover and refrigerate until cold, at least six hours.
  Makes two cups

Wynne Joyce

COCONUT-CRANBERRY CHEWS

Ingredients:

1 1/2 cups butter
2 cups sugar
1 Tbs. grated orange peel
2 tsp. vanilla
3 1/4 cups all-purpose flour
1 tsp. baking powder
1/4 tsp. salt
1 1/2 cups cranberries, dried
1 1/2 cups dried coconut, sweetened flaked

Steps:
- Preheat oven to 350°F.
- In a large bowl, using a mixer at medium speed, beat the butter, sugar, orange peel and vanilla until smooth.
- Separately, in a medium bowl, mix the flour, baking powder, and salt.
- Add the butter mixture to the dry mixture and stir. Beat on low until a dough comes together.
- Mix in the cranberries and coconut.
- Shape the dough into one-inch balls and place them two inches apart on a buttered 12x15-inch baking sheet.
- Bake until cookie edges begin to brown (eight to 11 minutes).
- Cool for five minutes before removing to a cooling rack.
  Makes 6 dozen

Helmi Viliesis

CRANBERRY-SWIRL CHEESECAKE

Bright ribbons of cranberry puree swirled through a creamy, white cheesecake create a pretty contrast. The cake can be made two days ahead, if kept refrigerated.

Ingredients For Cranberry Puree:

Nonstick vegetable-oil spray
2 3/4 cups butter-biscuit cookies or butter cookies
2 Tbs. sugar
1 tsp. ground cinnamon
1/2 cup (1 stick) unsalted butter, melted

Four 8-oz. pkgs. cream cheese, room temperature
1 cup sugar
4 large eggs
1 cup sour cream
1/2 cup whipping cream
1 Tbs. vanilla extract

Steps for Cranberry Puree:
- Combine all ingredients except the vanilla in a heavy, large saucepan. Cook over medium heat until the mixture thickens, stirring occasionally, about five minutes.
- Cool slightly and transfer to a food processor.
- Add the vanilla, and puree until smooth.
- Strain the puree into a medium bowl.
- Cover with plastic and refrigerate for at least six hours.

Ingredients for Cheesecake:

2 cups cranberries, fresh (or previously frozen and thawed)
2/3 cups sugar
2/3 cups fresh orange juice

2 Tbs. grated orange peel
1/2 tsp. ground cinnamon
1/4 tsp. ground nutmeg
4 tsp. vanilla extract

Steps:
- Spray a 10-inch-diameter springform pan with 2 3/4-inch-high sides with nonstick spray.
- Wrap the outside of the pan with two layers of heavy-duty aluminum foil.
- Finely grind the cookies, sugar and cinnamon in a food processor.
- Add the melted butter and continue to process until moist clumps form.
- Press the resulting crumb mixture onto the bottom and up the sides of the prepared springform pan. Chill this crust while preparing the filling.
- Position a rack in the center of the oven, and preheat to 350°F.
- Using an electric mixer, beat the cream cheese in large bowl until it is fluffy.
- Into the cream cheese, beat the sugar and eggs, one at a time.
- Mix in the sour cream, whipping cream and vanilla.
- Transfer one third of the cheesecake filling to the chilled, prepared crust.

▶

- Remove the pre-made Cranberry Puree from the refrigerator and dollop one third of it on top of the filling.
- Repeat this layering of filling and puree two more times.
- When finished, using a knife, swirl the puree through the filling, creating a marbled design.
- Place the springform pan inside a large roasting pan, and pour enough boiling water into the roasting pan to come halfway up the sides of the springform pan.
- Place the roasting pan containing the cheesecake pan in the oven until the cheesecake puffs around the edges (about 1 hour and 15 minutes).
- Turn off the oven and let the cake stand in the oven for another hour, leaving the door ajar.
- Transfer the cake to a rack. Run a knife around the sides of the pan to loosen.
- Cool completely!
- Remove the foil from the sides of the pan.
- Cover the cake and chill it overnight.
- Remove the pan sides and serve the cheesecake with Cranberry-Raspberry Compote (recipe on p. 75).
Serves 12

Wynne Joyce

CRANBERRY SQUARES*

Ingredients:

1/2 cup butter	1 1/2 cups flour, sifted
1 cup sugar	1 tsp. baking powder
1/2 cup brown sugar, packed	1/2 tsp. salt
2 eggs	1 cup cranberries, chopped
1 tsp. vanilla	1/2 cup nuts, chopped (optional)

Steps:
- Preheat the oven to 350°F.
- Cream the butter and sugars together.
- Add the eggs, one at a time and beat until fluffy.
- Stir in the vanilla.
- Blend in each of the dry ingredients.
- Stir in the cranberries and nuts (if desired).
- Spread the dough in a greased 9x13-inch pan.
- Bake for 25-30 minutes.
- Cool and cut into bars.

Kathleen Fulton

ORANGE-CRANBERRY-GINGER OAT BARS

Ingredients:

12 oz. whole cranberries
1 Tbs. ginger, grated fresh
3/4 cups water
1 tsp. grated orange zest
3/4 cups sugar
1 3/4 cups flour
1 tsp. baking powder

2 tsp. ground ginger
1/2 tsp. salt
1 cup (2 sticks) butter
1 cup brown sugar, packed
2 lg. eggs
1 1/2 cups old-fashioned oatmeal

Steps:
- In a medium-sized, non-aluminum saucepan, heat the first five ingredients until the berries "pop" (about 10 minutes).
- Remove the saucepan from the heat, and let it cool and thicken. (This may be done up to a day ahead.) This is your filling.
- Preheat the oven to 350°F.
- Lightly butter a 13x9-inch baking pan.
- In a large bowl, sift together the next four ingredients, and then set aside.
- Beat the butter and brown sugar together until light and fluffy.
- Add the eggs, one at a time, beating well after each addition.
- Beat the dry mixture and the oatmeal into the creamed mixture, just until all is blended into a dough.
- Reserve 1 1/2 cups of this dough to use as a topping. Then spread the remaining dough in an even layer in the prepared baking pan.
- Spoon the filling over the dough.
- Using floured fingertips, sprinkle small clumps of the reserved dough over the top.
- Bake for 35-40 minutes.
- Cool and cut into bars.
  Serves 24

Denise Ripley

CRANBERRY TURTLE BARS*

Ingredients for the base:

2 cups flour
1/2 cup light brown sugar, packed
1/2 tsp. salt

1/4 cup (1/2 a stick) unsalted butter, cold

▶

Ingredients for the topping:

1 cup unsalted butter
1/4 cup light corn syrup
1 2/3 cups sugar
1/2 tsp. salt

1 1/2 cups fresh cranberries
1 tsp. vanilla
3 cups pecans, toasted and chopped

Ingredients for decoration:
3 oz. bittersweet chocolate, finely chopped

Steps:
- Preheat the oven to 350°F.
- Line a 15x10-inch baking pan with foil, leaving an overhang. Butter the four edges, but not the bottom.
- Blend the flour, brown sugar and salt in a food processor. Add the butter, and pulse until it is reduced to small lumps.
- Sprinkle the resulting crumbs into the prepared baking pan, then press down evenly. This will be your base.
- Bake for 15-17 minutes, then cool.
- Next, begin the topping. Melt the butter in a large saucepan, and stir in the sugar, corn syrup and salt. Boil over moderately high heat, stirring occasionally until the temperature reaches 245°F on a candy thermometer (about eight minutes). You will have a caramel mixture.
- Stir in the cranberries, and boil until the caramel returns to 245°F. Remove it from the heat.
- Stir in the vanilla. Stir in the pecans until they are well coated.
- Working quickly, spread the caramel topping over the base. Cool completely.
- Lift the bars in foil from the pan and transfer to a cutting board. Cut into six crosswise strips, then six lengthwise strips to form 36 bars.
- Melt the chocolate on top of a warm double boiler, stirring until smooth.
- Drizzle warm chocolate over the bars, and let stand at room temperature for at least one hour.
Makes 36 bars

Dorothy Robertson

* *This recipe won First Place (Bars Category) in the Thornton W. Burgess Society Cranberry Bake-off 2002, held at Green Briar Jam Kitchen.*

OATMEAL-CRANBERRY-PECAN COOKIES*

Ingredients:

2 1/4 cups flour	2/3 cup brown sugar
1 cup oats	2 tsp. vanilla
1 tsp. baking soda	2 eggs
1/2 tsp. salt	1 cup Craisins (dried cranberries)
1 cup butter	1 cup white-chocolate chips
2/3 cup sugar	1 cup pecans, chopped

Steps:
- Preheat the oven to 350°F.
- Line baking sheets with parchment paper.
- Combine the flour, oats, baking soda, and salt. Set this dry mixture aside.
- With a mixer on low speed, cream the butter, sugar, brown sugar, and vanilla until light. Add the eggs one by one.
- With the mixer still set on low, beat in the dry mixture until all is well blended.
- Remove the bowl from the mixing stand, and stir in the Craisins, white-chocolate chips and pecans.
- Drop this batter by the heaping spoonful onto baking sheets, placing each cookie two inches apart.
- Bake for eight to 10 minutes.
- Let the cookies sit for a minute before transferring them to a cooling rack. Makes 36 cookies

Marie Grasso

DESSERTS - CAKES & PIES

This large brick building was originally the Company Store built for the families of the Boston and Sandwich Glass Company in early 1800. When the Boston and Sandwich Glass Company brought about 60 city families to work and live in the remote Sandwich village, they soon found that the stores and amenities available to them in Cambridge were not available here. The B & S immediately built this building and stocked it as a general store. Later it became The Corner Grocer and a source for home made pies and cakes. It was located at the corner of State Street and Harbor Street in Sandwich village.

Photo courtesy Sandwich Town Archives

MARK H. F. ELLIS
The CORNER GROCER

DEALER IN
Groceries, Provisions, Fruits and Vegetables

Ice Cream in season.   A choice line of Home Made Pies and Cake.

TELEPHONE CONNECTION   **State, cor. Dock St., Sandwich, Mass.**

81

*"With Weights and Measures Just and True
Oven of Even Heat.
Well Buttered Tins and Quiet Nerves,
Success Will be Complete."*

GOOD OLD APPLE PIE

From east to west,
From north to south,
There's nothing better
For your mouth
Than good old apple pie!

You can eat it
Hot or cold,
When you're young
And when you're old.
Eat it morning,
Night or noon
With your fingers,
Fork or spoon.
Eat it plain
Or a la mode,
In your abode
Or on the road!
Just grab a slice
And go to town,
Use some milk
To wash it down.
Once you start
It's hard to stop,
You'll want to eat it
Till you pop!
If you don't like it
You really must
Be flakier
Than any crust,
'cause any time
or any place
with anything,
in any case,
the greatest thing
to feed your face
is good old apple pie!

PUMPKIN CHEESECAKE

If you like, garnish this delicious cheesecake with whipped cream and crushed toffee candy.

Ingredients for the crust:

3/4 cup molasses cookies, crushed
1/3 cup pecans, finely chopped
1/4 cup dark brown sugar, firmly packed
1/4 cup granulated sugar
1/2 stick unsalted butter, melted and cooled

Ingredients for the filling:

1 cup canned pumpkin puree
3 lg. eggs, room temperature
1 1/2 tsp. ground cinnamon
1/2 tsp. ground ginger
1/2 tsp. nutmeg, freshly grated
1/2 tsp. salt
1 cup + 2 Tbs. granulated sugar
1 1/2 lb. cream cheese, softened
2 Tbs. heavy cream
1 Tbs. cornstarch
1 tsp. vanilla

Steps:

- To make the crust, combine the crumbs, pecans, brown sugar, granulated sugar, and butter in a bowl.
- Press the mixture into the bottom of a 10-inch springform pan, and freeze for 15 minutes.
- Preheat oven to 425°F.
- To make the filling, whisk together in a bowl the pumpkin, the eggs, the cinnamon, the nutmeg, the ginger, the salt, and 3/4 cup of the granulated sugar. Set aside.
- In another bowl, with the electric mixer, cream together the cream cheese and the remaining 6 tablespoons granulated sugar.
- Beat in the cream, the cornstarch, and the vanilla.
- Fold the pumpkin mixture into the cream-cheese mixture.
- Pour the filling into the crust, and bake the cheesecake in the middle of the oven for 25 minutes. Turn the oven down to 225°F. for another hour. (DO NOT OPEN THE OVEN DOOR!)
- When finished, let the cheesecake cool in the pan on a rack. Chill it, covered loosely, overnight.
- When ready to serve, run a knife around the inside edge and remove the side of the pan.
Serves 8-10

Tricia Daley

GRANDMA LEIGHTON'S BLUEBERRY CAKE

Ingredients:

1/2 cup butter or margarine
2 cups sugar
2 egg yolks
3 cups flour
2 tsp. baking powder
1 cup milk
2 egg whites, beaten
2 cups blueberries

Steps:
- Cream the butter with the sugar.
- Add the egg yolks.
- Sift together the flour and baking powder.
- Add the dry mixture alternately to the butter mixture with the milk.
- Fold in beaten egg whites. Fold in blueberries.
- Bake in a 9x13x2-inch greased pan at 375° for 35-40 minutes. Sprinkle with granulated sugar.
Serves 8-10

Barbara Lucas

CREAM-CHEESE CUPCAKES

Serve topped with frozen or fresh sweetened strawberries or your favorite pie filling!

Ingredients:

Two 8-oz. pkgs. cream cheese, softened
3/4 cup sugar
2 eggs
1 tsp. vanilla
16 vanilla wafers

Steps:
- Preheat the oven to 275°F.
- Beat the cream cheese with the electric mixer until light and fluffy.
- Add the sugar, eggs and vanilla, and beat thoroughly.
- Place one vanilla wafer in the bottom of a paper-lined muffin pan.
- Fill three-quarters full with batter.
- Bake for 30 minutes.

Barb Albers

BLACK-BOTTOM CUPCAKES

Ingredients for Cream-Cheese Mixture:

8 oz. cream cheese
1/3 cup sugar
1 egg
One 6-oz. pkg. chocolate chips

Ingredients for Chocolate Mixture:

1-1/2 cups flour
1 cup sugar
1/4 cup cocoa
1 tsp. baking soda
1/2 tsp. salt
1 cup water
1/3 cup vegetable oil
1 tsp. vanilla
1 Tbsp. vinegar

Ingredients for Topping:

1/2 cup sugar
Nuts, chopped

Steps:

- Begin with the cream-cheese mixture, combining the softened cream cheese, sugar and egg.
- Beat and stir in the chocolate chips. Set aside.
- Preheat the oven to 350°F.
- Next, prepare the chocolate mixture by mixing the dry ingredients together.
- Add the wet ingredients to the dry, and mix well.
- Fill greased or paper-lined muffin tins with 1/3 cup of the chocolate mixture.
- Drop one heaping teaspoon of the cream-cheese mixture on top.
- Sprinkle with a topping of sugar and chopped nuts, mixed together.
- Bake for 30 minutes.
  Makes 24 cupcakes

Helmi Viliesis

> "Aurelia Buck can take good flour and sugar, sweet butter and fresh eggs, and in ten strokes of her hand she can make 'em into something the very hogs'll turn away from."
>
> -Kate Douglas Wiggin, author, *The Village Watch-Tower*, 1895.
> Mrs. Wiggins was best known for her book *Rebecca of Sunnybrook Farm*.

FRESH-GINGER CAKE

Serve with ice cream or whipped cream.

Ingredients:

4 oz. fresh ginger, peeled, sliced and grated
2 1/2 cups flour
1 tsp. cinnamon
1/2 tsp. cloves
1/2 tsp. fresh-ground black pepper
1 cup mild molasses
1 cup sugar
1 cup vegetable oil
2 tsp. baking soda
1 cup boiling water
2 large eggs

Steps:

- Preheat oven to 350°F.
- Peel, slice and grate the ginger, to make 1/2 a cup; set aside.
- Whisk the flour and spices together.
- Beat the molasses, sugar and oil together.
- Dissolve the baking soda in boiling water and add it to the molasses mixture.
- Stir in the ginger.
- Gradually add the dry ingredients, then add the eggs and mix well.
- Pour the batter into a 9-inch springform pan that has a circle of parchment paper in the bottom.
- Bake for 1 hour.
- Cool for at least 30 minutes, then run a knife around the edge to loosen the cake.
- Remove cake from the pan, and peel off the parchment.

SWEET-POTATO POUND CAKE WITH ORANGE GLAZE

Ingredients for Pound Cake:

2 lbs. sweet potatoes, peeled and chunked
3 cups flour
1/4 tsp. salt
2 tsp. baking powder
1 tsp. baking soda
1/2 tsp. nutmeg
1 tsp. cinnamon
1 cup butter, at room temperature
2 cups sugar
4 large eggs
1 tsp. vanilla
1/2 cup pecans, chopped
1/2 cup unsweetened coconut, finely chopped

Steps:
- Preheat the oven to 325°F.
- Place the potatoes in a saucepan, add water to cover, and simmer until tender. Drain well and puree.
- Combine the flour, salt, baking powder and baking soda, nutmeg and cinnamon in a bowl and whisk together.
- Cream together the butter and sugar.
- Add the sweet potato mixture, and beat until fluffy.
- Add the eggs, one at a time, beating well after each egg.
- Stir in the vanilla.
- Add the flour mixture to make a stiff batter.
- Fold in the pecans and coconut, and spoon the batter into a greased Bundt pan.
- Bake for 90 minutes.
- Let cake stand on a rack, in the pan, for 10 minutes, then invert onto a serving plate.
- If you like, while cake is still warm, pour orange glaze on top (recipe follows).
- Let cake cool before slicing.
Serves 12-16

Ingredients for Orange Glaze:

2 cups confectioners' sugar
1 1/2 Tbs. orange zest, finely chopped
1 Tbs. lemon zest, finely chopped
1/4 cup fresh lemon juice

Steps for Orange Glaze:
- Combine all ingredients, adding more lemon or orange juice to dissolve all the sugar.
- Pour glaze on top of warm cake, spooning up any that pools around the edges.

"To invite a person into your home is to take charge of his happiness for as long as he is under your roof."

-Anthelme Brillat-Savarin, French author and gourmet

ONE-STEP YOGURT POUND CAKE WITH LEMON GLAZE

Ingredients:

2 1/4 cups flour
2 cups sugar
1/2 tsp. salt
1/2 tsp. baking soda
1 tsp. grated lemon rind
3 eggs
1 tsp. vanilla

1 cup butter, softened
One 8-oz. carton pineapple or orange yogurt (1 cup sour cream can be substituted)
1 cup confectioners' sugar, sifted
2 Tbs. lemon juice

Steps:
- Preheat the oven to 325°F.
- Blend all ingredients in a large mixing bowl, mixing at low speed until well blended. Beat at medium speed for 3 minutes.
- Pour batter into a 10-inch well-greased tube or Bundt pan.
- Bake for about 60-70 minutes.
- Cool the cake in the pan for 15 minutes upright.
- Combine the confectioners' sugar and lemon juice, and drizzle the resulting glaze onto the cooled cake.
Serves 8-12

Lorraine Gabellini

DUTCH APPLE CAKE

Serve warm, with ice cream or whipped cream.

Ingredients:

3 cups semisweet apple, peeled, cored and thinly sliced
2 Tbs. sugar
2 tsp. fresh lemon juice
1 tsp. cinnamon
1/2 tsp. nutmeg
1 cup flour

2 Tbs. sugar
1 1/2 tsp. baking powder
1/2 tsp. salt
4 Tbs. cold butter
1/2 cup half and half
1 egg
3 Tbs. butter, melted

Steps:
- Preheat oven to 400°F.
- Toss the apples with the next four ingredients and set aside.
- In a food processor, pulse the flour, sugar, powder and salt
- Cut the butter into eight pieces and add to processor.
- Pulse until the mixture resembles coarse cornmeal

> *"There's nothing better than a good friend, except a good friend with chocolate."*
>
> –Linda Grayson, author, *The Pickwick Papers*

- Beat the egg and cream together, and, with the machine running, add the liquid just until the batter comes together.
- Scrape into a greased 8-inch-square pan, spreading to the edges.
- Arrange the apple slices on top, drizzle with melted butter, and bake for 35-40 minutes. Cut into squares to serve.

RED-BEET CHOCOLATE CAKE

This cake's flavor improves overnight, so be sure to make it ahead of time.

Ingredients:

Two 1-oz. squares unsweetened chocolate	3 lg. eggs
	1 cup vegetable oil
1 3/4 cups flour, unbleached, sifted	1 1/2 cups beets, pureed
1 1/2 tsp. baking soda	1 tsp. vanilla extract
1/2 tsp. salt	1 cup confectioners' sugar, sifted
1 1/2 cups sugar	

Steps:

- Melt and cool the two 1 oz. squares of baking chocolate.
- Preheat the oven to 350°F.
- Sift together flour, baking soda and salt; set aside.
- Combine sugar, eggs and oil in a mixing bowl.
- Beat with an electric mixer set at medium speed for two minutes.
- Beat together the beets, cooled chocolate and vanilla.
- Gradually add the dry ingredients, beating well after each addition.
- Pour into a greased 13x9x2-inch baking pan and bake for 25 minutes or until the cake tests done.
- Cool the cake in the pan on a rack.
- Cover and let stand overnight to improve the flavor.
- Sprinkle with confectioners' sugar, and serve.

REGGIE'S KNOBBY APPLE CAKE

Ingredients:

1 cup sugar
6 Tbs. margarine
1 tsp. vanilla
1 egg
1 1/2 cups flour
3/4 tsp. each: baking soda, baking powder, cinnamon, nutmeg
1/3 cup raisins that have been covered with water and microwaved for two minutes
1/4 cup walnuts
3 med. apples, peeled and cubed

Steps:
- Preheat the oven to 350°F.
- Cream together the sugar and margarine.
- Add the vanilla and egg.
- Add the dry ingredients and mix well.
- Add the raisins and water, walnuts and chopped apples.
- Bake for 45 minutes.

Mary Williams

MOCHA CAKE WITH MOCHA FROSTING

Ingredients:

1 1/4 cups flour
1 cup brown sugar, packed
1/4 cup cornstarch
3 Tbs. cocoa
1 tsp. baking soda
1 tsp. instant coffee powder
1/2 tsp. salt
1/3 cup oil
1 Tbs. vinegar
1/2 tsp. vanilla
1 cup water

Steps:
- Preheat the oven to 350°F.
- In an 8- or 9-inch-square pan with a fork, mix the flour, brown sugar, cornstarch, cocoa, baking soda, instant coffee and salt.
- Add the oil, vinegar, vanilla and water.
- Mix briskly with a fork until thoroughly blended.
- Bake for 40 minutes or until toothpick inserted in the center comes out clean and the cake pulls away from the sides of the pan.
- Cool the cake in the pan on a rack.
- Frost with Mocha Frosting (recipe follows).
  Serves 9

Mocha Frosting Ingredients:

3 Tbs. butter or margarine, softened
1 1/2 cups confectioner's sugar
2 Tbs. cocoa
1/2 tsp. instant coffee powder
1/2 tsp. vanilla
1 Tbs. milk

Steps:
- With a wooden spoon, mix the butter, sugar, cocoa and instant coffee.
- Add the vanilla and milk.
- Beat until smooth.

Ellen Arrigo

CHOCOLATE BUTTER ICING

Ingredients:

1/4 cup semi-sweet chocolate morsels
1 Tbs. rum or strong coffee
2 Tbs. unsalted butter

Steps:
- Melt the chocolate with the rum or coffee over hot water.
- When perfectly smooth, remove from the water and beat the butter in bit by bit.
- Beat the icing over cold water until it is of spreading consistency.

Liz Desaulniers

FLUFFY "POOR MAN'S FROSTING"

For a large cake, you can double this recipe.

Ingredients:

2 Tbs. flour
1/2 cup milk
1/2 cup sugar
1/2 tsp. vanilla
1/2 cup margarine, softened

Steps:
- Cook the flour and milk until thick.
- When cool, add the sugar, vanilla and margarine.
- Beat all with an electric mixer until fluffy.

REINE DE SABA (QUEEN OF SHEBA) CAKE WITH CHOCOLATE BUTTER ICING

This melt-in-your-mouth chocolate-, rum- and-almond cake is baked so that its center remains slightly underdone. If overcooked, the cake loses its special creamy quality. Like most French cakes, this one is only an inch and a half high, which makes it easy to serve.

Ingredients:

2/3 cup semi-sweet chocolate morsels
2 Tbs. rum or strong coffee
1/4 lb. softened butter
2/3 cup granulated sugar
3 eggs, separated
Pinch of salt

1 Tbs. granulated sugar
Dash of cream of tartar
3/4 cup sifted cake flour
1/3 cup almonds, pulverized in an electric blender
1/4 tsp. almond extract

Steps:
- Butter and flour an 8x1 1/2-inch round metal cake pan.
- Preheat the oven to 350°F.
- In a small saucepan set in hot water, stir the chocolate and rum or coffee until the chocolate is melted and smooth. Set aside.
- Cream the butter and sugar together until pale yellow and fluffy.
- Beat in the egg yolks.
- In a separate bowl, beat the egg whites and salt until soft peaks form. Sprinkle in the sugar and cream of tartar and beat again.
- Beat the melted chocolate into the egg-yolk mixture,
- With a rubber spatula, stir in the flour, almonds, and almond extract.
- Stir in one quarter of the egg whites, then delicately fold in the rest.
- Turn the whole mixture into the prepared cake pan, and bake in the middle level of the oven.
- The cake will be done when it has puffed, and when 2 1/2 to 3 inches of the cake around the circumference is set, so that a toothpick plunged into that area comes out clean (about 25 minutes).
- The center should move slightly if the pan is shaken, and a toothpick inserted in the center should come out oily.
- Allow the cake to cool in the pan for 10 minutes.
- Run a knife around the edge of the pan and reverse the cake onto a rack.
- Allow the cake to cool for an hour or two before icing with Chocolate Butter Icing (see page 91).
- Decorate the iced cake with blanched almonds.
Serves 8

Liz Desaulniers

COCOA FUDGE FROSTING

Ingredients:

2 1/2 cups sifted powdered sugar
1/2 tsp. vanilla
1/4 cup cocoa
3 Tbs. milk
1/4 cup butter, melted

Steps:
- Combine all ingredients in a small mixing bowl, and beat until smooth and of a spreading consistency.
  Yields 1 1/2 cups

SOUR-CREAM COFFEE CAKE

Ingredients:

2 cups flour
1 tsp. baking powder
1/2 tsp. baking soda
1/2 tsp. salt
1 cup butter or margarine, softened
1 1/4 cups + 3 Tbs. sugar
2 eggs
1 tsp. vanilla
One 8-oz. carton sour cream
1 1/2 tsp. ground cinnamon
Powdered sugar, for sprinkling

Steps:
- Grease and flour a 10-inch fluted tube pan; set aside.
- In a medium mixing bowl, stir together the flour, baking powder, baking soda, and salt; set aside.
- Preheat the oven to 350°F.
- In a large mixing bowl, beat together the butter or margarine and 1/14 cups sugar with a mixer until combined.
- Beat in the eggs and vanilla until combined.
- Add the flour mixture and sour cream alternately to butter mixture, beating just until combined after each addition.
- Spread half of this mixture into the prepared pan.
- Stir together the remaining 3 Tbs. sugar and cinnamon. Sprinkle this over the batter in the pan.
- Spread the remaining batter over the sugar-and-cinnamon mixture.
- Bake for 45 to 50 minutes, or until a toothpick inserted near the center comes out clean. Cool in the pan on a wire rack for 15 minutes.
- Remove from the pan, and let cool.
- Sprinkle with sifted powdered sugar.
  Serves 14-16

Christina Evans

BLUEBERRY STREUSEL COFFEE CAKE

Serve warm.

Ingredients:

2 cups + 3 Tbs. flour flour
2 tsp. baking powder
1/2 tsp. salt
1/4 cup + 3 Tbs. butter
3/4 cup sugar
1 large egg
1/2 cup milk
1 pint blueberries
1/2 cup firmly packed light brown sugar
1 Tbs. cinnamon
1/2 cup walnuts, finely chopped

Steps:

- Preheat the oven to 375°F.
- Stir together the 2 cups of flour, baking powder and salt. Set aside
- In a separate bowl, cream the 1/4 cup of butter and the sugar; beat in the egg until blended.
- Add the flour mixture and the milk to the butter mixture. Stir only until the flour mixture is moistened.
- Fold in the blueberries.
- Turn the batter out into a buttered 9x9x2-inch cake pan.
- To make the streusel topping, stir together the brown sugar, remaining 3 Tbs. flour and the cinnamon.
- Cut in the remaining 3 Tbs. butter until the particles are fine.
- Stir in the walnuts.
- Sprinkle the streusel over the cake batter in the pan.
- Bake until a cake tester comes out clean (45-50 minutes).
- Cut into squares to serve.
  Serves 8-10

Christina Evans

APPLE CRUMB CAKE

Serve with a whipped topping.

Ingredients:

1 lb. butter or margarine
2 cups sugar
6 cups flour - unsifted
Pinch of salt
3 tsp. baking powder
1 tsp. vanilla
3 eggs
2 cans Comstock Apple Pie Filling, drained
1 lb. broken walnuts
Confectioner's sugar

Steps:
- Preheat the oven to 375°F.
- Cream the butter and sugar together until light and fluffy.
- Mix the dry ingredients together and add to the butter and sugar mixture. Mix with a fork blending well.
- Add the vanilla and eggs, blending with a fork to resemble coarse meal.
- Butter a 12-inch springform pan, and place one half of the mixture in it, lining the bottom and sides of pan.
- Place the apple pie filling over the crumb lining.
- Crumble the remaining flour mixture lightly on top of the apples.
- Sprinkle the top with walnuts, and press them down lightly into the crumb mixture.
- Bake for 30 minutes, then reduce the heat to 325°F for another 30 minutes. The cake is done when a toothpick inserted in the center comes out clean.
- Cool the cake completely in the pan.
- Sprinkle the top with confectioner's sugar.

NOTE: If cutting this recipe in half, use a 9-inch springform pan and bake for about the same amount of time.

Serves 12-14

Sue Czel

Thornton W. Burgess Museum

SWEDISH TORTE

Ingredients:

1/2 cup shortening
1/2 cup + 3/4 cup sugar
3 eggs, separated
1/2 tsp. vanilla
1 cup flour
1 tsp. baking powder
1/4 cup milk

1/4 tsp. cream of tartar
Nuts, chopped
1/2 pint heavy cream
1/4 cup sugar
One sm. can crushed pineapple, drained (or strawberries or raspberries)

Steps:
- Preheat the oven to 375°F.
- Cream the shortening, the 1/2 cup sugar, egg yolks and vanilla.
- Add the flour and baking powder alternately with the milk.
- Spread the batter into two 8-inch greased cake pans.
- Beat the egg whites, gradually adding the cream of tartar and the 3/4 cup sugar, until a stiff meringue forms.
- Spread the meringue on top of the cake batter in the pans.
- Sprinkle meringue with chopped nuts
- Bake for about 25 minutes.
- Let the cakes cool.
- Beat the heavy cream and sugar until peaks form.
- Fold in the fruit.
- Place the first cake layer meringue-side down, and spread it with all of the fruit-filled whipped cream.
- Top with the second cake layer, so that the meringue-side is on top of the finished cake.
Serves 6 to 8

Judy Koenig

FROZEN CHOCOLATE-SUNDAE PIE

Ingredients:

1 1/2 cups chocolate cookie crumbs
3 Tbs. sugar
1/3 cup butter, melted
1 qt. coffee ice cream, slightly softened
Two 1-oz. squares unsweetened chocolate

1 Tbs. butter
1/2 cup sugar
One 5-oz. can evaporated milk
1 cup whipping cream
1 oz. or more Kahlua or creme de cacao liqueur
Grated chocolate

Steps:
- Combine the cookie crumbs, sugar and melted butter, and press into a 9-inch pie plate. Freeze.
- Fill the frozen crust with the coffee ice cream and freeze again.
- Meanwhile, in a double boiler, melt the chocolate squares with the butter and sugar.
- Slowly stir in the evaporated milk. Cook and stir until thick, then let cool.
- Spread the cooled chocolate mixture on top of the ice cream and freeze the pie again.
- Whip the cream until stiff.
- Fold the liqueur into the whipped cream.
- Spread the whipped cream over the chocolate layer and freeze for three to four hours.
- Sprinkle with the grated chocolate.
- Remove the pie from the freezer 10-15 minutes before slicing.
Serves 8

Pat Maguire

SWEDISH APPLE PIE

Ingredients:

6-8 apples, sliced	1 egg
1 tsp. cinnamon	1 cup sugar
1 tsp. sugar	1 cup flour
1 stick oleo margarine or butter	Nuts, chopped

Steps:
- Preheat the oven to 350°F.
- Mix the apples with the cinnamon and sugar, then put into a pie plate.
- Cream together the butter, egg and sugar.
- Add the flour. Mix and roll out the resulting dough for a crust.
- Cover the apples with the crust and sprinkle the top with chopped nuts.
- Bake for 45 minutes.

Jodie Jacobson

PEACH-BLUEBERRY CREAM PIE

Ingredients:

1 cup graham-cracker crumbs
1/4 cup pecans or walnuts, ground
2 Tbs. sugar
1/4 cup butter, melted
One 21-oz. can blueberry-pie filling
Two 3-oz. pkgs. cream cheese, room temperature
1/3 cup sugar
1 Tbs. milk
1/2 tsp. ground nutmeg
1 cup heavy cream
One 16-oz. can sliced peaches, drained
1/2 cup apricot preserves, melted and strained

Steps:
- Preheat the oven to 350°F.
- Combine the graham-cracker crumbs, ground pecans or walnuts, sugar and melted butter in a bowl until well blended. Press evenly over the bottom and sides of a 9-inch pie plate.
- Bake the graham-cracker crust for eight to 10 minutes, or until lightly colored. Let cool.
- Pour the blueberry filling into the cooled crust.
- Beat together the cream cheese, sugar, milk and nutmeg in a medium bowl until well blended.
- Beat the heavy cream in a small bowl until stiff.
- Fold the whipped cream into the cream-cheese mixture, and spread the whole thing evenly over the blueberry layer. (Better yet, spoon the cream-cheese mixture into a pastry bag fitted with large star tip and pipe it decoratively over the blueberry layer.)
- Arrange the peach slices over the cream-cheese layer.
- Spoon the apricot preserves over the peaches.
- Chill for several hours or overnight.

Jennie Zantuhos

CHOCOLATE-MOUSSE PIE WITH CHOCOLATE LEAVES

Ingredients:

3 cups chocolate-wafer crumbs
1/2 cup (1 stick) unsalted butter, melted
1 1/2 lbs. semisweet chocolate
6 eggs (2 whole, 4 separated)

4 cups whipping cream
6 Tbs. powdered sugar
1 scant Tbs. vegetable shortening
Camellia or other waxy leaves
Sugar, to taste

Steps:
- Combine the chocolate crumbs and melted butter. Press onto the bottom and completely up the sides of a 10-inch springform pan. Refrigerate for 30 minutes (or chill in freezer).
- Soften 1 lb. of the chocolate in the top of a double boiler over simmering water. Let the chocolate cool to lukewarm (95°F).
- Add the 2 whole eggs and mix well.
- Add the 4 egg yolks and mix until thoroughly blended.
- Whip 2 cups of the cream with the powdered sugar until soft peaks form.
- Beat the 4 egg whites until stiff but not dry.
- Stir a little of the cream and egg whites into the chocolate mixture to lighten it.
- Fold in the remaining whipped cream and egg whites until they are completely incorporated.
- Pour this mixture into the crust. Chill for at least six hours or, preferably, overnight.
- Prepare the Chocolate Leaves for garnish by melting the remaining 1/2 lb. chocolate along with the shortening on top of a double boiler.
- Using a spoon, generously coat the underside of the leaves. Chill or freeze them until firm.
- When ready to garnish the pie, loosen the crust on all sides using a sharp knife, and remove the springform pan.
- Whip the remaining 2 cups of cream with sugar to taste until the cream is quite stiff.
- Spread all but about half a cup of the whipped cream over top of the mousse.
- Pipe the remaining whipped cream into rosettes in the center of the pie.
- Separate the chocolate from the leaves, starting at the stem end of each leaf.
- Arrange the chocolate leaves in an overlapping pattern around the rosettes. Serves 10-12

Monique Galipeau

EISENHOWER STRAWBERRY PIE

Garnish with whipped cream.

Ingredients:

9-inch baked pie shell
4 cups strawberries (3 cups whole smaller ones or sliced, plus 1 cup mashed)

3/4 cup water
3 Tbs. cornstarch
1 cup granulated sugar
1 tsp. lemon juice

Steps:
- In a baked pie shell, pack the whole or sliced berries.
- Cook the mashed berries in the water for about four minutes.
- Mix the cornstarch and sugar together and add to the boiling berry mixture. Let cook for one or two minutes, until the mixture becomes clear.
- Remove the mashed berry mixture from the heat and add the lemon juice.
- Pour this mixture over the uncooked berries in the shell.
- Dip several whole uncooked berries into the thickened, cooked berry mixture to glaze them. Use these to decorate the top of the pie, if desired.
- Cool in the refrigerator until set.
Serves 6-8

Wilhelmina Stover

CREAM-CHEESE PECAN TARTS

These tarts look great topped with whipped cream or powdered sugar. They also freeze very nicely.

Ingredients:

6 oz. cream cheese, softened
1/2 lb. butter, softened
2 cups flour
1/3 cup brown sugar, packed
2 eggs

2 Tbs. melted butter
2 tsp. vanilla
Dash of salt
1/4 cup pecans, finely chopped

Steps:
- Preheat the oven to 350°F.
- Mix the cream cheese, softened butter and flour. Chill for about an hour.
- Press this mixture on the bottom and sides of tiny muffin tins.
- Beat the brown sugar, eggs, melted butter, vanilla and salt until smooth.
- Add the pecans, then fill the shells halfway.
- Bake for about 25 minutes or until just set.
- Cool before serving.
Makes 36 tarts

Sally Bates

BAVARIAN APPLE TORTE

Ingredients:

3/4 cup butter, softened
1 1/4 cups sugar
1 1/2 cups all purpose flour
1/2 + 3/4 tsp. vanilla extract
Two 8-oz. pkgs. cream cheese, softened

2 eggs
3 cups thinly sliced tart apples (peeled and sliced)
1 tsp. cinnamon

Steps:

Preheat the oven to 350°F.
Combine the butter, 1/2 cup of the sugar, all of the flour and 1/2 tsp. of the vanilla. Press into the bottom of an ungreased 9-inch springform pan, and set aside.
In a mixing bowl, beat the cream cheese and sugar together.
Add the eggs and remaining 3/4 tsp. vanilla, and mix well.
Pour this filling over the crust.
Combine the apples, cinnamon and the remaining 1/2 cup sugar, and spoon this over the filling.
Bake for 55-60 minutes or until the center is set.
Cool on a wire rack, and store in the refrigerator.
Serves 8
HINT: Place a baking sheet in the oven under the pan, to catch drips.

Susan Stover

PLUM OR PEACH KUCHEN

This wonderful summer dessert can be served warm or at room temperature.

Ingredients:

2 cups sifted flour
1/4 tsp. baking powder
1/2 tsp. salt
1 cup sugar
1/2 cup sweet butter

12 to 14 peaches or plums (halves), enough to cover the pan's bottom
1 tsp. cinnamon
1 cup sour cream or heavy cream
2 egg yolks

Steps:
- Preheat the oven to 400°F.
- Sift the flour, baking powder, salt and 2 Tbs. of the sugar together.
- Cut the butter into small chunks, and blend it into the dry ingredients to form a dough.
- Press the dough into a well greased 8- or 9-inch glass pan.
- Arrange the fruit on top of the dough and sprinkle with the rest of the sugar and cinnamon.
- Bake for 15 minutes.
- Combine the egg yolks and sour cream (or heavy cream) in a small bowl.
- Remove the fruit pan from the oven and spread the cream-yolk mixture over the fruit.
- Return the pan to the oven and bake for 30 minutes more.
Serves 8 to 10

Marilyn Vinecour-Goldberg

Cuts as Clean as a Pair of Shears

The cutting action of the "ENTERPRISE" Chopper is positive. Nothing gets past the four sharp blades of steel, which revolve against the inside surface of the perforated steel plate, without being actually *cut*.

"Enterprise" MEAT and FOOD Chopper

The ordinary cheap food chopper grinds and tears — the "ENTERPRISE" Meat and Food Chopper *cuts* as clean as a pair of shears.

Made in 45 sizes and styles for hand, steam and electric power. No. 5, small family size, $1.75. No. 10, large family size, $2.50.

No. 5 Price $1.75
No. 10 Price $2.50

Sold by all dealers

"The Enterprising Housekeeper," a book of 200 recipes sent to anyone for 4 cents in stamps.

THE ENTERPRISE MFG. CO. OF PA.
DEPT. 14, PHILADELPHIA, PA.

Cookies make us think of children. This photo shows Paul Wing's Spring Hill Academy which in 1841 accommodated a total of 73 boys and 30 girls. The large vegetable garden and fruit trees surely helped to feed the children. One of the most famous pupils of this school was the Quaker girl from New Bedford who became Hetty Green the Witch of Wall Street.

Photo courtesy of the Wing Family Assoc.

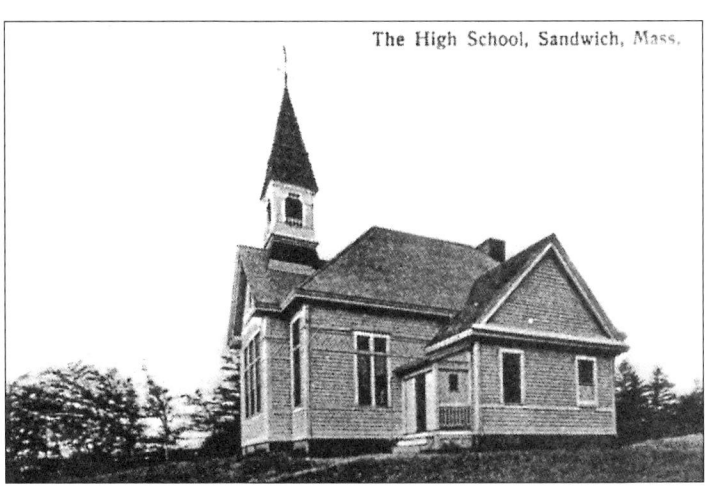

Sandwich High School about 1910. This school was built by the trustees of the Sandwich Academy, using proceeds from the sale of the old Academy on Water Street plus the sale of the land in Maine granted to the Academy, and other assets. The school was leased to the town of Sandwich, and was popular with students because it had steam heat and indoor toilets.

103

Jelly Cake

½ lb. of Sugar, 6 oz. of Butter, 8 egg. 1 lb of sifted Flour, 1 fresh Lemon, grated rind and juice. Turn this mixture on Scolloped tin plates, well buttered, not more than ¼ of an inch thick on each plate. Bake them directly in a quick oven till a light brown. Pile them on a plate, with a layer of Jelly, or Marmalade, between each of the cakes and a layer on top.

Sugar Drops

3 oz. of Butter, 6 oz. of Sugar, 3 eggs. ½ lb of Flour, ½ a Nutmeg. Drop this mixture with a large spoon on buttered plates several inches apart, sprinkle small sugar plums on the top and bake them directly

Page from a nineteeth century hand-written book of recipes.

GREAT-GREAT GRANDMA EMMA'S SUGAR COOKIES

Ingredients:

1 cup butter
3 eggs
2 cups sugar
2 tsp. baking powder

Lemon or almond flavoring
3 cups flour
2 Tbs. milk

Steps:
- Preheat oven to 350°F.
- Cream the butter, eggs, sugar and baking powder until smooth.
- Add the lemon or almond flavoring, according to your taste.
- Dissolve enough of the flour into the milk to make a stiff paste, and then add that to the creamed ingredients. Add the rest of the flour until the mixture is smooth. If the dough is not firm enough, you may want to add a little more flour.
- Drop the dough by the teaspoon onto a cookie sheet, and bake in the oven until brown around the edges (10 to 12 minutes).

Mae Foster

RAISIN-OATMEAL COOKIES

Ingredients:

3/4 cup raisins
1/4 cup water
1/2 cup Crisco shortening
1 tsp. vanilla
1 cup brown sugar

3/4 cup flour
1/2 tsp. baking soda
1/2 tsp. salt
1/2 tsp. cinnamon
1 1/2 cups oats

Steps:
- Combine the raisins, water and shortening. Heat this mixture in a saucepan until the shortening melts, then let cool.
- Preheat the oven to 350°F.
- Stir in the vanilla and brown sugar. Add the flour, baking soda, salt and cinnamon, then blend.
- Stir in the oats.
- Drop the dough by the teaspoon onto greased baking sheets and bake the cookies for 10 minutes.

Avis Clay

SWEDISH FARMER COOKIES

The dough for these cookies needs to chill for a bit after it's been mixed, so be prepared to start a little ahead of time.

Ingredients:
1 cup butter
3/4 cup sugar
1 Tbs. Karo corn syrup
2 cups flour
1 tsp. baking soda

Steps:
- Cream the butter and sugar.
- Blend in the corn syrup.
- Add the rest of the ingredients to the butter-sugar mixture.
- Shape the resulting dough into two logs, and wrap them each in wax paper to chill in the refrigerator for a bit.
- Preheat the oven to 350°F.
- When the dough logs are quite firm, cut them into cookie slices, and place the cookies on an ungreased baking sheet.
- Bake the cookies for about eight to 10 minutes.

Carolyn Nelson

ALMOND SPRITZ COOKIES

Ingredients:
1 cup (2 sticks) unsalted butter
1/2 cup plus 2 Tbs. superfine sugar
3 oz. imported almond paste*
1 large egg, beaten
2 cups all purpose flour
1 tsp. vanilla
1 tsp. almond extract
Dash of salt
Sliced cherries, finely chopped nuts, sugar sprinkles, etc. (for decoration)

Steps:
- Preheat the oven to 375°F.
- Cream the butter until light and fluffy.
- Add the sugar, almond paste and egg, and beat thoroughly.
- Add the flour gradually, then the flavorings and salt, blending each completely.
- Put the dough through a cookie press or in a pastry bag fitted with a #5 star tube. (NOTE: When not working with the remaining dough, keep it in the refrigerator.) Squeeze out cookies in an "S" or other shape onto an ungreased cookie sheet.
- Decorate your cookies as desired, with sliced cherries, nuts or sugar sprinkles.

- Bake the cookies for eight to 12 minutes, or until the edges are slightly golden. Remove them to a rack and cool.

* Imported almond paste has less sugar then the domestic variety, thus it makes a better cookie.
  Makes 5 to 6 dozen

Christina Evans

BLACK DOG'S GINGER COOKIES

People have been known to stand in line for these cookies at The Black Dog Bakery on Martha's Vineyard. This recipe makes a lot, so you'll have plenty of delicious treats to show for your effort. They're good for keepers, and great for a bake sale!

Ingredients:

1/2 cup fresh ginger, coarsely chopped
1 1/2 cups canola oil
4 cups granulated sugar (reserve 1 cup in which to roll the dropped cookie dough)
3/4 cup molasses

3 eggs
1 1/2 tsp. salt
1 Tbs. cinnamon
5 1/4 tsp. baking soda
3/4 tsp. ground cloves
7 cups pastry flour

Steps:
- Preheat the oven to 350°F.
- Mix the fresh ginger with 1/2 cup of the oil in a food processor until it is well minced.
- In a large mixing bowl, blend 3 cups of the sugar, as well as the molasses and eggs.
- Strain the minced ginger/oil mixture, reserving the liquid. Add this liquid, plus the remaining cup of oil to the egg mixture and blend it until smooth.
- In a separate bowl, mix together the salt, cinnamon, baking soda, cloves and flour. Add this dry mixture to the wet mixture, and blend well.
- Either line the cookie sheets with parchment paper or grease them with butter, then scoop up the cookie dough by the teaspoon, rolling each scoop in the reserved cup of granulated sugar.
- Place the rolled, sugared dough balls onto the prepared cookie sheets, and bake for about eight to 12 minutes, or just until the tops crack and the cookies are flat.
- Cool the cookies completely on wire racks.
  Makes about eight dozen

Stan Moszka

CHERRY-NUT COOKIES

Ingredients:

1 cup sugar
3 eggs
1/2 cup oil
2 tsp. almond or vanilla extract (according to your taste)
3 1/4 cups flour
2 tsp. baking powder
Two 10-oz. bottles of maraschino cherries, drained and cut in half
1/2 cup chopped almonds (or other nuts, according to your taste)
16 oz. confectioners' sugar
Water
Almond extract

Steps:

- Preheat the oven to 350°F.
- Combine the sugar, eggs, oil, and extract and mix with a mixer until well blended.
- Combine the flour and baking powder into the wet mixture.
- Put the cherries and nuts in by hand, and stir them in gently.
- Spoon the dough onto ungreased cookie sheets and shape it into two narrow loaves. Bake the loaves for 25 minutes.
- Cool the loaves a little, then slice them diagonally into cookies.
- When the cookies are completely cooled, mix the confectioners' sugar with enough hot water and almond extract to form a thin frosting, and drizzle the cookies with the frosting.

Jennie Zantuhos

CHOCOLATE SPRINKLE COOKIES

Ingredients:

10 Tbs. butter or margarine
1 cup sugar
1 egg
1 tsp. vanilla
1 cup flour
6 Tbs. cocoa
1/2 tsp. baking soda
1/2 tsp. salt
Rainbow sprinkles

Steps:

- Preheat the oven to 350°F.
- Cream the butter and sugar.
- Add the egg and vanilla.
- Add the dry ingredients (except for the sprinkles).
- Scoop up the dough by the teaspoon, and dip the tops into the sprinkles, then placing the scoops on a baking sheet, sprinkles-side up.
- Bake for about 10 minutes. These cookies are best if not overbaked!

Nancy Ockers

COCONUT-ALMOND BISCOTTI

After many experiments with biscotti recipes, my sister and I have perfected this one. They're delicious, and last for a long time in a sealed container.

Ingredients:

2 1/4 cups all-purpose flour
1 1/2 tsp. baking powder
1/4 tsp. salt
1/2 cup (1 stick) butter
3/4 cups brown sugar, packed
2 large eggs
1 cup sweetened flaked coconut
1 cup chopped almonds
1/2 can almond filling
2 tsp. almond extract

Steps:

- Preheat the oven to 350°F.
- Grease a cookie sheet, or line it with parchment paper.
- Mix the flour, baking powder and salt, and set aside.
- In a large bowl, using an electric mixer, cream the butter and sugar together. Add the eggs one at a time, beating well after each addition.
- Beat in the coconut.
- On low speed, gradually add the flour mixture to the dough.
- Stir in the almonds, almond filling and almond extract by hand.
- Turn the dough onto a floured surface and divide it in half. Shape each half into a two-inch-wide log the length of a rolling pin.
- Transfer the dough logs to a cookie sheet, and pat them down by hand to make each dough log flat and the same thickness for its entire length.
- Bake for 30 minutes, until the logs are golden brown and firm to the touch, and a tester inserted in the centers comes out clean.
- Cool the logs for 20 minutes and reduce the oven temperature to 325°F.
- Cut the logs into 1/2-inch slices and arrange the slices on the cookie sheet. Bake another 10 minutes, until golden brown, watching carefully.
- Turn the biscotti and bake them until the other side is browned.
  Makes 36 biscotti

Marsha Supranovicz

CRANBERRY-OATMEAL COOKIES

Ingredients:

1 cup flour
1/2 tsp. baking powder
1/2 tsp. baking soda
1/2 tsp. salt
1 egg
1/2 cup shortening
1 Tbs. water
1 tsp. vanilla
1/2 cup brown sugar
3/4 cup granulated sugar
1 1/2 cups rolled oats
1 1/2 cups fresh or dried cranberries, chopped

Steps:
- Preheat the oven to 375°F.
- Sift the flour, baking powder, baking soda and salt into a bowl.
- Add the next six ingredients, and beat until smooth.
- Fold the oats and cranberries into the dough.
- Shape the dough into small balls, and place them on a greased cookie sheet two inches apart. Bake for 12-15 minutes.
Makes 3 dozen

Evelyn Broadbridge

ICEBOX FINGER COOKIES

These cookies are supposed to be crispy thin, and are a big hit—especially at teatime!

Ingredients:

1 cup butter, melted
1 cup sugar
1/2 cup molasses, heated
1 tsp. baking soda
1 tsp. salt
1 tsp. vanilla
3-4 tsp. ginger
2 1/2 cups flour

Steps:
- Pour the melted butter over the sugar and mix.
- Add the molasses.
- Add the rest of the ingredients and mix.
- Form the dough into two rolls (about a half-dollar diameter).
- Wrap the dough logs in waxed paper or foil, and chill well.
- Preheat oven to 375°F.
- When cold, slice thin and place on a greased cookie sheet.
- Bake for seven to nine minutes.
- Makes about six dozen

Rosemary J. Morse (Granddaughter of Thornton W. Burgess)

SHORTBREAD COOKIES WITH LAVENDER ICING

The dough for these shortbread cookies needs to chill after it's been mixed, so begin ahead of time. If you want to decorate them with this very special lavender icing, start a day in advance. It's worth it!

Ingredients for Shortbread:

1 cup unsalted butter, softened
2/3 cup granulated sugar
1 tsp. vanilla extract
1/4 tsp. lemon extract
2 cups all-purpose flour
1/8 tsp. salt

Steps for Shortbread:

- In a medium mixing bowl, cream the butter, sugar, vanilla and lemon extract.
- Mix the flour, lavender and salt together, then add these dry ingredients to the creamed mixture. Stir until the dough is smooth. If the dough feels sticky, add an additional 1/4 cup of flour. The dough should be soft, but not sticky.
- Chill the dough for one to two hours, or until firm.
- Preheat the oven to 325°F.
- On a lightly floured surface, roll the dough out about 1/4-inch thick. Cut out shapes with your favorite cookie cutters, and place them on an ungreased cookie sheet. (The dough and resulting scraps may be re-rolled.)
- Bake the cookies for 10 to 15 minutes, or until they are light brown around the edges. Place cookies on a cooling rack to cool completely, then decorate with Lavender Icing (if you wish).
  Makes 1 1/2 to 2 dozen cookies

Ingredients for Lavender Icing:

1 or 2 Tbs. dried lavender flowers, crumbled
1 cup confectioners' sugar
2 tsp. milk
2 tsp. light corn syrup
Food coloring (optional)

Steps for Lavender Icing:

- One day before baking the cookies, mix the lavender flowers with confectioners' sugar in a small plastic bag. Let this stand for a day.
- In a bowl, combine a cup of the lavender-sugar with milk and corn syrup. Stir well.
- If desired, tint the icing with food coloring to make a violet color, then spread on cooled cookies.

Christina Evans

JAM JEWELS

Ingredients:

2 sticks butter, softened
1 cup confectioners' sugar
1 egg yolk
3 oz. cream cheese (softened)
1 1/2 tsp. vanilla
1 tsp. grated lemon rind

2 1/4 cups flour
Scant 1/2 tsp. baking soda
1/4 tsp. baking powder
1/4 tsp. salt
2/3 cup chopped almonds
Jam of your preference

Steps:
- Preheat the oven to 350°F.
- Cream the butter, sugar, and egg yolk until fluffy.
- Beat in the cream cheese, vanilla, and grated lemon rind.
- Combine the flour, baking soda, baking powder and salt, and stir to thoroughly combine. Beat in the flour mixture until the dough is smooth. Wait five minutes for the batter to firm up.
- Shape the dough into one-inch balls, then dip the balls slightly in the nuts, and place on a buttered cookie sheet.
- Press your thumb into the center of each dough ball to make a depression, then fill it with 1/4 tsp. of your favorite jam.
- Bake for nine to 12 minutes, or until cookies are lightly browned.

Jennie Zantuhos

HERSHEY-BAR SQUARES

A favorite in our family for over 40 years!

Ingredients:

1 cup butter
1/2 cup sugar
1/2 cup brown sugar
1 egg

1 cup flour
1 cup Quaker oats
6 oz. Hershey chocolate (equivalent of four 1.5-oz. Hershey bars)

Steps:
- Preheat the oven to 350°F.
- Cream the butter and sugars together.
- Add the egg.
- Stir in the flour and oats.
- Grease and flour a 9x13-inch pan, then spread the batter in the pan.
- Bake for 18-20 minutes.

- Remove from the oven and place the Hershey bars on top, allowing them to melt.
- Spread the melted chocolate over the top evenly.
- Cool and cut into squares.

Carolyn Nelson

SANDWICH "STAR" COOKIES

These are called Sandwich "Star" cookies because the pretty star pattern on the cookies is achieved by pressing the dough with the bottom of a drinking glass whose base is star-shaped. In the 19th century, the Boston & Sandwich Glass factory of Sandwich, Massachusetts made scores of tumblers with star-shaped bottoms. If you don't have an old Sandwich Glass tumbler among your glassware, you can use any glass or crystal drinking vessel with a star pattern on the bottom.

Ingredients:

1 1/2 cups sugar	1 tsp. baking powder
1/2 cup butter (creamed)	1/2 tsp. salt
1/2 cup Crisco shortening (creamed)	2 tsp. vanilla
2 eggs (beaten)	Sugar and flour mixed together for topping
3 cups flour	

Steps:

- The dough for this recipe should chill overnight, so begin making the cookies one day ahead of when you want to bake them.
- Combine the sugar, butter and Crisco. Add eggs.
- Sift together the flour, baking powder and salt, then stir this dry mixture into the sugar-shortening mixture.
- Add the vanilla. The resulting dough will be stiff. Chill it overnight.
- Preheat the oven to 400°F.
- Roll the dough into 1-inch-wide balls, and place them on greased cookie sheets, 20 balls to a sheet.
- Dip the bottom of a Sandwich Glass tumbler in equal amounts of sugar and flour. Press the glass down hard on the dough balls to make thin, star-patterned cookies.
- Bake for 10 to 15 minutes.
  Makes about 80 cookies

Mae Foster

SNICKERDOODLES

These large, crinkly-topped cookies have been popular in the United States since at least the 1800s. Early cookbooks from areas settled by German immigrants often referred to cookies of this type as "Schneckenoodles," which eventually turned into the nonsense name "Snickerdoodles."

Ingredients:

3 1/2 cups all-purpose or unbleached flour
1 Tbs. baking powder
2 tsp. baking soda
1/4 tsp. salt
1/4 tsp. + 1/2 tsp. ground cinnamon

1 cup (2 sticks) unsalted butter
2 cups + 3 Tbs. granulated sugar
2 large eggs
1 Tbs. light corn syrup
2 1/2 tsp. vanilla extract

Steps:
- Preheat the oven to 375°F.
- Thoroughly stir together the flour, baking powder, baking soda, salt and 1/4 tsp. cinnamon, and set aside.
- In a large mixing bowl, place the butter and 2 cups of the sugar, and beat with an electric mixer on medium speed until light and smooth.
- Add the eggs and corn syrup, and continue beating until they are thoroughly blended and smooth. Beat in the vanilla.
- Gradually beat in about half of the dry ingredients. As the dough stiffens, stir in the rest of the dry ingredients by hand, using a large wooden spoon.
- In a small bowl, combine the remaining 3 Tbs. sugar and 1/2 tsp. cinnamon for decorating the tops of the cookies.
- Pull off generous portions of dough and roll them between your palms to form 1 3/4-inch balls. Then, roll the balls in the sugar-cinnamon mixture to coat.
- Space the balls about three inches apart on greased baking sheets. With a flat-bottomed drinking glass, press down on the balls to flatten them. Dip the bottom of the glass back in the sugar-cinnamon mixture after each cookie to prevent sticking.
- Bake the cookies for about 10 minutes, or until the cookie bottoms are lightly golden. Remove the baking sheets from the oven and let them stand for one to two minutes, then transfer the cookies to a wire rack to cool. Makes 35 to 40 cookies

Christina Evans

RUSSIAN KISSES (RUM BALLS)

These freeze well, and everyone loves them on a Christmas cookie plate.

Ingredients:

1/2 lb. oleo margarine (2 sticks)
2 cups flour
1 cup sugar

1 lb. ground pecans
1 to 2 tsp. rum extract
Confectioners' sugar

Steps:
- Preheat the oven to 300°F.
- Cream the margarine with a mixer.
- Add the flour and sugar.
- Add the remaining ingredients and blend well.
- Knead by hand, then form the dough into balls the size of small walnuts. Place on an ungreased cookie sheet.
- Bake for 25 minutes or until lightly browned.
- When cool, roll the rum balls in confectioners' sugar. (If you're freezing them, omit the powdered sugar until you're ready to serve.) Makes 5 or 6 dozen

Joyce Losh

FRUIT-FILLED HORNS

Ingredients:

1 lb. oleo margarine
1 lb. cottage cheese, small curd
4 cups flour

2 cans Solo-brand fruit filling
2 egg whites, slightly beaten
Ground nuts with sugar

Steps:
- Form a dough by blending the ingredients together with your hands (unless you have a heavy-duty mixer).
- Shape the dough into one-inch balls, and refrigerate overnight. (These balls will last in the refrigerator for up to a month.)
- Roll the balls out into three-inch rounds (only roll out 10 at a time, keeping the rest in fridge).
- Place 1 teaspoon of filling in the center of each round. By hand, roll the filled round into the shape of a crescent.
- Preheat the oven to 375°F.
- Dip the crescents in the egg whites and then into the nut-sugar mixture. (I use colored sugars to identify the different fruit fillings.)
- Bake on a dark cookie sheet for 25 to 30 minutes or until golden brown.

Joyce Losh

COCONUT & ALMOND MACAROONS

The world's easiest cookie recipe!

Ingredients:

2 2/3 cups (7 oz.) Angel Flake coconut
2/3 cup granulated sugar
1/4 cup unbleached flour
1/4 tsp. salt
4 egg whites

1 tsp. pure almond extract
1 cup almonds, sliced
Two 1-oz. squares of semi-sweet chocolate (optional, for drizzling on top of macaroons)

Steps:
- Preheat the oven to 325°F.
- Mix the coconut, sugar, flour and salt together.
- Stir in the egg whites and almond extract, and mix well. Add the sliced almonds and mix well again.
- Drop dough by the teaspoon, about two inches apart, onto baking sheets lined with parchment paper.
- Bake cookies for 20 minutes, or until edges are golden brown, then let cool on the parchment paper. Remove to a wire rack and let cookies cool completely for a few minutes.
- If you would like chocolate drizzle on your macaroons, melt the chocolate in a double boiler over slowly boiling water.
- Spoon the melted chocolate into a plastic sandwich baggie, and cut the tiniest slice from one corner of the baggie. Drizzle the chocolate over the macaroon tops (it will turn dull). Let the chocolate cool completely before storing the macaroons in a tightly sealed container.
Makes 30 cookies

Karyn Frances Gray

TREASURE-CHEST BARS

Ingredients for Bars:

2 cups flour
1 tsp. vanilla
1/2 cup sugar
2 eggs
1/2 cup brown sugar
3/4 cup milk

1 1/2 tsp. baking powder
1/2 cup margarine or butter
Three 1.45-oz. bars milk-chocolate candy, cut into small pieces
1 cup maraschino cherries, halved
1 cup walnuts, chopped

Steps for Bars:
- Preheat oven to 350°F.
- Combine all ingredients except the chocolate, cherries and nuts. Blend on medium speed for two minutes.
- Stir in the chocolate, cherries and nuts by hand.
- Spread the mixture in a 15x10x1-inch pan and bake for 25 to 30 minutes or until golden brown.
- Spread the bars with Icing (recipe follows) while they are still warm. Makes 48 bars

Ingredients for Icing:

1/4 cup butter	1/2 tsp. vanilla
2 cups confectioners' sugar	2 to 3 Tbs. milk

Steps for Icing:
- Combine ingredients until well mixed.

Margaret Welsh

BLACK-EYED SUSANS

Ingredients:

1/2 cup butter or margarine, softened	1 lg. egg
	1 1/2 Tbs. warm water
1/2 cup sugar	1 1/2 cups all-purpose flour
1/2 cup firmly packed brown sugar	1/2 tsp. salt
1 cup creamy peanut butter	1/2 tsp. baking soda
1 tsp. vanilla extract	1/2 cup semisweet chocolate morsels

Steps:
- Beat the butter and sugars at medium speed with an electric mixer until light and fluffy.
- Add the peanut butter and the next three ingredients, beating well.
- Combine the flour, salt, and baking soda, then add this to butter mixture, beating until blended.
- Preheat the oven to 350°F.
- Use a cookie gun fitted with a flower-shaped disc to make these cookies, following the manufacturer's instructions. Place cookies on lightly greased baking sheets.
- Place a chocolate morsel in the center of each cookie.
- Bake the cookies for eight minutes or until lightly browned. Remove them to wire racks to cool, then chill them in the refrigerator for 30 minutes.
- These cookies can be frozen for up to one month. Makes 8 dozen

Christina Evans

HOLIDAY CHOCOLATE-ALMOND BARS

Serve these bars in decorative paper "cupcake cups," or wrap them in ribbon for a festive gift.

Ingredients:

1 1/2 cups unsifted flour
2/3 cup sugar
3/4 cup (1 1/2 sticks) cold butter or margarine
1 1/2 cups semi-sweet chocolate chips
One 14-oz. can Eagle Brand sweetened condensed milk (not evaporated milk)
1 egg
2 cups almonds, toasted and chopped
1/2 tsp. almond extract
1 tsp. solid shortening

Steps:
- Preheat the oven to 350°F.
- Combine the flour and sugar.
- Cut in the cold butter until the mixture is crumbly.
- Press the resulting crumb mixture into the bottom of a 13x9-inch baking pan, and bake for 20 minutes or until lightly browned.
- Melt 1 cup of the chocolate chips with the can of condensed milk. Remove from heat when thoroughly melted.
- Cool the condensed milk-chocolate mixture slightly, then beat in the egg.
- Stir in the almonds and almond extract.
- Spread this mixture over the crust, then bake for 25 minutes (or until set).
- Cool bars.
- Melt the remaining 1/2 cup of chocolate chips with the shortening and drizzle melted mixture on top of the bars.
- Chill for 10 minutes or until glaze is set.
- Cut into bars, and store covered at room temperature. Makes 24 to 36 bars

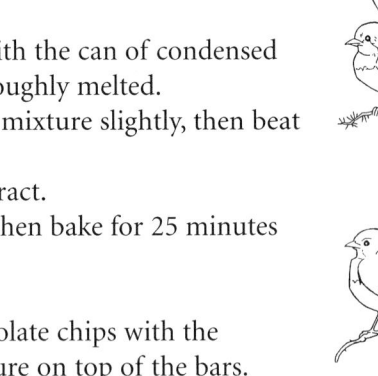

PUMPKIN BARS WITH CREAM-CHEESE ICING

Ingredients for Pumpkin Bars:

4 eggs
1 2/3 cups sugar
1 cup oil
One 16-oz. can pumpkin
2 cups flour
2 tsp. baking powder
2 tsp. cinnamon
1 tsp. salt
1 tsp. baking soda

Steps for Pumpkin Bars:
- Preheat oven to 350°F.
- In a mixing bowl, beat together the eggs, sugar, oil and pumpkin until light and fluffy.
- In a separate bowl, stir together the rest of the ingredients. Add the dry mixture to the pumpkin mixture, and mix thoroughly.
- Spread the batter in an ungreased 15x10-inch pan, and bake in the oven for 25-30 minutes.
- Cool, then frost with Cream Cheese Icing (recipe follows).
- Cut into bars.

Ingredients for Cream-Cheese Icing:

One 3-oz. pkg. cream cheese
1/2 cup butter or margarine, softened
1 tsp. vanilla
2 cups confectioners' sugar

Steps for Cream-Cheese Icing:
- Cream together the cream cheese and butter.
- Stir in the vanilla and confectioners' sugar a little at a time, beating until smooth.

Jennie Zantuhos

"Oh weary mothers rolling dough, don't you wish that food would grow? How happy all the world would be, with a cookie bush and a doughnut tree!"

—Unknown

CRUSTY CARAMEL "CREED" BARS

Ingredients for Crust:

1 1/2 cups flour
1 1/4 cups oatmeal
3/4 cup butter (melted)
3/4 cup brown sugar
1/2 tsp. salt

Ingredients for Caramel Filling:

1 bag of caramels
4-5 Tbs. milk
1 cup chocolate chips
1 cup pecans, chopped

Steps:
* Preheat oven to 350°F.
- Mix all crust ingredients together, and pat all except one cup of crumb mixture into a 9x13 inch pan (save the one cup for topping).
- Bake for 10 minutes.
- Let cool.
- Melt the caramels with the milk.
- Spread the chocolate chips and pecans on top of the cooled crust, then pour the caramel over the top of them.
- Sprinkle the reserved cup of crust mixture on top.
- Bake again for 15 minutes.
- Cut into bars when cool.

Julie Ruatti

LEMON SQUARES

These squares are easier to cut when entirely cool.

Ingredients:

1 stick (1/2 cup) softened butter
1/4 cup confectioners' sugar, plus a little more for dusting
1 cup + 2 Tbs. flour
2 eggs
1 cup granulated sugar
3 Tbs. lemon juice (bottled is fine)

Steps:
- Preheat the oven to 350°F.
- Blend the butter and confectioners' sugar.
- Add 1 cup of the flour and mix.
- Press this crust mixture evenly in the bottom of an 8-inch-square glass pan.
- Bake for 20 minutes and then cool.

- While the crust is cooling, thoroughly beat the eggs, granulated sugar, remaining 2 Tbs. flour, and the lemon juice. Pour the mixture over the cooled crust.
- Bake for 20 minutes until the top is dry and barely brown around the edges.
- Cool completely, then dust the top well with confectioners' sugar.

Joyce Losh

HERSHEY'S ULTIMATE CHOCOLATE BROWNIES WITH FROSTING

Hershey's best-loved recipe!

Ingredients for Brownies:

3/4 cup Hershey's cocoa
1/2 tsp. baking soda
2/3 cup butter or margarine, melted and divided in two equal portions
1 cup Hershey's semi-sweet chocolate chips

2 cups sugar
2 eggs
1/4 tsp. salt
1/2 cup boiling water
1 tsp. vanilla extract
1 1/3 cups all-purpose flour

Steps for Brownies:
- Preheat oven to 350°F.
- Grease a 13x9x2-inch baking pan or two 8-inch-square baking pans.
- Stir together the cocoa and baking soda in a large bowl.
- Add in half of the butter.
- Add boiling water. Stir until the mixture thickens.
- Stir in the sugar, eggs and the remaining half portion of butter. Stir until smooth.
- Add the flour, vanilla and salt, and blend completely.
- Stir in the chocolate chips and pour into the prepared pan(s).
- Bake the brownies for 35 to 40 minutes for a rectangular pan, or 30 to 35 minutes for square pans. Brownies begin to pull away from the sides of pans when done.
- Cool completely in their pans on a wire rack.
- Meanwhile, prepare Chocolate Buttercream Frosting (recipe follows).
- Frost brownies and sprinkle with additional chocolate chips, if desired.
- Cut into squares.
  Makes about 36 brownies

Ingredients for Chocolate Buttercream Frosting:

6 Tbs. butter or margarine, softened
2 2/3 cups confectioners' sugar
1/2 cup Hershey's cocoa
4 to 6 Tbs. milk
1 tsp. vanilla extract

Steps for Chocolate Buttercream Frosting:
- Beat softened butter in a medium bowl.
- Add the powdered sugar and cocoa alternately with the milk, beating to a spreading consistency.
- Stir in vanilla.

Mary Beaudain

COFFEE-GLAZED BROWNIES

Making a good brownie—one that is moist and fudgy—requires great self-restraint. The melted butter must be cool when it is added or it will cook the eggs. If you beat the eggs and sugar too vigorously, too much air will be incorporated, and the brownies will be more like cake. The final mixture should be gently stirred rather than beaten, or the brownies will be tough and dry. Most important of all, it is vital to avoid overbaking! Test by inserting a skewer halfway between the center and the side of the pan—the center should remain quite moist. It is also good to wrap the cooled brownies and keep them overnight before cutting them into squares—if you can wait!

Ingredients:

4 lg. eggs
Four 1-oz. squares of unsweetened chocolate
2 Tbs. instant coffee
2 cups granulated sugar
1 tsp. vanilla extract
1 cup all-purpose flour
3/4 cup (1 1/2 sticks) butter or margarine
1 cup nuts, toasted and coarsely chopped (optional)

Steps:
- Preheat the oven to 350°F.
- Line a 13x9-inch baking pan with foil, and lightly butter the foil.
- Stir the eggs, instant coffee and vanilla in a small bowl until well blended; set aside.
- Microwave the butter and chocolate in a microwavable bowl on High for 2 minutes or until the butter is melted. Stir until the chocolate is completely melted.
- Stir the sugar into the chocolate mixture until well blended. Mix in the egg mixture. Stir in the flour and nuts.

➤

- Spread the batter in the prepared pan.
- Bake for 30 minutes or until a toothpick inserted in the center comes out with fudgy crumbs. (Do not overbake!)
- Cool completely in the pan on a wire rack.
- Spread Bittersweet Coffee Glaze (recipe follows) over the brownies, if desired.
- Cut into squares. Store in a tightly covered container.
  Makes 24 brownies

Ingredients for Bittersweet Coffee Glaze:

Six 1-oz. squares bittersweet chocolate
5 Tbs. corn syrup
1 Tbs. butter or margarine
1 tsp. instant coffee

Steps for Bittersweet Coffee Glaze:
- Microwave the chocolate, corn syrup, butter, and instant coffee in a medium microwaveable bowl on High for 2 minutes or until the butter is melted. Stir until the chocolate is melted.
- Cool slightly.

> They're homemade, Jack, old man, homemade!
> No baker's truck, these, for the trade,
> But just the real old homely brand;
> Molasses from the brown jug close at hand,
> Flour from the barrel sifted in,
> Carefully measured lest they be too thin;
> Sugar, eggs, assorted kinds of spice,
> And things whereof we only know they're nice;
> All mixed and stirred, and kneaded to a dough,
> And rolled out thin and cut out so;
> Then comes a slamming of the oven door,
> A wait, a whiff, a wish for more
> And then—well Jack, you know the kind
> They never used to be so hard to find.
> They're homemade, Jack, old man, homemade,
> No baker's truck, these, for the trade.
>
> -Thornton W. Burgess, excerpted from
> "Homemade," Good Housekeeping, July 1902

BIRD NESTS IN SYRUP (FOLITSES)

For a holiday version I call "The Belly Dancer's Navel," place half a maraschino cherry in the center of the nest.

Ingredients for Syrup:

1 cup water
1/4 tsp. lemon juice
1 cup sugar
1 Tbs. honey
1 cinnamon stick

Ingredients for Bird's Nests:

Walnuts, roasted or ground
Pistachios, unsalted
Almonds, ground and blanched
Mixture of sugar and cinnamon*
1 lb. premade, refrigerated filo dough
1 lb. unsalted butter
Ground pistachios (for garnish)

*For 1 cup nuts, add 1/4 cup sugar and 1/2 tsp. ground cinnamon.

Steps:

- Bring all syrup ingredients to a boil and simmer for 15 minutes.
- Begin to prepare the Birds' Nests by combining a mixture of nuts, cinnamon and sugar for filling the nests.
- Prepare the filo dough by cutting the sheets in half. Brush them with butter and double them over, being sure to brush each filo sheet again.
- Sprinkle the nut mixture generously on the filo, and squeeze or roll the filo into a nest.
- Place each nest on a greased baking sheet and bake at 350°F for 15 minutes or until nests are golden.
- When nests are cooled, dip them quickly into the warm syrup, and sprinkle ground pistachios on the top for garnish.

Jasmine P. Andrews

BIRD'S NESTS

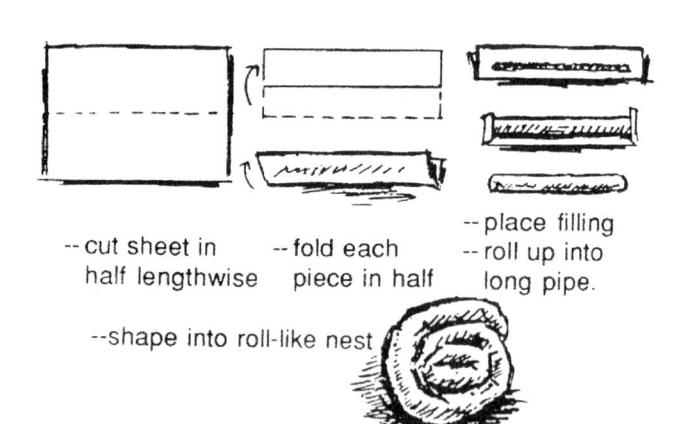

-- cut sheet in half lengthwise
-- fold each piece in half
-- place filling
-- roll up into long pipe.
--shape into roll-like nest

R. Frank Armstrong and his ca. 1910 Flanders Milk Truck. Mr. Armstrong ran Mill Pond Farm on Old County Road and had two milk routes. One route was Sandwich village and the other was a summer route in Hyannisport. In the 1920s there were 20 farms in Sandwich delivering milk. Orders stopped when pasteurization was legally required.

Photo courtesy of Rosanna Cullity

WILLIAM M. RILEY
Blacksmith, Wheelwright and Horse Shoeing

Automobile Repairing and Supplies
A SPECIALTY

DESSERTS - PUDDINGS & DESSERTS

Rusk Pudding.

5 Rusk sliced thin and buttered put in a deep dish with alternate layers of Rusk and Zante Currants. 1 qt of Milk, 4 eggs a little Nutmeg. To be eaten with wine sauce.

A. Williams

Albany Cake.

1½ lbs of Flour, ½ lb. of Butter, 1 lb. of Sugar, 2 eggs, a teaspoonfull of Pearlash dissolved in Milk, Carroway seed, add a little milk, enough to make it a stiff dough, roll them out in thin cakes, a very few minutes will bake them.

Small plain Cake

3 eggs, 1 cup Sugar, 1 cup of Butter mix it soft with Flour.

Page from a nineteeth century hand-written book of recipes.

QUICK-AND-EASY CORN-FLAKE PUDDING

Ingredients:

1 egg
1/2 cup sugar
1/2 cup molasses
1 qt. milk

4 cups Corn Flakes
Butter
1 Tbs. sugar
1 Tbs. cinnamon

Steps:
- Preheat the oven to 350°F.
- Beat egg, sugar and molasses together.
- Add milk and Corn Flakes.
- Pour the mixture into a baking dish, and put small pieces of butter on top.
- Mix sugar and cinnamon, and sprinkle on top.
- Bake in the oven for 30 to 45 minutes.

Mae Foster

GRAPENUT PUDDING

Ingredients:

2 cups cold milk
2 eggs
1/4 cup sugar

1/4 cup Grapenuts cereal
1 tsp. vanilla
Pinch ground nutmeg

Steps:
- Mix all ingredients except nutmeg, and let stand for 20 minutes.
- Preheat the oven to 350°F.
- Place mixture in a greased casserole or individual custard cups.
- Sprinkle the nutmeg on top.
- Place the pudding dish in a pan filled halfway with hot water, and bake in the oven about one hour.
Serves 4 to 6

Evelyn Broadbridge

"My advice to you is not to ask why or whither, but just to enjoy your ice cream while it's on your plate."

-Thornton Wilder, writer

LEMON SPONGE PUDDING

Ingredients:

1 cup sugar
1/4 cup flour
1/8 tsp. salt
2 Tbs. oleo margarine, melted
4-5 Tbs. lemon juice
2 egg yolks
1 cup milk, scalded
2 egg whites, beaten until stiff

Steps:
- Preheat the oven to 325°F.
- Combine the first four ingredients.
- Add the lemon juice.
- Stir in the egg yolks and scalded milk. Mix.
- Fold in the beaten egg whites.
- Pour all into a greased 1 1/2- to 2-qt. shallow casserole.
- Place the casserole in a pan of water so that the water surrounds the casserole pan.
- Bake in the oven for one hour.

Jackie Jacobson

BREAD PUDDING

Ingredients:

3 Tbs. butter
1/2 cup brown sugar
6 slices buttered white bread, cut into cubes
1/3 cup raisins
2 eggs
1 1/2 cup milk
Pinch salt
1/4 cup granulated sugar

Steps:
- Butter the top pan of a double boiler, and add the brown sugar to the double boiler.
- On top of the brown sugar place the buttered bread cubes and raisins. DO NOT STIR!
- In a mixing bowl, beat eggs, milk, salt, and granulated sugar well. Pour over the bread cubes in top of the double boiler. DO NOT STIR!
- Have the water boiling in the bottom portion of the double boiler, then lower slightly.
- Cook until set (about 30-45 minutes). Test for doneness with a knife.
- While the bread pudding is still warm, invert it onto a serving plate and spoon the sauce from the bottom of pan over top of it.
  Serves 4 to 6

Carol Horan

CREAMY RICE PUDDING

Serve warm!

Ingredients:

1 1/2 cups water
3/4 cup white rice, uncooked*
2 cups milk, divided
1/3 cup granulated sugar
1/4 tsp. salt

1 egg, beaten
2/3 cup golden raisins
1 Tbs. butter
1/2 tsp. vanilla extract
Pinch ground nutmeg or cinnamon

Steps:
- In a medium saucepan, bring the water to a boil. Add the rice and stir. Reduce heat, cover and simmer for 20 minutes.
- In a separate saucepan, combine 1 1/2 cups of the cooked rice, 1 1/2 cups of the milk, and all of the sugar and salt. Cook over medium heat until thick and creamy (15-20 minutes).
- Stir in the remaining 1/2 cup milk, the beaten egg and the raisins. Cook for two minutes more, stirring constantly.
- Remove pudding from the heat, and stir in the butter and vanilla extract.
- Sprinkle with nutmeg or cinnamon before serving, if desired.
  Serves 4
   * For creamier pudding, use short- or medium-grain rice

Steven Hauck

BLUEBERRY CRUMBLE

Ingredients:

4 cups blueberries
1 1/4 cups sugar
Juice of 1 lemon
Dash of cinnamon
1/3 cup butter

1 cup flour
1/4 tsp salt

Steps:
- Preheat the oven to 375°F.
- Mix the blueberries with half the sugar in a casserole. Sprinkle with lemon juice and cinnamon.
- Blend the remaining ingredients and sprinkle them over the berries.
- Bake for 40 minutes.
  Serves 6

Frances Meigs (Thornton W. Burgess's granddaughter)

CITRUS SPONGE PUDDING

Ingredients:

1 cup low-fat milk
1/2 cup pineapple juice
1/3 cup fresh lemon juice
2 Tbs. margarine, melted
1 tsp. grated lemon rind
1 tsp. grated orange rind
3 egg yolks

3/4 cup sugar
1/3 cup all-purpose flour
1/4 tsp. salt
3 egg whites, room temperature
Vegetable cooking spray
1 tsp. powdered sugar

Steps:
- Combine the first seven ingredients, stirring with a wire whisk; set aside.
- In a large bowl, combine the sugar, flour, and salt.
- Gradually add the milk mixture to the dry mixture, stirring well (batter will be thin).
- Beat the egg whites at high speed with a mixer until stiff peaks form.
- Gently stir one-fourth of the egg whites into the batter; gently fold in remaining egg whites.
- Pour the batter into a 1 1/2-qt. casserole dish that has been sprayed with vegetable spray, and place the dish into in an 8-inch-square baking pan that contains hot water to a depth of one inch.
- Bake at 350°F for 50 minutes or until golden brown.
- Sprinkle with powdered sugar.

Ann McDonnell

COLD LEMON SOUFFLE

Ingredients:

1 envelope gelatin
1/2 cup cold water
8 egg yolks, lightly beaten
1 3/4 cups sugar
1 cup lemon juice

1 tsp. salt
1/4 tsp. cream of tartar
8 egg whites, stiffly beaten
Almond slivers
Chocolate, grated

Steps:
- Soften the gelatin in the cold water.
- Beat the egg yolks lightly, then add 1 cup of the sugar, lemon juice and salt. Cook in a double boiler, stirring constantly until the mixture coats a spoon.
- Add the gelatin and blend thoroughly.
- Cool
- Add the cream of tartar to the egg whites, beating well. Add the

remaining sugar to the egg whites and continue beating until stiff peaks form.
- Fold both the egg-white mixture and the lemon mixture together and pour into a 2-qt. souffle dish.
- Chill for at leaast three hours.
- Garnish with almond slivers and chocolate curls.

Nancy McMaster

RHUBARB AND STRAWBERRY COMPOTE

This is a great way to cook rhubarb!

Ingredients:

4 cups fresh or frozen rhubarb, sliced
1 cup sugar
1/8 tsp. salt

2 cups fresh or frozen strawberries, hulled and halved
2 med. oranges, optional

Steps:
- In a large skillet, mix the rhubarb, sugar and salt. Cover and cook over low heat without stirring for 20-25 minutes, or until rhubarb is tender, shaking skillet occasionally.
- Cool.
- Stir in strawberries and oranges.

Carolyn Nelson

SWEDISH CREAM

Serve with fresh or frozen raspberries.

Ingredients:

1 envelope Knox gelatin
1 cup sugar

1 pint heavy cream
1 pint sour cream

Steps:
- Dissolve gelatin and sugar in cream over very low heat.
- Remove from heat and cool slightly.
- Stir in the sour cream.
- Pour into individual dishes or a bowl and chill for three hours or more.

Carolyn Nelson

KAHLUA MOUSSE

Ingredients:

1 lb. dark sweet chocolate
3 oz. butter or margarine
1/2 cup confectioners' sugar, sifted
3 eggs, separated

1/4 cup Kahlua liqueur
1 tsp. instant coffee
2 cups heavy whipping cream

Steps:
- In the top of a double boiler, melt the chocolate and butter over simmering water.
- In a separate bowl, combine the sugar, egg yolks, Kahlua and coffee powder.
- Blend the Kahlua mixture into the melted chocolate.
- Whip the cream until stiff peaks form; then, fold it into the chocolate mixture.
- Beat the egg whites until soft peaks form; fold into the chocolate mousse.
- Spoon mousse into a serving bowl or dessert glasses and refrigerate for four hours or overnight.

Ann McDonnell

FUDGE-BATTER PUDDING

Serve warm, spooning each portion of cake with cocoa syrup. Then pass the cream!

Ingredients:

1 cup flour
1/2 cup packed brown sugar
1/2 cup chopped nuts
3 Tbsp. cocoa
2 tsp. baking powder

1/2 tsp. salt
1/2 cup milk
2 Tbsp. oil
1 tsp. vanilla
Cocoa syrup, cream or half and half

Steps:
- Preheat the oven to 350°F.
- In a greased 2-quart casserole, stir together the flour, sugar, nuts, cocoa, baking powder and salt.
- Separately, combine the milk, oil and vanilla. Stir the wet mixture into the dry mixture until well blended.
- Pour cocoa syrup on top.
- Wipe the edges of the casserole and bake it in the oven for 40 minutes or until a pick inserted in the center comes out clean.
  Serves 6

Ann McDonnell

CREAM PUFFS

Fill these wonderful cream puffs with custard, ice cream or whipped cream for a delicious dessert—or fill them with chicken salad, shrimp salad or turkey salad for a tasty buffet item.

Ingredients:

1 cup water
1/2 tsp. salt
1/2 cup butter

1 cup flour
4 eggs

Steps:

- Preheat the oven to 425°F.
- Bring the water to a boil.
- Add the salt and butter. (Break the butter up to speed melting, as it's important that as little as possible of the water boil away.)
- Dump the flour into the boiling liquid and stir rapidly. As soon as the mixture holds together and looks like corn-meal mush, remove it from the heat.
- Beat in the eggs, one at a time, until the mixture is smooth.
- Drop batter by the tablespoon onto a shiny cookie sheet. Allow room for expansion.
- Bake for 20 minutes, then reduce the heat to 325°F and bake for 20 minutes longer, or until golden and crisp.
- Remove to cooling racks. Make a slit in each puff or cut off the top to speed cooling and drying.

Ann McDonnell

CRISPY EASTER NESTS

Ingredients:

One 7-oz. jar marshmallow creme (about 2 cups)
1/4 cup creamy peanut butter
2 Tbs. butter or margarine, melted

One 5-oz. can chow-mein noodles (about 3 cups)
1 cup chopped chocolate candies
Confectioners' sugar

Steps:

- Combine the marshmallow creme, peanut butter and butter, and mix until well blended.
- Add the noodles and chopped candies.
- Drop by rounded tablespoons onto greased cookie sheets. Shape with greased fingers to form nests. Let stand until firm.
- Dust the bottom of the nests lightly with confectioners' sugar, and fill the nests with chocolate candies before serving.

Ann McDonnell

HEATH-BAR CHOCOLATE TRIFLE

Ingredients:

1 pkg. chocolate-cake mix
1 cup Kahlua liqueur
2 pkgs. (4-serving size) instant chocolate pudding mix
Two 8-oz. containers Cool Whip
6 Heath bars, crushed

Steps:
- Prepare the cake as directed on the box, and bake it in a 13x9x2-inch pan. Cool.
- Crumble the chocolate cake into chunks. Put half the chunks into a clear, glass serving bowl.
- Sprinkle half of the Kahlua over the cake in the bowl.
- Make the pudding as directed on the box, and pour half the pudding over the liqueur-soaked cake.
- Add half of the Cool Whip to the top of the pudding in the bowl.
- Sprinkle with half of the Heath bars.
- Repeat the layers with the other half of the ingredients.
- Chill until ready to serve.

Wynne Joyce

COFFEE-ALMOND TORTONI

Ingredients:

1 cup whipping cream
1/2 cup sugar, divided
1/4 tsp. almond extract
1 tsp. vanilla extract
2 egg whites (at room temperature)
1/4 cup almonds; finely chopped and toasted
1/4 cup flaked coconut, toasted
1 tsp. instant coffee granules

Steps:
- Combine the whipping cream, 1/4 cup sugar and flavorings in a medium mixing bowl. Beat at high speed until soft peaks form. Set aside.
- Beat egg whites at high speed with an electric mixer just until foamy. Gradually add the remaining 1/4 cup sugar, one tablespoon at a time, beating until soft peaks form a meringue.
- Into the meringue, fold the whipped cream mixture, 2 Tbs. almonds and 2 Tbs. coconut to make a tortoni. Spoon half of the tortoni into eight muffin cups with foil liners.
- Stir the coffee granules into the remaining half of the tortoni left in the bowl; then spoon it into the muffin cups.
- Sprinkle the tops with the remaining almonds and coconut.

- Cover tightly and freeze for eight hours.
- Remove the frozen tortoni from the muffin pans and place them in a Ziploc heavy-duty bag, placing the bag back in the freezer to store.
- Remove tortoni from the freezer 15 minutes before serving.
Serves 8

Ann McDonnell

BAKED APPLES

Ingredients:

2 large Rome or Fuji apples
2 heaping Tbs. raisins
1/2 tsp. ground cinnamon
2 tsp. light brown sugar
1 tsp. lemon zest

Steps:
- Preheat the oven to 350° F.
- Grease a small loaf pan.
- Core the apples and use a knife to make a shallow "X"-shaped slit over the top hole, to prevent skin from bursting.
- Place the cored apples snugly in the pan. Stuff the raisins, cinnamon and brown sugar into their cavities.
- Sprinkle all with lemon zest.
- Pour about a half inch of water into the bottom of the pan and bake for 30-40 minutes.
- Cool slightly and enjoy!

Regina Murphy Silvia

CHOCOLATE DESSERT CREPES

Ingredients:

1 cup all-purpose flour
2 eggs
1 1/2 cups milk
1 Tbs. oil
1/3 cup instant cocoa powder, presweetened
1 tsp. vanilla

Steps:
- Combine all ingredients, beating until blended.
- Heat a greased 6-inch skillet.
- Pour two tablespoons of batter into the skillet for each crepe.
- Lift and tilt the skillet quickly to spread the batter. Brown on one side, then flip to brown second side.
Yields 16 to 18 crepes

Ann McDonnell

GRAND MARNIER CHOCOLATE MOUSSE

This is an elegant dessert for chocolate lovers everywhere. Serve with a generous dollop of whipped cream!

Ingredients:

21 oz. semi-sweet chocolate morsels
1 1/2 cups heavy cream
15 egg whites
7 Tbs. sugar
3 Tbs. Grand Marnier

Steps:
- Combine the chocolate and heavy cream in a double boiler over low heat until smooth. Let cool.
- Beat the egg whites until stiff peaks form, adding the sugar gradually.
- Add the Grand Marnier to the chocolate mixture.
- Once the egg whites are stiff, fold them gently into the chocolate mixture until evenly dispersed (use a rubber spatula to get the chocolate off the bottom).
- Chill for four hours before serving.
  Serves 15 or more
    Timothy Burgess Hikade (Great great grandson of Thornton W. Burgess)

Bread, men say, is the staff of life;
But they will oft concede
That were it not for our dainty desserts,
The staff would be heavy indeed.

—Unknown

DESSERTS - CONFECTIONS

CAPE COD VIEWS. N. & S.

Early view across Shawme Pond toward Grove St. in Sandwich village, showing Isaiah Tobey Jones and Charles H. Chapouil, great uncle of Thornton W. Burgess, the author of "Old Mother West Wind" and 160 books for children.

Thornton W. Burgess wrote in his autobiography, "Now I Remember", that as a young boy growing up on Cape Cod, he sold candies that his mother made to the glass factory workers. Maybe he used a wagon like this boy has in the picture - or maybe this boy could be young Thornton W. Burgess.

Photo credit
Sandwich Town Archives

"RULES OF AN EXPERT CANDY-MAKER"

by Mrs. Frances (Fannie) Hayward Burgess (mother of Thornton W. Burgess)
Good Housekeeping, December, 1900

"Use your judgment, child, use your judgment," was the sound but rather unsatisfactory advice of an old aunt of mine when besought for aid in the realms of pots and kettles. Since then I have learned what she meant, and many a time I have been tempted to repeat it to perplexed new candy-makers. But judgment without experience is impossible, and for that reason the experience of others may save many a bitter disappointment.

Fondant

Many a disappointment did I suffer until I took into account the weather. Then I had found the source of the greater part of my trouble and the keynote of success. All French cream candy has as its foundation fondant, and it is in the making of this that the weather plays so important a part. Nothing is more easily affected by the atmosphere than sugar. Therefore, I take advantage of the most favorable dry and clear days to make up my fondant, for in glass jars it will keep indefinitely. Then when I want to make up my bonbons just before the holidays I am sure that they will be just what they should be.

For the beginner it is easier to work with small quantities. To a pound of fine granulated sugar add a small cup of water and set to boil. When the first bubbles appear, add as much cream of tartar as you can take up on the point of a penknife, dissolved in a teaspoonful of water saved from the cup. Better too little tartar than too much, for in the latter case you will not be able to bring your fondant at all. Boil without stirring until upon dipping a fork into it and holding in the air a hair-like thread will hang from the tines. Then test a little in ice-cold water. If it gathers at the bottom in a soft ball, take from the fire, pour into a bowl and set to cool in a dry place away from water.

When I can bear a finger in it I begin to stir it with a large spoon. It soon thickens into a cream and when too thick to stir longer, I work it quickly and hard in my hands, like bread dough, until it is a smooth, stiff paste. There should be no grains whatever. If it granulates it probably has been boiled too long, and with a cup of boiling water added must be boiled over again with greater care. The perfect fondant melts instantly in the mouth. My fondant made, I have done enough for one day and find I enjoy the work more if I put it away and leave the making up into the various bonbons until another day. Pressed into a glass jar and covered it will keep for weeks.

Fourteen years of candy-making has convinced me that all the world likes chocolate. Therefore I find nothing more satisfactory than chocolate creams. Personally I prefer, and I have found many others do also, my creams made with plain, unsweetened chocolate, the filling being so very sweet that the slight bitterness of the chocolate is just what is needed. Candy-making requires quickness; everything must be ready to hand. So, on chocolate day I first crack a number of walnuts, taking care to retain the halves of the meat whole. I have also a dish of almonds shelled and skinned, such flavoring extracts as I am to use and a deep colored orange.

Orange and Nut Chocolates

Putting some of the fondant in a bowl, set in a pan of hot water on the stove, I grate enough orange peel into it to flavor it, adding just a speck of tartaric acid to give it tartness. If the fondant is very stiff it will stand a little juice from the orange, but if inclined to be soft it will not stand the extra moisture. As the fondant melts, I stir it constantly until the orange is thoroughly mixed in. If not stirred the fondant would go back to plain syrup. When thoroughly mixed I remove from the stove, stirring it until stiff enough to work with the hands. Breaking off small bits I mold them into small balls the size of marbles, putting them on a sheet of wax paper. When this is used up I treat another batch of fondant in like manner, save that this time I flavor with extract of vanilla instead of orange. When it cools so that I can work it with my hands I work the chopped nuts in.

They are now ready for dipping. The chocolate must be melted slowly in a cup or small bowl set in hot water on the back part of the stove or in the top of the teakettle. Turning a baking pan bottom up, I cover it with waxed paper. Taking a cream on the end of a fork I dip it into the melted chocolate, taking care that it is thoroughly covered, and then drop onto the pan, working as quickly as possible. On the top of each of the large creams I place the half of a walnut or an almond after dipping. When all are dipped, I set away to cool in as cold a place as I can find. All other flavors are made in the same manner.

Frances Burgess • 1900

ALMOND BUTTER CRUNCH

A Christmas favorite!

Ingredients:
1/2 lb. blanched almonds (chopped fine)
1 cup butter
1 cup sugar
One 12-oz. pkg. semi-sweet chocolate morsels

Steps:
- Toast the nuts lightly.
- Cook the butter and sugar together over low heat until the sugar melts.
- Add half the nuts.
- Cook until a candy thermometer inserted into the mixture reads 31F, stirring occasionally. Do not allow the mixture to burn!
- Pour into a lightly buttered 8x8-inch pan. Cool.
- Heat the chocolate over boiling water until nearly melted.
- Stir and spread half of the chocolate over the cooled nut mixture.
- Sprinkle with half the reserved nuts. Cool.
- Invert the candy and spread it with the remaining melted chocolate and nuts in the same way. Cool.
- Break into irregular shaped pieces to serve.
  HINT: Use the best quality chocolate you can find.
  Makes about 1 1/2 pounds

Sarah Burgess Morse (Great granddaughter of Thornton W. Burgess)

ALMOND BUTTER CRUNCH

This is the original recipe, but you can use any nut you want. Be careful, as the mixture is very hot.

Ingredients:
1 cup blanched slivered almonds
1/2 cup butter
1/2 cup sugar
1 Tbsp. light corn syrup

Steps:
- Line the bottom and sides of an 8-inch pan (square or round) with foil, and butter the pan heavily.
- Combine almonds, butter, sugar and corn syrup in a heavy 10-inch skillet, and bring to a boil over medium heat, stirring constantly. Boil until the mixture turns a golden brown (six or seven minutes).
- Work quickly to spread the candy in the prepared pan. Cool for 15 minutes or until firm.
- Remove the foil from the pan and peel off the candy.
- Cool thoroughly, then break into pieces.
  Makes 1 lb. of candy

Mary West

BARK

Top with chopped nuts if you like.

Ingredients:
2 Tbs. butter
3 sticks of butter
1 1/2 cups sugar
1 large box of Saltine-type crackers
Two 12-oz. bags of any baking morsels: semi-sweet chocolate, milk chocolate, white chocolate, peanut butter or butterscotch

Steps:
- Preheat the oven to 400°F.
- Line two cookie sheets with foil.
- Melt 2 Tbs. of butter and spread each cookie sheet with 1 Tbs. of it.
- Place crackers in a single layer on the cookie sheets.
- In a saucepan, melt the three sticks of butter and sugar, and bring to a boil for one minute. Spread the butter-sugar mixture over the Saltines, and cover the crackers on both sheet pans.
- Bake at 400°F for five minutes or until the crackers are brown and puffy. Remove baking trays from the oven and sprinkle one 12-oz. bag of baking morsels over the contents of each cookie sheet and let them melt for a few seconds. Spread the morsels completely over the crackers.
- Refrigerate trays for one hour, then break the candy into pieces.

Paula Looney (A similar recipe was also contributed by Nancy Bourdeau.)

CHURCH WINDOWS

Great for Christmas.

Ingredients:

One 12-oz. pkg. of chocolate chips
1/2 cup butter or margarine
One 10-oz. pkg. colored miniature marshmallows
1/2 cup chopped nuts (optional)
Coconut (shredded or flaked)

Steps:
- Melt butter and chocolate chips until soft. Cool slightly.
- Add marshmallows and nuts to the melted chocolate mixture.
- Place the coconut on wax paper.
- Drop the chocolate mixture onto the coconut, and roll into a log shape until the log is covered in coconut.
- Place chocolate log in the refrigerator for about one hour or until solid.
- Cut into slices like a jelly roll.

Cindy Dejardin and Samantha Schmechel

WHITE CRANBERRY-WALNUT FUDGE

Ingredients:

1 tsp. + 1/2 cup butter, divided
2 cups sugar
3/4 cup sour cream
1 cup dried cranberries, coarsely chopped
1 jar (7 oz.) marshmallow Fluff
1 tsp. vanilla
3 cups coarsely chopped walnuts
1 pkg. vanilla or white-chocolate baking morsels

Steps:
- Line an 8-inch square pan with foil and grease the foil with 1 tsp. butter.
- In a heavy saucepan, bring the sugar, sour cream and remaining butter to a boil. Cook and stir until a candy thermometer inserted into the mixture reads 234°F (about 15 minutes.)
- Remove mixture from heat. Add baking morsels, marshmallow Fluff and vanilla, and stir until smooth.
- Fold in the walnuts and cranberries, and pour into the prepared pan. Cool.
- When cooled, lift the fudge out of the pan and remove the foil. Cut into squares.
  Makes 3 pounds of candy

Norma Coleman

CREAMY CHOCOLATE CRESCENTS

I got this recipe from Better Homes and Gardens. It was a contest winner!

Ingredients:
Two 8-oz. bars milk chocolate
One 8-oz. container frozen whipped dessert topping, thawed
2/3 cup finely crushed vanilla wafers

Steps:
- In a heavy 2-qt. saucepan, melt the chocolate bars over low heat, stirring often. Cool to room temperature.
- Fold in dessert topping. Mixture will thicken.
- Cover and chill mixture for at least one hour
- Form chilled chocolate mixture into 1-inch crescent shapes.
- Roll crescents in cookie crumbs.
- Chill thoroughly.

Microwave Directions:
- Break chocolate bars into small squares in a 2-qt. microwave-safe casserole dish. Microwave uncovered on 100% power (high) for 2 1/2 minutes, stirring once.
- Stir until smooth.
- Continue as directed above.
  Makes about five-and-a-half dozen crescents

Pat Maguire

CHOCOLATE-COATED PECAN PRALINES

Ingredients:
1 lb. soft caramels   1 1/2 cups chopped pecans
2 Tbs. heavy cream   One 12-oz. bag of chocolate chips

Steps:
- Melt caramels and heavy cream in a double boiler.
- Add chopped pecans to the caramel-cream mixture.
- Drop the praline mixture by the teaspoonful onto a lightly greased baking sheet and let cool for at least 30 minutes.
- Melt the chocolate chips in a double boiler, and, when melted, dip the cooled pralines in the chocolate. Place the candies on wax paper to harden.
- Makes three to four dozen pralines.

Mary West

DAN'S MILLION-DOLLAR FUDGE

My son made this first when he was in middle school, and went up and down our street giving away small packages to neighbors at Christmas. He's had to make some every season since! Enjoy!

Ingredients:

4 1/2 cups sugar
12-oz. can evaporated milk
2 sticks margarine
3 cups semi-sweet chocolate chips
1 1/2 tsp. vanilla
1 cup chopped nuts

Steps:
- Mix together the sugar and evaporated milk in a pan.
- Bring milk mixture to a boil over medium heat, boil and stir for 10 minutes (set the timer), then remove from the heat.
- Stir in the chocolate chips and margarine, and heat until smooth.
- Add vanilla and nuts and blend.
- Pour into an 8x12-inch or a 9x9-inch pan or into individual 1-lb. pans.
- Cool completely. Remember, fudge cuts easier when it has been refrigerated. Makes 5 lbs. of candy

Daniel Bourdeau

PEANUT-BUTTER FLAKES

Ingredients:

2 cups light Karo corn syrup
2 cups sugar
2 cups peanut butter
2 Tbs. butter
1/2 tsp. vanilla
12 cups Corn Flakes cereal

Steps:
- Mix corn syrup with the sugar, and boil together.
- Add the peanut butter, butter and vanilla, and pour the whole mixture over the Corn Flakes. Mix.
- Drop the cereal mixture by spoonfuls onto wax paper or press into a pan. When cool, they are ready to be eaten. If pressed into a pan, you must cut into bars.

Tina VanKauwenberg

PEANUT-BUTTER BARS

Ingredients:

16 oz. confectioners' sugar
1 cup graham-cracker crumbs
1 cup peanut butter

2 sticks of melted butter or margarine
One 12-oz. pkg of chocolate chips, melted

Steps:
- Mix together the confectioners' sugar, graham-cracker crumbs, peanut butter and melted butter. Press firmly into a lightly greased 9x12-inch pan.
- Pour the melted chocolate chips evenly over the top of the crumb mixture and refrigerate for 10 minutes.
- Cut into squares and return to the refrigerator for one hour before removing from the pan.
  Makes appoximately 48 squares

Christina Evans

QUICK PEANUT-BUTTER FUDGE

Ingredients:

2 cups sugar
1/2 cup milk
3 Tbs. butter (lightly salted)

1/2 cup peanut butter
1/2 cup marshmallow Fluff
1 tsp. vanilla

Steps:
- Combine the sugar, milk and butter in a saucepan, and cook for three minutes.
- Next whip in the peanut butter, marshmallow Fluff and vanilla.
- Put mixture into a greased pan and refrigerate until stiff.
- Cut into squares when cooled.
  Makes appoximately 25 squares

Mae Foster

"Christmas-with its lots and lots of candies, cakes and toys-was made, they say, for proper kids, and not for naughty boys."

-Eugene Fields, poet

TEMPT-ME TRUFFLES

Ingredients:

4 cups powdered sugar (plus extra for dusting)
One 8-oz. pkg. cream cheese, softened
Five 1-oz. squares unsweetened chocolate, melted
1 tsp. vanilla
Almonds, chopped, toasted
Cocoa (for dusting)

Steps:
- Gradually add 4 cups powdered sugar to cream cheese, mixing well after each addition.
- Add the chocolate and vanilla; mix well.
- Chill mixture for several hours.
- Shape into 1-inch balls when cold.
- Roll balls in chopped almonds, cocoa or powdered sugar to decorate.
- Chill again.
  Makes 4 dozen truffles.

Pat Maguire

CHRISTMAS-JEWEL WHITE FUDGE

Ingredients:

Three 6-oz. pkgs. premium white chocolate
One 14-oz. can Eagle Brand sweetened condensed milk (not evaporated milk)
1 1/2 tsp. vanilla extract
1/8 tsp. salt
1/2 cup chopped green candied cherries
1/2 cup chopped red candied cherries

Steps:
- Over low heat, melt the white chocolate with sweetened condensed milk, vanilla and salt.
- Remove the chocolate mixture from the heat and stir in the green and red cherries.
- Spread fudge mixture into a foil-lined 8- or 9-inch square pan. Chill for two hours or until firm.
- Turn fudge onto a cutting board; peel off foil and cut into squares.
- Store covered in the refrigerator.

Optional:

- Rum-Raisin White Fudge
  Omit the vanilla and cherries and add 1 1/2 tsps. white vinegar, 1 tsp. rum flavoring and 3/4 cup of raisins. Proceed as above.

- Toasted Nutty White Fudge
  Omit the cherries and add 1 cup of chopped toasted nuts.
  Proceed as above.
  Makes about 2 1/4 pounds of fudge.

Jennie Zantuhos

PENUCHE FUDGE

Ingredients:

2 cups brown sugar
1/2 cup of cream or evaporated milk
Butter (the size of a large egg)

1 tsp. vanilla
3 Tbs. marshmallow Fluff

Steps:

- Cook brown sugar, cream and butter together until the mixture forms a soft ball when dropped in cold water.
- Add vanilla and marshmallow.
- Mix all ingredients and pour into a flat shallow pan (buttered).
- When the mixture is set, cut the candy into pieces.
  Makes appoximately 25 squares

Mae Foster

DIVINITY FUDGE

Ingredients:

2 cups sugar
1/2 cup Karo syrup

2 egg whites stiffly beaten
3/4 cup chopped walnuts

Steps:

- Boil sugar and Karo syrup until, when a fork is dipped into it and held in the air, a brittle thread will spin from the tines. (This takes about 15 minutes.)
- Beat in the egg whites.
- Add walnuts just before mixture is stiff enough for the pan.
- Pat the mixture into a flat shallow pan (buttered).
- When mixture is set, cut into pieces.
  Makes appoximately 25 squares

Mae Foster

Green Briar Jam Kitchen about 1905. Ida Putnam started the Jam Kitchen in 1903 in the small kitchen beyond the porch. This was a summer operation with just a cast iron stove for the first few years. In 1916 when sugar was rationed during WW1, the Jam Kitchen found its access to sugar allowed a large expansion of its business, and added the present large kitchen with multiple kerosene stoves. In the 1920s, an addition to the main house provided space for a tea room for the new tourists who came to Cape Cod.

Photo: Rosanna Cullity

INDEPENDENT, Sandwich, Mass. 20 September 1898

NEW TROUT TRUST

A company of well-known sportsmen, including Messrs. Grover Cleveland, Joseph Jefferson, C.B. Jefferson, E.C. Taft, and C.H. Taylor of Buzzards Bay, Edson J. White of Boston, J.L.Wesson, H.A. Belcher, A.H. Armstrong, and J.H. Foster of Sandwich have leased the "Springs" at Green Briar and will stock the same with trout. This minature lake is a beautiful sheet of water, about a half a mile in length, and but a few rods wide. It is pronounced an ideal place to grow trout. Three thousand fish will be put in the first of the month and in the spring a still larger number will be added. The work will be superintended by S.S. Chipman.

The Springs at Green Briar later became the magical "Smiling Pool" in the wonderful stories of Peter Rabbit and his animal friends by Thornton W. Burgess.

Beach Plum

"Even now after more than threescore years I could go to the exact spot where once blossomed the earliest and the pinkest mayflowers; to the very bush, if it still survives, that bore exceptionally large beach plums; and to the distant, partly fallen old stone wall smothered under the tangled vines that also climbed the neighboring tree and bore the biggest bunches of rich purple fruit to make the finest grape jelly in the world."

-Thornton W. Burgess, excerpted from *Now I Remember*, 1960

PRESERVING THE PAST

Jams, jellies, pickles and preserves have been made at the Green Briar Jam Kitchen for over 100 years. Ida Putnam first started cooking up batches of jams like strawberry, peach, cranberry and blueberry for use in her tearoom.

The Jam Kitchen today looks very similar to when it was first added on to Green Briar in 1916, once Ida's business started to flourish. Thornton Burgess would often stop by the Jam Kitchen when visiting his hometown of Sandwich, MA.

The Thornton W. Burgess Society purchased the property from Martha Blake in 1979. Martha had worked in the kitchen under Ida's direction for over forty years, and continued the tradition of making jams until her retirement at the age of 75.

Today, the Society operates the kitchen in the same way that Ida and Martha did—using only the freshest ingredients, and preparing products in small batches. Visitors can walk through the kitchen from April through December and see firsthand how our products are made. Profits from the sale of the Jam Kitchen products support the Society's mission of "inspiring reverence for wildlife and concern for the natural environment" through its environmental education programs.

GETTING STARTED ON PRESERVING AT HOME

To make jams, jellies, etc. at home, you will need certain pieces of equipment. These include jelly jars, lids, a funnel, ladle, knife, cheesecloth and, for jellies, a jelly bag. An eight-to-nine-quart pot (sometimes called a kettle in this section) is the correct size for our recipes. These items are readily available at supermarkets and hardware stores.

To ensure that the products you make will keep properly, certain precautions must be taken. The jars must be sterilized. Jars may be sterilized in the dishwasher, using the full wash cycle and full dry cycle with full heat. They can also be sterilized by hand, using hot soapy water with some ammonia added and scrubbing the jars with a bottle brush. To rinse by hand, run the jars under tepid water to remove the soap, then place them in the sink and pour boiling water over each, making sure the water goes around the rim of each jar, inside and out. Once this has been done, using a potholder or rubber gloves, shake the water around in each jar and pour it over the remaining jars. The jars can then be placed upside down on a clean towel on a tray or on a rack.

At the Jam Kitchen, we sterilize the one-piece lids by wetting a piece of clean cloth or cheesecloth with brandy (or any alcohol product), using it to wipe the inside of each lid. Once this has been done, we place lids in a clean container with the rubber side down. (The covers for two-piece lids can be sterilized just as the jars are when done by hand.)

Once the jars and lids are sterilized and the product is made, the jars are filled, using a funnel, ladle and knife. Fill each jar full, so that a kitchen knife placed horizontally on the top of the jar will touch the product in the jar. When using the two-piece lids, the manufacturer suggests processing them in a hot-water bath after the jars have been sealed. (You need to leave 1/2— to 1/4-inch of space—called "headroom"—between the lid and the top of the jam or jelly when you are filling those jars.)

Using the knife, go around the inside edge of the jar, knifing up and down as you go, to get rid of any air bubbles. When the bubbles are removed and the jar is full, use a piece of cheesecloth (dipped in water and wrung) to wipe the upper outside edge of the jar and the screw edge, to remove any juice or pieces of fruit. Place the lid on the jar and screw it on tight. The jars are then sealed, and will keep for up to one year on a cupboard shelf. Washing the full jars in soapy water and ammonia will make them shine. Remember to refrigerate jars once they have been opened!

Many of the recipes provided for this section are from our jam classes. The Society offers jam-making classes throughout the year for adults and families. Class participants learn the ins and outs of jam making, and take home between four and six jars from each class. Consider joining us sometime!

JAMS - Jams are made from crushed fruit.

TIP FOR NEW JAM MAKERS: One way to tell if jam is at the setting point is by using the "cold saucer" test. Put a saucer or small plate in the freezer for 15 minutes while you're getting started on making your jam. When you think the jam might be close to ready, take the saucer out of the freezer and place a small amount of jam (a drop or two) on it. Put the plate back in the freezer until the jam is cooled (just to to room temperature). The jam is ready if it jells when you touch it.

STRAWBERRY JAM

Ingredients:

3 pints strawberries, hulled and washed
4 cups sugar

Steps:
- Place strawberries in a pan. Crush slightly (do not puree), and add sugar. Bring to a boil.
- Reduce heat and boil gently until the jam has reached its setting point (about 15 to 20 minutes). Skim foam from surface.
- Pour the jam into sterilized jars and seal.
  Yields five 6-oz. jars

PEAR-PINEAPPLE-LEMON JAM

Ingredients:

3 lemons
2 lbs. pears, cored and sliced
1 1/2 cups crushed pineapple
5 cups sugar
1/4 cup Kirsch liqueur

Steps:
- Grate lemon rinds and juice the lemons. Set aside the gratings and juice. Discard pulp.
- Put the pears, pineapple, lemon juice and lemon-rind gratings in a saucepan and simmer for 10 minutes.
- Add sugar and cook over low heat, stirring constantly, until the sugar has dissolved.
- Bring to boil and boil until the setting point is reached.
- Add the Kirsch and mix well.
- Pour the jam into sterilized jars and seal.
  Yields five 6-oz. jars

PEACH JAM

Ingredients:
3 lbs. peaches, peeled and pitted
3 1/3 cups sugar

Steps:
- Cut the peaches up according to your preference and place them in a pan. Add sugar. Bring the contents of the pan to a boil.
- Reduce heat to maintain a moderate boil. Cook jam until thick and glossy.
- Pour the jam into sterilized jars and seal.
  Yields four 6-oz. jars

BLUEBERRY-PEACH JAM

Ingredients:
2 pints blueberries
2 lbs. peaches, peeled and pitted
4 cups sugar

Steps:
- Pick over and wash the blueberries; remove stems. Place in a pan.
- Cut up peaches according to your preference, and place them in the pan with the blueberries. Add sugar and bring to a boil.
- Reduce heat and boil moderately until the jam is thick and glossy.
- Pour the jam into sterilized jars and seal.
  Yields five 6-oz. jars

FALL-FRUIT JAM

Ingredients:

1 lb. pears, peeled, cored and diced
1/3 cup water
1 lb. apples, peeled, cored and diced
3 /4 lb. cranberries or pitted diced plums
3 cups sugar

Steps:
- Put the pears in a kettle with water, and cook gently. Add the apples and cranberries or plums, as well as the sugar to the pan and bring to a boil.
- Reduce heat and boil jam moderately until it is thick and glossy.
- Pour the jam into sterilized jars and seal.
  Yields five 6-oz. jars

CRANBERRY JAM

Ingredients:
2 lbs. cranberries
3 cups sugar

Steps:
- Wash and de-stem the cranberries. Cook them in a small amount of water until their skins break.
- Put the cranberries through a blender or food processor and return the puree to the kettle.
- Add sugar and cook for about 15 minutes.
- Pour jam into hot, sterilized jars and seal.
  Yields three pints

STRAWBERRY-RHUBARB JAM

Ingredients:
2 pints strawberries, washed and hulled
1 lb. rhubarb, washed and diced
4 cups sugar

Steps:
- Place the strawberries in a pan and crush slightly. Do not puree!
- Add sugar to the strawberries in the pan and bring to a boil.
- Reduce heat and boil gently for 15 minutes.
- Add the rhubarb to the strawberry mixture and return to a boil. Boil gently until jam is thick and glossy and has reached the setting point.
- Skim foam from the top.
- Pour into sterilized jars and seal.
  Yields five 6-oz. jars

APRICOT-PEAR JAM

Ingredients:

1/2 lb. dried apricots, chopped or quartered, and soaked in water overnight
1 1/2 lbs. pears, peeled, cored and chopped
1/4 cup lemon juice
3 cups sugar

Steps:
- Put the chopped apricots and pears in a pan and cook over low heat for ten minutes.
- Add sugar and cook, stirring over low heat until the sugar is dissolved.
- Bring the jam to a boil and cook until thick.
- Pour the jam into sterilized jars and seal.
  Yields four 6-oz. jars

NO-COOK FREEZER PEACH OR RASPBERRY JAM*

Ingredients:

2 1/4 cups crushed peaches
  (peel and pit before crushing)
2 Tbs. lemon juice
2 cups sugar
3/4 cups water
1 box fruit pectin

Steps:
- Place the fruit and lemon juice into a large bowl.
- Stir the sugar into the fruit.
- Set the fruit aside for ten minutes, stirring occasionally.
- Mix water and fruit pectin in a small saucepan. (It may be lumpy before cooking.) Bring the water-pectin mixture to a boil over high heat, stirring constantly. Continue boiling and stirring for 1 minute.
- Stir the hot pectin mixture into the fruit mixture, and stir constantly for three minutes. A few sugar crystals may remain.
- Fill all jars to within 1/2 an inch of the jar top. Wipe off the top edges of the jars, and quickly cover them with lids.
- Let the jars stand at room temperature for 24 hours, then place them in the freezer.
- After opening, store the jars in the refrigerator.
  Yields five cups of jam

* A similar recipe was submitted for No-Cook Red Raspberry Jam. Use 3 cups of crushed red raspberries, 5 1/4 cups sugar and omit the lemon juice. Follow steps as above. Makes six cups.

JELLIES - Jellies are made from strained fruit juices.

APPLE JELLY

Ingredients:
4 lbs. apples
Water
3/4 cup sugar

Steps:
- Wipe the apples, and remove any stems and blossom ends. Cut the apples into quarters.
- Put the apples into a kettle and add water to nearly cover the apples. Cover the kettle and cook slowly until the apples are soft.
- Put the cooked mixture into a jelly bag and hang it until the juice stops dripping.
- Measure the juice into a jelly kettle and boil it for twenty minutes.
- Add 3/4 cup of sugar, and boil for an additional five minutes. Skim the top for foam and ladle the jelly into jars.
- Put the jars in a sunny window and let them stand for twenty-four hours.
- Put a thin layer of paraffin wax on the top of the jars and cap them.
- Store in a cool place.

- For Mint Jelly: After skimming, add green food coloring and mint flavoring to taste.
- For Cinnamon Jelly: After skimming, add red food coloring and cinnamon flavoring to taste.
- For Quince or Crab Apple Jelly, replace the apples in the above recipe with either quince or crab apples.

Mae Foster

JALAPENO JELLY

Ingredients:

1/2 cup bell peppers, washed and seeded
1 cup jalapeno peppers, washed and seeded
6 1/2 cups sugar
1 1/2 cups cider vinegar
2 packages Certo liquid fruit pectin
Green food coloring

Steps:
- Chop the peppers together in a blender or food processor.
- Place the peppers, sugar and vinegar in a large pot and bring to a rolling boil. Cook until mixture is transparent, about 25 minutes.
- Remove mixture from heat and let stand for five to ten minutes.
- Add fruit pectin and food coloring, and stir well.
- Pour into sterilized jars and seal.
  Yields six small jars

GRAPE JELLY

Ingredients:

3 1/2 lbs. grapes (enough to make 5 cups of juice), washed, stems removed
7 cups of sugar
1 1/2 cups water

Steps:
- Crush grapes and place in a saucepan. Add water and bring to a boil. Cover and simmer for ten minutes.
- Place a jelly bag in a large bowl. Pour the cooked fruit into the bag, then tie it and hang it to let the juice drip into the bowl.
- Measure juices and, if necessary, add up to 1/2 cup of water to reach an exact measure.
- Combine the juice and sugar, and bring to a full rolling boil over high heat, stirring constantly.
- Skim the top for foam, and ladle the jelly into sterilized jars.
- Put the jars in a sunny window, and let stand for twenty-four hours.
- Put a thin layer of paraffin wax on top of the jars and cap them.
- Keep them in a cool place.

Mae Foster

MARMALADES - Marmalades are jellies with small pieces of fruit in them.

SPRING MARMALADE

Ingredients:

1 seedless orange
1 cup water
2 lbs. rhubarb, washed and diced
2 cups crushed pineapple
4 cups sugar

Steps:
- Cut the ends from the orange and discard. Slice the orange in half lengthwise, then slice each half lengthwise into thirds. Remove the white center pith and slice each wedge crosswise as thin as possible.
- Place water and orange in a pan and cook the orange gently until the water is almost evaporated.
- Place the rhubarb in the pan with the orange. Add the pineapple and sugar, and bring to a boil.
- Reduce heat and boil gently until the marmalade is thick and glossy.
- Pour the marmalade into sterilized jars and seal.
- Yields four to five 6-oz. jars

CRANBERRY MARMALADE

Ingredients:

1 grapefruit
1 orange
1/2 a lemon
3 cups water
3 cups cranberries
5 cups sugar

Steps:
- Cut the ends from the grapefruit, orange and lemon and discard. Cut each fruit in half lengthwise, then cut each half into three lengthwise wedges. Remove the white center pith and slice each wedge crosswise into thin wedges.
- Place the grapefruit, orange and lemon wedges in a pan. Add water and cook gently until the water is almost evaporated.
- Pick over the cranberries and wash them. Add the cranberries and sugar to the pan with the citrus fruit. Bring to a boil.
- Reduce the heat and cook marmalade until it's thick and glossy, 20 to 25 minutes.
- Pour marmalade into sterilized jars and seal.
  Yields six 6-oz. jars

APRICOT AND GINGER MARMALADE

We use fresh ginger in our Jam Kitchen recipes, but you can also substitute crystallized ginger. Below, please find our method for preserving fresh ginger.*

Ingredients:
2/3 lb. dried apricots, rinsed and chopped, then soaked in 2 cups water for 24 hours
1/3 cup preserved ginger*
2 1/2 cups sugar

Steps:
- Place the apricots, their water and the ginger in a pan. Bring them to a boil and simmer for twenty minutes.
- Add the sugar and stir over a low heat until dissolved.
- Bring the mixture to a boil and boil rapidly for about ten minutes, stirring occasionally, until the marmalade is thick and glossy and the setting point is reached.
- Pour marmalade into sterilized jars and seal.
  Yields five 6-oz. jars.

* Preserving fresh ginger-Peel fresh ginger and cut it into crosswise slices. Cover the sliced ginger with water and bring to a boil. Reduce heat and cook until tender. Drain and save the cooking liquid. Put the ginger through a food processor, grinder or chop finely by hand and set aside. Use 2 cups of sugar for every pound of ginger before it was cooked. Using the reserved cooking liquid, use 1 cup of liquid for every 2 cups of sugar used. Add the liquid to the sugar in the pan. Bring the pan to a boil and cook for fifteen minutes until it has become syrup. Add the ginger to the syrup and bring it back to a boil. Put into jars and seal.

PINEAPPLE-ORANGE MARMALADE

Ingredients:
1 orange, washed
1 lime, washed
1 cup orange juice
2 medium ripe pineapples (about 4 lbs. total), washed, peeled and chunked, with "eyes" and core removed or 1 can (20 oz.) crushed pineapple in its juices
4 cups sugar

Steps:
- Remove the peels from both the orange and the lime, and discard the white pith. Cut the citrus peels into very thin strips. Set aside the fruit.
- In a saucepan combine the peels and the orange juice and bring to a boil. Reduce heat, cover and simmer for twenty minutes. Do not drain.
- Section the fruit of the orange and the lime over a bowl to catch the juices. Add the sections and the juice to the pan with the peels.
- Add the pineapple and sugar to the pan. Bring slowly to a boil until the sugar dissolves. Reduce the heat and cook until the marmalade is thick and glossy, and pineapple is tender (20 to 25 minutes).
- Keep cooking until the marmalade thickens up. Stir frequently to prevent sticking.
- Pour into sterilized jars and seal.
  Yields four to five 6-oz. jars

SPICED ORANGE MARMALADE

Ingredients:

1 grapefruit	Water
6 oranges	1/3 cup ginger
2 lemons	Sugar

Steps:
- **Day One:** Cut and discard the ends from the grapefruit, the oranges and the lemon. Cut each fruit in half lengthwise. Next, cut each orange and lemon half into three further lengthwise wedges, and each grapefruit half into four lengthwise wedges. Remove the white center pith and slice each wedge crosswise into thin wedges.
- Measure the fruit into a bowl, and add 2 cups of water for each cup of pulp.
- Let stand overnight.

- **Day Two:** Bring fruit and water to a boil, reduce heat and cook at a medium boil until mixture is reduced by half. Again, let stand overnight.

- **Day Three:** Measure the fruit, and add 2 cups of sugar for each cup of pulp. (Use no more than 8 cups of pulp for each batch of marmalade.)
- Bring the marmalade to a boil, reduce heat and cook at a medium boil for about 20 minutes, or until thick.
- Pour into sterilized jars and seal.
  Yields five 6-oz. jars

CONSERVES - Conserves usually consist of two or more fruits, as well as nuts and raisins.

CRANBERRY CONSERVE

Ingredients:

1 orange	2/3 cup raisins
3 cups cranberries, picked over and washed	2/3 cup water
1 cup sugar	1/3 cup nuts of your choice

Steps:
- Cut the ends from the orange and discard them, then cut the orange in half lengthwise. Cut each half into three lengthwise wedges. Remove the white center pith and slice each wedge crosswise into thin wedges.
- Place all ingredients, except nuts, into a pan and bring to a boil. Cook for about twenty minutes.
- Add nuts and stir in well.
- Pour into sterilized jars and seal.
  Yields three 6-oz. jars

PLUM CONSERVE

Ingredients:

1 orange	1 cup raisins
1 cup water	2 2/3 cups sugar
2 lbs. plums, washed and pitted and chopped small	3/4 cup nuts

Steps:
- Cut the orange lengthwise in half. Cut each half into three further lengthwise wedges. Remove seeds and white center pith, and discard them. Cut each orange wedge into thin slices and place the fruit in a kettle.
- Add water and cook the orange slices over low heat for about 10 minutes.
- Place the plum fruit in the kettle with the orange. Add remaining ingredients and bring conserve to a boil.
- Reduce heat and boil over moderate heat until thick and glossy.
- Remove from heat. Add nuts and stir well.
- Pour conserve into sterilized jars and seal. Yields five 6-oz. jars

BLUEBERRY CONSERVE

Ingredients:

1/2 a lemon	1 qt. blueberries, washed and stemmed
1/2 an orange	
1 cup water	3 cups sugar
1/2 cup raisins	

Steps:
- Cut the ends from the lemon and orange halves and discard. Cut each fruit half into three lengthwise wedges. Remove the white center pith, and slice each wedge crosswise into thin slices. Place the slices in a pan and add the water.
- Cook the citrus fruit over low heat until the water is almost gone.
- Add the blueberries, raisins and sugar to the citrus and bring to a boil.
- Reduce heat and cook, stirring frequently, for about 20 minutes or until conserve is thick and shiny.
- Pour conserve into sterilized jars and seal. Yields five 6-oz. jars

STRAWBERRY CONSERVE

Ingredients:

1 orange
1 lemon
1 qt. strawberries, washed and hulled
4 1/2 cups sugar
1/3 cup almonds, blanched and sliced

Steps:
- Grate the peels from the orange and lemon, and squeeze the juice from each. Put the rind gratings and the juice in a pan.
- Add the strawberries and sugar to the rinds and juices in the pan and bring to a boil.
- Reduce heat to medium and cook for about 35 minutes, or until conserve is thick and shiny.
- Add the almonds, and cook for a few minutes longer.
- Pour the conserve into sterilized jars and seal.
  Yields five 6-oz. jars

CRANBERRY-PINEAPPLE CONSERVE

Ingredients:

1 orange
1 1/2 cups water
3 cups cranberries
1 cup pineapple, crushed
2 1/2 cups sugar
3/4 cup raisins
1/2 cup nuts of your choice

Steps:
- Cut the ends from the orange and discard. Cut the orange in half lengthwise and cut each half into three further lengthwise wedges. Remove the white center pith and slice each wedge crosswise into thin slices. Place the orange slices in a pan, add the water and cook gently while preparing the cranberries.
- Pick over the cranberries and wash them. Add them and the remaining ingredients-except the nuts-to the pan and bring to a boil. Reduce heat and cook until the conserve is thick and glossy.
- Add nuts and stir well.
- Put into sterilized jars and seal.
  Yields six 6-oz. jars

PICKLES & RELISHES

BREAD-AND-BUTTER PICKLES

Ingredients:

2 English or 5 pickling-size cucumbers
5 small white onions, sliced thin
2 Tbs. coarse pickling salt
1 1/2 cups white grape juice, simmered down from 3 cups

2/3 cup cider vinegar
1/3 tsp. whole mustard seed
1/4 tsp. celery seed
1/2 tsp. black pepper
1/4 tsp. turmeric powder
1 cup sugar

Steps:
- Score the cucumbers lengthwise with the tines of a fork. Cut them into medium-thick slices (about five slices per inch), and discard the hard ends.
- Put both cucumber and onion slices into a bowl and cover them with the pickling salt. Mix so that all slices are covered with the salt, and let them stand for 30 minutes.
- Rinse the cucumber and onion slices in cold water.
- Combine the cucumbers, onions, sugar, juice and seasonings in a large, non-aluminum kettle. Heat to boiling, and boil for five minutes.
- Pack the pickles immediately into clean, hot jars and seal with lids.
- Process the pickles in a water bath for 10 minutes after the water returns to boiling.
  Yields two pints

RIPE-TOMATO RELISH

Ingredients:

3 lbs. firm, ripe tomatoes, peeled and sliced
1 large onion, chopped
1 large red pepper, chopped
1 large green pepper, chopped
1 1/2 cups of celery, chopped
2 1/2 tsp. salt

1/2 tsp. ginger
1/2 tsp. nutmeg
2/3 cup vinegar
1/2 tsp. cloves
1/2 tsp. allspice
1/4 tsp. dry mustard
1 cup sugar

Steps:
- Place sliced tomatoes in a pan and bring to a boil. Cook for ten minutes and drain, then return tomatoes to pan.
- Add the vegetables, spices and vinegar to the tomatoes and mix well. Bring to a boil and cook for fifteen minutes.

➤

- Add the sugar and cook for an additional fifteen to thirty minutes, or until relish is thick.
- Put into sterilized jars and seal.
  Yields five 6-oz. jars

"SWEET" PEPPER RELISH

Ingredients:

2 1/2 lbs. red peppers (or half red and half green), washed, cored and seeded and cut into a fine dice
1 lb. onions, peeled and cut into a fine dice

1 1/2 tsp. mustard seed
1 Tbs. salt
3/4 cup sugar
1 cup vinegar
1/4 cup water

Steps:
- Place the peppers and onions in a pan with the rest of the ingredients and bring to a boil. Boil gently until the onions are transparent but still hold their shape.
- Put the relish into sterilized jars and seal.
  Yields six 6-oz. jars

ZUCCHINI RELISH

Ingredients:

6 cups zucchini, chopped
1/2 a red pepper, chopped
3 to 4 onions, chopped
2 1/2 Tbs. salt
2 cups sugar

1 1/2 cups vinegar
1 1/2 tsp. dry mustard
1/4 tsp. celery seed
1/4 tsp. ground red pepper
1/4 tsp. turmeric

Steps:
- Place the first four ingredients into a large bowl and let sit for one hour.
- Rinse the vegetables with cold water and drain well.
- Place the drained vegetables into a kettle with the remaining ingredients and bring to a boil. Cook for ten minutes.
- Put the relish into sterilized jars and seal.
  Yields six 6-oz. jars

APPLE & LEMON RELISH

Ingredients:

6 good-sized apples, peeled and quartered
1 lemon, sliced
Water
1 1/2 cup sugar

Steps:
- Cover the quartered apples and sliced lemon with water and add 1 cup of sugar. Boil gently until the apples are tender.
- Add the other 1/2 cup sugar, and cook slowly until the syrup thickens.
- Put into sterilized jars and seal.
  Yields five 6-oz. jars

Grace Chipman

CORN RELISH

Ingredients:

2 cups vinegar
1/4 cup cold water
1 1/2 cups sugar
3/4 cup flour
2 Tbs. salt
1 tsp. dry mustard
1/2 tsp. turmeric
4 ears worth of fresh corn, cut off the cob
1/4 bunch celery, diced
2 white onions, sliced thin
1 green pepper, diced
1/2 a red pepper, diced

Steps:
- Place all ingredients except the vegetables into a pan. Stir the mixture until smooth, then bring to a boil.
- Add the vegetables and cook for 25 minutes, stirring frequently.
- Put into sterilized jars and seal.
  Yields five 6-oz. jars

YELLOW-SQUASH PICKLES

Ingredients:

2 qts. yellow squash, thinly sliced
1 qt. onion, thinly sliced
1 large green pepper, cored, seeded and cut into pieces
1 cucumber, unpeeled and thinly sliced
1/4 red pepper, cut into small pieces

1/4 cup coarse salt
2 cups cider vinegar
3 cups sugar
2 tsp. celery seed
1/2 tsp. dill weed
2 tsp. mustard seed
1/2 tsp. turmeric

Steps:
- Layer the squash, onions, cucumbers and red peppers in a large bowl and sprinkle with salt as you layer. Put some ice cubes on top and let stand for one hour or more. Drain in a colander.
- Combine the remaining ingredients in a pan and bring to a boil. Stir well and simmer for 5 minutes.
- Add the drained vegetables and bring to a full boil. Boil until the cucumber becomes transparent.
- Put into sterilized jars and seal.
  Yields six 6-oz. jars

CHUTNEYS - Chutneys are a combination of vegetables and/or fruits, spices and vinegars.

ORANGE CHUTNEY

Ingredients:

4 navel oranges
3 apples, peeled and cored
2 medium onions
2/3 cup raisins
1 1/3 cups brown sugar

1/4 cup preserved ginger
1/2 tsp. crushed hot pepper
1/2 Tbs. salt
1/8 tsp. black pepper
2 1/2 cups vinegar

Steps:
- Grate the orange rind and set aside. Peel the orange and section the fruit. Cut the sections into small chunks.
- Cut the apples into small pieces.
- Put the grated rind, orange chunks, apple pieces and all other ingredients into a pan and mix well. Bring to a boil.
- Reduce heat and simmer until the mixture is thick, stirring frequently.
- Pour the chutney into sterilized jars and seal.
  Yields five 6-oz. jars

CRANBERRY, GINGER AND LEMON CHUTNEY

This chutney can be prepared up to one week ahead, covered tightly and refrigerated.

Ingredients:

1 lemon
One 12-oz. bag fresh or frozen cranberries
2 cups sugar
1/2 cup diced crystallized ginger or preserved ginger
1/3 cup onion, finely chopped
1 clove garlic, minced
1 jalapeno pepper, seeded and minced
1 cinnamon stick
1/2 tsp. dry mustard
1/2 tsp. salt

Steps:
- Grate the yellow zest from the lemon and set aside. Cut the lemon crosswise in half, pick out the seeds and remove the white pith. Dice the lemon pulp into 1/4-inch pieces.
- Combine all ingredients in a pan and bring to a boil over medium heat, stirring often to help dissolve the sugar.
- Reduce the heat to low and simmer until the sauce is thick and the cranberries have burst (10 to 15 minutes).
- Let the chutney cool completely to room temperature and remove the cinnamon stick before serving.
  Makes about three cups or 12 servings

PINEAPPLE CHUTNEY

Ingredients:

1 cup cider vinegar
1 cup light-brown sugar
2 1/2 cups crushed pineapple
4 tsp. minced garlic
2 hot peppers, seeded and minced or 1 tsp. crushed red pepper
2 tsp. salt
2 tsp. gingerroot, fresh, peeled and chopped
2/3 cup nuts of your choice, chopped

Steps:
- Boil the vinegar and sugar together for five minutes.
- Add all remaining ingredients, except nuts, and cook for about 30 minutes.
- Add the nuts and mix well.
- Put into sterilized jars and seal.
  Yields five or six 6-oz. jars

K. T. BROWN

DEALER IN

CHOICE MEATS and PROVISIONS

FRUITS and VEGETABLES

ITALIAN MEATS AND CANNED GOODS

Choice Farm Poultry a Specialty

Telephone Orders Promptly Attended to.

Telephone at House and Market

SAGAMORE,   MASS.

MEAT & POULTRY

From the Bourne, Falmouth, & Sandwich Business Directory 1905

Note the Telephone orders listed. In 1908 there were 2 public phones available in Sandwich, one in Town Hall and the other at J.A. Hall's gasoline station on Route 6A, East Sandwich.

167

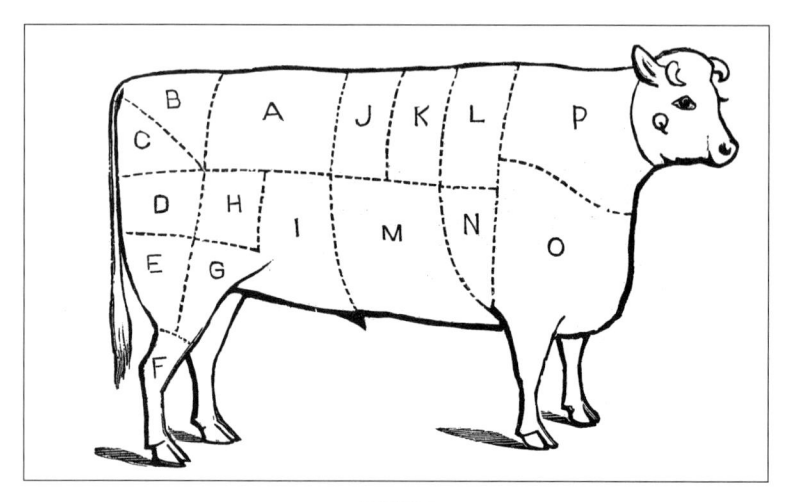

BEEF

FORE QUARTER
- J. Fore ribs, a prime roast piece.
- K. Middle ribs, for roasts.
- L. Chuck ribs, for second choice roasts.
- M. Brisket, for soups, corned beef, etc.
- N. Shoulder, for pot roasts, stews.
- O. Sticking piece (neck), for sausages, stock, soups, etc.
- P. Same as O in name and uses.
- Q. Cheek.

HIND QUARTER
- A. Porterhouse and sirloin steaks.
- B. Rump, for corned beef, stews and steaks.
- C. Aitch bone, for pot roasts, stews, etc.
- D. Round or buttock, for steaks, pot roasts and boiling.
- E. Round, for boiling and stewing.
- F. Shin, for hashes, soups, etc.

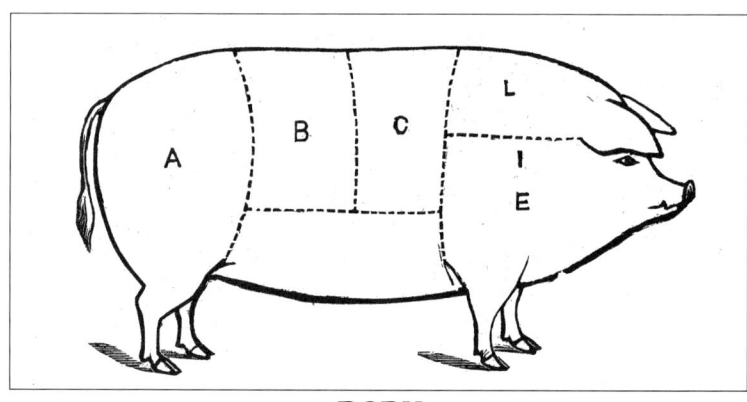

PORK

- A. The leg, for roasts and smoked hams.
- B. Sirloin, for chops and roasts, furnishing the choicest.
- C. Fore loin, furnishes second choice roasts, chops, etc.
- L. Neck, furnishes inferior roasts, and boiling pieces; to be used for corning.
- E. Shoulder, used mostly for pickling and smoking, and is fine for boiling, whether fresh or corned.

ORANGE MANDARIN CHICKEN

Ingredients:

2 Tbs. sesame oil
4 boneless chicken breasts, halved
1/2 tsp. salt
1/4 tsp. black pepper
One 11-oz. can mandarin oranges in light syrup, undrained
1/2 cup green onions, chopped
1 Tbs. jalapeno pepper, finely chopped and seeded
1 tsp. garlic, minced
1/2 cup fat-free less-sodium chicken broth
1 Tbs. low-sodium soy sauce
2 tsp. cornstarch

Steps:
- Heat the sesame oil in a nonstick skillet over medium-high heat.
- Sprinkle the chicken breasts with salt and pepper, then add the chicken to the pan. Cook for four minutes on each side, or until browned.
- While the chicken cooks, drain the oranges in a colander over a bowl, reserving two tablespoons of their liquid.
- To the chicken in the pan, add the oranges, the two tablespoons of reserved orange syrup, the onions, jalapeno and garlic. Reduce the heat and simmer for two minutes.
- Combine the broth, soy sauce and cornstarch, then add this mixture to the pan and bring to a boil. Cook for one minute or until slightly thickened.

Christine Maguire

TARRAGON CHICKEN

Delicious served with rice. For more flavor, prepare a day before serving.

Ingredients:

7 or 8 boneless chicken breasts, halved
2 cans cream-of-chicken soup
1 cup Hellman's mayonnaise
3 Tbs. dried tarragon, crushed

Steps:
- Cut the chicken into bite-sized chunks.
- Boil the chicken in water for 10 minutes or until done.
- Put the cooked chicken into a large bowl with the other ingredients.
- Microwave until very hot.
- Stir well and serve.

Mary Cosgrove

HONEY-GLAZED BROILERS

I put the garlic in this recipe through a press, and use cut-up chicken pieces rather than broiler halves. Often I partially pre-bake the chicken in the oven to assure that it's done on the grill without being burned to a crisp.

Ingredients:

1/2 cup honey
1/2 cup soy sauce
Juice of two lemons
3 cloves garlic, finely chopped
2 tsp. dry mustard
4 broiler halves or 2 whole chickens
Olive oil

Steps:
- Combine the honey and soy sauce, stirring until the honey thins out. Add the lemon juice, garlic and dry mustard, and blend well.
- Brush the chicken with the olive oil, then broil or grill.
- Turn and baste with the honey mixture.
- Brush with the honey mixture from time to time until the chicken is cooked and glazed.

Mimi McConnell

PARMESAN CHICKEN

This chicken gets its flavor from marinating overnight.

Ingredients:

1/2 cup Dijon mustard
2-4 Tbs. dry white wine
4 chicken breasts, skinned and boned
1 cup grated Parmesan cheese
1 cup grated Romano cheese
1 cup bread crumbs
1/4 cup minced parsley
Salt and pepper

Steps:
- Mix the mustard and wine together to the consistency of cream, then pour it over the chicken pieces. Cover or seal the chicken in a plastic bag; refrigerate overnight.
- When ready to cook, mix the cheeses and breadcrumbs with the parsley.
- Preheat the oven to 375°F.
- Season the marinated chicken with salt and pepper, and dredge it in the crumb mixture.
- Bake the chicken in the oven on a foil-lined baking sheet for 20 minutes, or until cooked through.

Pat Maguire

CHICKEN CHEESE ROLLS

Ingredients:

3 lg. chicken breasts, boned and split
8 oz. whipped cream cheese with chives, divided
1 Tbs. butter or margarine, divided
6 slices bacon

Steps:
- Place the chicken breasts between waxed paper, then pound them to a 1/2-inch thickness.
- Spread each chicken breast with about three tablespoons of the cream cheese, then dot with half a teaspoon of butter.
- Preheat the oven to 400°F.
- Fold the ends of the chicken breast over the filling (some will ooze out during baking).
- Wrap a slice of bacon around each roll, then place them seam-side down in a shallow baking pan.
- Bake on the top rack of the oven for 40 minutes, or until chicken is tender and juice runs clear when the meat is pierced.
- Finally, broil for about five minutes or until bacon turns crispy and golden.
  Serves six

CHICKEN CASSEROLE

Ingredients:

1 cup rice, uncooked
1 cup celery, chopped
3/4 cup onion, chopped
2 tsp. parsley, chopped
1 can cream-of-mushroom soup mixed with 1 1/2 cups water
3 whole boneless chicken breasts, split
Seasoning to taste

Steps:
- Preheat oven to 350°F.
- Put the rice, celery, onion and parsley in the bottom of a 9x12-inch baking dish.
- Pour half of the soup mixture into the baking dish.
- Put the chicken breasts in and cover them with the remaining soup mixture.
- Bake for one hour.

ORIENTAL CHICKEN CASSEROLE

Ingredients:

2-3 cups cooked chicken meat, diced
1 egg, hard-boiled, chopped
1/4 cup mushrooms, sliced
1/4 cup almonds, slivered or water chestnuts
1 Tbs. onion, chopped
1 can cream-of-mushroom soup
1/2 cup low-fat mayonnaise
Chow Mein noodles

Steps:
- Preheat the oven to 350°F.
- Combine all ingredients in a casserole dish except for the Chow-Mein noodles, and mix well.
- Sprinkle the noodles on top of the casserole.
- Bake for 30 minutes.

Charlene Sinko Evans

CHICKEN RUBY

Ingredients:

One 2 1/2- to 3-lb ready-to-cook broiler/fryer chicken, cut into pieces
1/3 cup all-purpose flour
1 tsp. salt
4 Tbs. butter or margarine
1 1/2 cups fresh cranberries
3/4 cup sugar
1/4 cup onion, chopped
1 tsp. orange peel, grated
3/4 cup orange juice
1/4 tsp. ground cinnamon
1/4 tsp. ground ginger

Steps:
- Coat the chicken pieces with a mixture of the flour and salt.
- Brown the chicken in a skillet with the butter, turning once.
- Meanwhile, combine the remaining ingredients in a saucepan; bring to a boil and pour over the chicken.
- Cover the skillet and cook slowly for 35-40 minutes, or until chicken is tender.
Serves 4

Brenda Wood

HAMBURG STEW

Ingredients:

1 lb. hamburger meat
1 Tbs. butter
1 onion, sliced
1/2 tsp. salt
1/4 tsp. pepper
1 can tomatoes

1 sm. can Hunt's tomato sauce
3 potatoes, sliced
3 carrots, sliced
2 stalks celery, diced
Parsley, chopped

Steps:

- In a large, non-stick pot or Dutch oven, brown the hamburger meat lightly in the butter.
- Add the onion and cook a little longer.
- Add the rest of the ingredients except for the parsley, and cover. Simmer for half an hour or until vegetables are done.
- Sprinkle with fresh parsley before serving.

Claire McGourthy

MEXICAN CHICKEN

From my daughter Amy, who knows I like to keep it short. This is quick and easy. Enjoy!

Ingredients:

1 1/2 lbs. boneless chicken breasts
One 8-oz. jar Old El Paso taco sauce
6 to 8 oz. shredded cheese

Steps:

- Preheat oven to 350°F.
- Place the chicken pieces in a glass baking dish, and cover with the taco sauce.
- Bake for 20 minutes uncovered.
- Sprinkle the cheese over the chicken, then bake for another 15 minutes uncovered.

Sarah Salois

MOUSSAKA

A Greek dish, moussaka is an excellent choice for entertaining. It can be prepared the day before and reheated in a 200°F oven. Cut it into squares just before reheating.

Ingredients:

3 med. eggplants (approx. 2 lb. each)	1/2 tsp. salt
Oil for frying	1/4 tsp. pepper
2 lbs. lean ground beef	1/4 cup bread crumbs
10 Tbs. butter (1 1/4 sticks)	1/2 tsp. cinnamon
2 onions, sliced thin	4 eggs (divided into whites and yolks)
1/2 cup white wine	1 cup Parmesan cheese, grated
2 lg. tomatoes, skinned, seeded and chopped	5 Tbs. flour
3 Tbs. parsley, chopped	4 cups milk
	Hot sauce, a few dashes, if desired

Steps:
- Cut the eggplant into 1/4-inch slices, lengthwise, then immerse in salted water for about 15 minutes.
- Rinse and drain the slices, then squeeze out any excess moisture. Pat dry.
- Heat the olive oil and lightly fry the eggplant slices, adding olive oil if necessary. Set the fried eggplant aside.
- Next, fry the ground beef, breaking up the clumps until all red color disappears. Pour off the fat and push the beef to one side of the pan.
- Add four tablespoons of the butter and melt it. Add the onions and sauté them until soft, then stir the onions and meat together.
- When the meat begins to sizzle, add the wine. Stir.
- Add the tomatoes, parsley, salt and pepper.
- Cook slowly, uncovered, for half an hour.
- Remove the meat mixture from the heat and stir in the bread crumbs, cinnamon and egg whites.
- Place half the eggplant in a 9x13-inch baking pan, and cover it with the meat mixture. Sprinkle the meat with half of the Parmesan cheese.
- Top with remaing eggplant.
- In a saucepan, melt the remaining six tablespoons of butter over low heat. Using a wire whisk, stir in the flour and blend it well. Remove from heat.
- Gradually pour in the milk, stirring vigorously. Return the sauce to the heat and cook, stirring constantly, until it is thick and smooth.
- Add salt to taste and stir a little of the hot sauce into the egg yolks.
- Stir the yolks into the sauce and cook over very low heat for two minutes, stirring constantly.
- Pour sauce over top and finish with remaining Parmesan.
- Bake for 45 minutes at 375°F.

Monique Galipeau

BURGUNDY POT ROAST

In this healthier version, the meat and sauce are refrigerated overnight so that the solidified fat can be removed. Great taste, less fattening.

Ingredients:

4- to 5-lb. good-quality beef roast, boneless
1 envelope dry onion-soup mix
1 sm. can Dawn Fresh steak sauce with mushrooms
1 Tbs. Worcestershire sauce
1/2 cup red Burgundy wine

Steps:
- Brown the meat on all sides in a heavy kettle.
- Spread the onion-soup mix over the meat.
- Mix the steak sauce with the Worcestershire sauce and pour over the meat.
- Cover with a tight lid and cook on low heat for 2 1/2 to 3 hours, or until the meat is fork tender.
- Remove the meat and refrigerate overnight. Pour the sauce into a bowl and chill it.
- The next day, the fat will have risen to the top and become solidified. Remove the fat.
- To serve, slice the meat into serving slices and place them in a shallow, ovenproof dish. Spoon some the sauce over the slices.
- Heat until warmed through (about 30 minutes at 250°F).

Helmi Viliesis

OVEN POT ROAST

Ingredients:
4-lb. beef chuck roast
1 can cream-of-mushroom soup
1 envelope dry onion-soup mix

Steps:
- Preheat oven to 350°F.
- Put two large pieces of heavy-duty foil into a deep roasting pan.
- Place the beef on the foil, and pour the can of soup and the envelope of soup mix over the meat
- Fold the foil loosely around the roast, making sealed folds.
- Roast in the oven for about two hours, or until meat is fork tender.
- Remove the roast and stir the gravy that's "magically" appeared in the pan, serve over the roast.

Barbara Lucas

HUNGARIAN STUFFED PEPPERS

This is typical Hungarian dish that was often on the menu in my home when I was growing up in Zimbabwe. Expatriate Hungarians like us were always filled with nostalgia when it was served, and we ate it a lot. Serve this dish over broad noodles with grated Parmesan cheese.

Ingredients:

6 smallish, thin-skinned bell peppers
1 lb. ground beef
1/2 cup uncooked rice
1 med. onion, chopped
2 sm. garlic cloves, minced
1/4 cup fresh parsley, chopped
1 egg
1 tsp. salt
3 Tbs. butter or margarine
3 Tbs. flour
Two 28-oz. cans tomato puree
One 8-oz. can tomato paste
1 Tbs. sugar

Steps:
- Wash, seed and core the peppers for stuffing.
- In a large bowl, mix the beef, rice, onion, garlic, parsley, egg and salt.
- Stuff the peppers with the meat mixture, lightly packing it in, but not tamping it down too hard.
- In a deep four-quart saucepan, melt the butter and stir in the flour.
- Add a little water.
- Add the tomato puree, tomato paste and sugar.
- Add the stuffed peppers, making sure they are completely covered by the sauce.
- Simmer for one to two hours, or until tender.

Monique Szechenyi

FIVE-HOUR BEEF STEW

Five hours is how long this stew stays in a 250°F oven. Do not peek! Keep the foil on until it's done.

Ingredients:

2 lbs. stew meat, cut into bite-sized pieces
2 lg. onions, chopped
2 cups celery, chopped
3 cups carrots, chopped
5 or 6 potatoes, peeled and chopped
2 Tbs. brown sugar
2 Tbs. tapioca
2 cans tomato soup
1 cup water
Salt and pepper

Steps:
- In a roasting pan, put the stew meat, then layer the vegetables on top of the meat.
- Mix the brown sugar, tapioca, tomato soup, water, salt and pepper, then pour it over the meat and vegetables in the pan.
- Cover with heavy-duty aluminum foil, sealing well.
- Bake at 250°F for five hours.

Nancy Bourdeau

ITALIAN POT ROAST

Ingredients:

4-lb. round roast, trimmed
Salt and pepper, to taste
2 Tbs. oil
1 garlic clove, minced
1 med. onion, sliced
1 jar Ragu Italian Cooking Sauce

Steps:
- Sprinkle the meat with salt and pepper.
- Brown the meat on all sides in oil.
- Add the onion and garlic, and brown lightly. Pour off any excess oil.
- Add the Italian Cooking Sauce, then cover and simmer for 2 1/2 hours or until tender.

Ann McDonnell

> "Some have meat and cannot eat,
> Some can not eat that want it;
> But we have meat and we can eat,
> Sae let the Lord be thankit."
>
> -Robert Burns, Scottish poet

SWEDISH MEATBALLS

Ingredients:

1/4 cup onion, finely minced
4 Tbs. butter or margarine, melted
1 egg, slightly beaten
1/2 cup milk
1/2 cup soft, fine bread crumbs
2 1/2 tsp. salt
1/2 tsp. allspice
1/4 tsp. nutmeg

1 lb. lean ground beef
1/4 lb. ground veal or pork
3 Tbs. flour
1 tsp. sugar
1/4 tsp. black pepper
1 cup water
3/4 cup light cream or evaporated milk

Steps:
- Sauté the onion in one tablespoon of the butter.
- Combine the egg with the milk and bread crumbs, and let them stand for five minutes.
- To the soaked breadcrumbs, add one and a half teaspoons of the salt, all of the spices, meat and sautéed onion. Blend well.
- Melt the remaining butter in a large skillet.
- Using two teaspoons, form the meat mixture into small balls about half an inch in diameter. Drop some of the meatballs into skillet, and brown them well on all sides. Remove them to a warm casserole dish when browned.
- Repeat until all meatballs are cooked.
- Preheat the oven to 350°F.
- Stir the flour, sugar, the remaining teaspoon of salt and all of the pepper into the butter left in the skillet from frying the meatballs.
- Slowly add the water and cream.
- Cook and stir until the mixture is thickened, about five minutes.
- Pour the sauce over the meatballs.
- Cover the casserole dish and bake in the oven for 25 to 30 minutes. (Or, if you prefer, simply return the meatballs to the skillet, and simmer them, covered, until tender.)
Makes about 36 meatballs

Cape Cod Personal Chef

STEAK DIANE

Ingredients:

2 filet mignons (or other type of steak)
1/8 tsp. salt
1/8 tsp. freshly ground pepper
3 Tbs. butter
1 tsp. Dijon-style mustard

1 Tbs. shallots, minced
1 Tbs. lemon juice
1 1/2 tsp. Worcestershire sauce
1 Tbs. fresh chives, minced
1 tsp. brandy
1 Tbs. fresh parsley, minced

Steps:
- Season both sides of the steaks with salt and pepper.
- Melt two tablespoons of the butter in a heavy skillet; add the mustard and shallots. Sauté over medium heat for one minute.
- Add the steaks and cook for approximately three minutes on each side (this will give you medium rare steaks).
- Remove the steaks to a serving plate and keep them warm.
- To the pan drippings, add the remaining tablespoon of butter, as well as the lemon juice, Worcestershire sauce and chives. Cook for two minutes.
- Add the brandy.
- Pour the sauce over the warm steaks and sprinkle the steaks with parsley.

Cape Cod Personal Chef

ORIENTAL-MARINATED STEAK STRIPS

Ingredients:

1/2 cup fresh orange juice
1/4 cup soy sauce
2 Tbs. very dry sherry
2 sm. cloves garlic, minced
2 dashes ground ginger
2 boneless strip-sirloin steaks

Steps:
- Combine the first five ingredients to make a marinade, then place the steaks in the marinade.
- Marinate the steaks in the refrigerator for two to three hours, turning occasionally.
- Remove the steaks from the marinade, and place them on a preheated grill over medium heat for approximately seven to nine minutes for a medium-rare steak.

Cape Cod Personal Chef

"A man seldom thinks with more earnestness of anything than he does of his dinner."

-Samuel Johnson, writer

CHICKEN AND MUSHROOM CREPES

Ingredients for Crepes:

2 Tbs. butter or margarine melted
1 1/2 cups milk
3 eggs

2/3 cup all-purpose flour
1/2 tsp. salt

Steps for Crepes:
- Using a whisk, beat the melted butter in a large bowl with the crepe ingredients until smooth. Cover and refrigerate for at least three hours.
- Brush both a 7-inch crepe pan and a 10-inch skillet with butter, and place over medium heat.
- Pour a scant 1/4 cup batter into the crepe pan; cook until the underside is browned
- Now invert the crepe into the skillet to cook for 30 seconds.
- Slip the finished crepe onto waxed paper. Repeat.

Ingredients for Chicken Filling:

5 Tbs. Butter or margarine
3/4 lb. mushrooms
1/4 cup all-purpose flour
1/2 tsp. salt
1 cup chicken broth
1/4 cup dry sherry

2 egg yolks
1 cup + 2 Tbs. milk, divided
1 cup Swiss cheese, shredded
3 cups chicken, cooked and diced
Parsley, chopped

Steps for Chicken Filling:
- Melt 2 tablespoons of the butter.
- Cook the mushrooms, and remove them to a bowl.
- In the same bowl, melt 3 more Tbs. of butter. Stir in the flour and salt.
- In a bowl mix the broth, sherry, egg yolks and the 1 cup of milk. Stir this into the flour mixture, then cook until thickened.
- Stir in the shredded Swiss.
- Preheat the oven to 325°F.
- Reserve half a cup of the sauce.
- Add the chicken and all but 1/4 cup of the mushrooms to remaining sauce; heat through.
- Spoon 1/3 cup filling onto a crepe. Roll up and place the crepe in a 13x9-inch baking dish.
- Repeat until all crepes are in the baking dish.
- Stir the remaining two tablespoons of milk and the saved mushrooms into the reserved sauce. Pour this mixture over the crepes in the dish, and bake for 20 minutes.
- Top with parsley before serving.
  Serves 6

Monique Galipeau

ITALIAN MEATBALLS AND SAUCE

Serve this dish with your favorite pasta. It tastes even better if it's made the day before being served.

Ingredients:

2 or 3 garlic cloves, minced
5 lbs. lean ground meat
4 or 5 eggs
2 cups Italian-style breadcrumbs
Coarse black pepper
2 cups freshly shredded Parmesan cheese
Olive oil
Six 15-oz. cans Italian-style tomato sauce
5 2/3 cups water (or fill three of the empty sauce cans with water)
Two 6-oz cans tomato paste

Steps:

- Combine the garlic, ground meat, eggs, breadcrumbs, pepper and Parmesan. Mix well, adding additional breadcrumbs or eggs so that the mixture holds together well.
- Roll the meat mixture into individual balls.
- In a deep saucepan, put enough olive oil to generously cover the bottom of the pan. Brown the meatballs and set them aside as you go, until all are browned. If necessary, add more olive oil.
- Place the meatballs back into the same saucepan used for browning, and add the tomato sauce, water and tomato paste.
- Simmer for four to six hours.
  Makes approximately three dozen meatballs

Jack Mondin

BEER MARINADE

A delicious marinade for beef, and it tenderizes, too!

Ingredients:

2 cups beer (use a 12-oz. or a 10-oz can)
2 tsp. salt
1/2 cup olive oil
1 tsp. ground cayenne pepper
1 Tbs. wine vinegar
1 Tbs. prepared horseradish
1 tsp. onion powder
2 Tbs. lemon juice
1 tsp. garlic powder

Steps:

- Mix all ingredients together.

LOBSTER-STUFFED TENDERLOIN OF BEEF

The tenderloin can be stuffed and tied ahead of time, then refrigerated until you're ready to cook it.

Ingredients:

4-lb. beef tenderloin, whole
Two 4-oz. lobster tails, frozen
1 Tbs. butter, melted
1 1/2 tsp. lemon juice
6 slices bacon, partially cooked
1/2 cup green onions, sliced
1/2 cup butter
1/2 cup dry white wine
1/8 tsp. garlic salt

Steps:
- Cut the tenderloin in half lengthwise, to within half an inch of the bottom.
- Preheat the oven to 425°F.
- Place the frozen lobster tails in enough boiling water to cover them. Simmer for five minutes.
- Remove the lobster meat from the shells and cut in half.
- Open the tenderloin and place the lobster end-to-end inside the beef tenderloin.
- Combine the melted butter and lemon juice and drizzle it on top of the lobster.
- Close the meat back up over the lobster, and tie the roast together with string.
- Place the meat in a roasting pan on a rack, and roast in the oven for 30 minutes.
- Place the bacon on top of the roast and cook for five minutes longer.
- Sauté the onions in the half cup of butter in a saucepan. Add the wine and garlic salt, and heat through.
- Slice the roast and spoon the wine sauce over the sliced beef to serve.

Ann McDonnell

BANGLADESH KEBABS

Ingredients:

1 1/2 tsp. salt
8 to 10 oz. onion, minced
1/2 tsp. ground clove
1 or 2 jalapeno peppers, minced
1/2 tsp. ground nutmeg
2 1/2 tsp. red hot-pepper flakes
1/2 tsp. black pepper
1 1/2 tsp. ground cumin
1 to 3 garlic cloves, minced
1 tsp. coriander, chopped
1 Tbs. fresh ginger, minced
3/4 tsp. cardamom
1/4 cup oil
1/2 tsp. cinnamon
2 lbs. chicken breast, cubed and sprinkled with meat tenderizer

Steps:
- Blend all ingredients except the chicken to make a paste.
- Marinate the chicken in the paste for at least four hours.
- Skewer and grill.

Beth Gebhardt

MEATLOAF WITH BROWN SUGAR-AND-TOMATO GLAZE

Ingredients for Meatloaf:

2 Tbs. oil
1 med. onion
2 garlic cloves, minced
2 eggs
1/2 tsp. thyme
1 tsp. salt
1/2 tsp. pepper
2 tsp. Dijon mustard
2 tsp. Worcestershire sauce
1/4 tsp. hot sauce
1/2 cup milk
2 lbs. ground-meat mixture (veal, pork and beef)
2/3 cup Saltine crackers, crushed

Ingredients for Brown Sugar-and-Tomato Glaze:

1/2 cup ketchup
4 Tbs. brown sugar
4 tsp. vinegar

Steps:
- Preheat the oven to 350°F.
- Heat the oil in a skillet, and sauté the onion and garlic until softened. Set aside.
- Mix the eggs with the thyme, salt, pepper, mustard, Worcestershire sauce, hot sauce and milk.
- Combine the sautéed onion and garlic, the egg mixture, the ground meat and the cracker crumbs in a large bowl.
- Pat the whole mixture into a 9x5-inch loaf shape, and place on a foil-lined shallow baking pan.
- Mix the glaze ingredients in a small saucepan, and brush the meatloaf with half of the glaze.
- Bake in the oven until a meat thermometer inserted into the middle registers 160°F.
- Meanwhile, heat the rest of the glaze on the stovetop.
- Slice the meatloaf, and serve with drizzles of the heated glaze.

Nancy Ockers

STUFFED CALZONE

Ingredients:

1 3/4 cups recipe-ready tomatoes, drained
1 1/4 cups spinach, drained and chopped
3/4 cup pepperoni, chopped
3/4 cup salami, chopped
1 cup mozzarella cheese, shredded
1 cup ricotta cheese
1/2 cup olives with pimientos
1/3 cup Parmesan cheese
1 1/2 tsp. garlic powder
1 1/2 tsp. basil leaves, crushed
1 1/2 tsp. oregano
1 tsp. seasoned pepper
2 loaves frozen bread dough, defrosted
2 Tbs. olive oil

Steps:
- Preheat the oven to 350°F.
- In a large bowl, combine all ingredients except for the bread dough and olive oil. (This is the filling.) Set aside.
- On a lightly floured board, roll one half of a loaf of defrosted bread dough into a 12-inch circle; place it on a pizza pan.
- Spread 1 1/3 cups of the filling on half of the dough circle, to within a half inch of the edge of the dough.
- Fold the dough over the filling, creating a half circle. Press the edges with a fork to seal, then cut three slits in the top of the dough to allow steam to escape.
- Repeat the process to make three more calzones.
- Bake in the oven for 20 minutes.
- Remove the tray and brush the calzones with olive oil, then bake an additional five to 10 minutes, or until golden brown.
- Let stand 10 minutes before cutting.

Annmarie Tatelbaum

BRAZILIAN PORK LOIN IN GENY'S STYLE

As prepared by Geny for Frank Sinatra

Ingredients:

1 sm. onion, finely chopped
Several cloves of garlic, minced
4 limes, 3 of which have been juiced
1 pkg. boneless pork tenderloin
2 or 3 tsp. salt
Olive oil for frying

Steps:
- Mix the onion, garlic, several tablespoons of lime juice, and salt.
- Work this mixture into the surface of the pork tenderloin with your fingers.
- Fry the tenderloin in olive oil over medium heat, turning frequently to brown evenly and to prevent burning.
- Continue frying gently until the internal temperature registers "done" on a meat thermometer. (Do not overcook!)
  Serve sliced, with additional lime wedges for garnish.

M. Mauney

SPICE-RUBBED ROAST PORK LOIN WITH CRANBERRY-CORIANDER CHUTNEY

This moist roast has a delicious crust.

Ingredients for Roast:

2 Tbs. ground coriander	2 tsp. dried red pepper, crushed
2 Tbs. coarse salt	1 tsp. ground cumin
1 Tbs. black pepper	One 8-lb. bone-in pork loin roast

Steps for Roast:
- Preheat oven to 350°F.
- Blend the first five ingredients in a small bowl
- Place the pork on a large rack in a roasting pan and drizzle with a little olive oil; rub it in.
- Rub the spice mixture over the pork.
- Roast until a meat thermometer registers 150°F (about two and a half hours).
- Let stand for ten minutes.
- Carve the roast, and serve with chutney (recipe below).

Ingredients for Chutney:

4 cups cranberries	1 cup apple cider
3/4 cup packed brown sugar	2 cinnamon sticks
2 cups orange juice	1 cup sugar
1/4 cup cider vinegar	1 Tbs. ground coriander

Steps for Chutney
- Combine all ingredients in a large saucepan over medium heat.
- Cook, stirring frequently, approximately one hour and fifteen minutes.
- Discard the cinnamon sticks before serving.

Wendy Harte

SKEWERED BABY BEEF AND MUSHROOMS

Serve these skewers on beds of hot cooked rice with a green vegetable and garnish of tomato wedges and parsley.

Ingredients:

1 1/2 lbs. beef round cut into 1/4-inch-thick slices
1 clove garlic mashed
1 Tbs. minced onion
1 1/2 Tbs. A-1 Steak Sauce
1 tsp. Worcestershire sauce
2/3 cup catsup
1 dash pepper
1/4 tsp. salt
3 Tbs. sherry
Green pepper, cut into squares 1 1/2-x 1 1/2-inch
12 slices onion, 1/4-inch thick or cut into wedges
36 mushroom crowns

Steps:
- Cut meat in 1 1/2-inch squares. (There should be 36.)
- Mix the next eight ingredients; stir. Let stand for several hours.
- Parboil the green pepper, onion and fresh mushrooms separately in small amounts of lightly salted water; drain.
- On six skewers, string the meat and vegetables, beginning and ending each skewer with green pepper.
- Broil slowly until browned on all sides.

Cape Cod Personal Chef

"Oh, those picnic lunches at the nooning, while backs straightened and fingers relaxed! Mother made cold roast-pork sandwiches of homemade bread and slices of chicken-tender meat from the sweetest pigs that ever grunted, and there was plenty to satisfy the cranberry-bog appetite of a hungry boy. There was the spice of good stories and old-time familiar songs."

-Thornton W. Burgess, excerpted from *Now I Remember*, Little, Brown & Co., Boston, 1960.

Sandy Neck Light • Barnstable, MA

Bathing Beach, 1910 • Sandwich, MA

FLETCHER CLARK

DEALER IN

Groceries ❧ and ❧ Hardware

AMMUNITION, PAINTS, OILS, VARNISHES,
WINDOW GLASS AND PUTTY . . . .

Agricultural Implements, Field and Garden Seeds

Drain-pipe and Fire-brick, Crockery, Stoneware
and Woodenware, Poultry and Mosquito Netting

AGENTS FOR BRADLEY FERTILIZER CO.

READY MIXED PAINTS

JARVES ST.   SANDWICH, MASS.

From the Bourne, Falmouth and Sandwich Business Directory 1905

American Beach Grass

RIGATONI WITH VEGETABLES

This is a great side dish for a crowd. It may be served hot or cold.

Ingredients:

1/4 cup red-wine vinegar
1 Tbs. mustard
1 tsp. sugar
1 tsp. salt
1/3 cup + 3 Tbs. olive or salad oil
One 16-oz. pkg. rigatoni
1 lg. onion, cut into chunks

1/2 lb. snap peas or Chinese pea pods, stems and strings removed
4 med. carrots, sliced
1 bunch broccoli, cut into 2 1/2x1-inch pieces
1/4 cup water
3 sm. tomatoes, cut into wedges
1/2 cup fresh basil, chopped
3/4 cup Parmesan cheese, grated

Steps:

- In a small bowl, with a fork, mix vinegar, mustard, sugar, salt and 1/3 cup olive oil
- Prepare rigatoni as label directs.
- Meanwhile, in 5-quart Dutch oven, over high heat, in 1 Tbs. hot olive oil, cook the onion for two minutes.
- Add the peas, and cook for two to three minutes until the vegetables are tender-crisp. Remove to a large bowl.
- In the same Dutch oven, in 2 Tbs. hot oil, cook the carrots and broccoli, stirring until coated with oil. Add the water and reduce heat to medium. Cover and cook for three minutes.
- Uncover and cook for five more minutes, or until vegetables are tender-crisp.
- Drain the rigatoni and add the onion mixture to broccoli mixture. Pour vegetables, dressing, tomatoes, basil, and Parmesan over the pasta and toss.

Karel Huber

"You two can be what you like, but since I am the big fromage in this family, I prefer to think of myself as the Gorgon Zola."

-Ogden Nash

ORZO, WILD RICE, AND PIGNOLA PILAF

This is great for picnics or buffets, or just plain leftovers.

Ingredients:

1/2 cup wild rice
1 cup Orzo pasta (any good imported Italian brand)
4 scallions, green and white parts, cleaned and sliced thinly into rounds

One 16-oz can chicken broth
1/3 cup pignola (pine nuts), lightly toasted*
1 Tbs. extra-virgin olive oil

Steps:
- In a 1 1/2 qt. saucepot, bring three cups of water to a boil.
- Rinse the wild rice in a small colander, then add it to the boiling water and let it boil slowly for 20 minutes or until the grains open.
- Drain the rice and place it in a 2- or 3-qt. mixing bowl. Add the sliced green onions and pine nuts to the bowl, too
- Bring the chicken broth and 1/2 cup water to a boil, and add the orzo pasta. Let the pasta cook until it is al dente. (The pasta water should be soupy; if not, add a bit of water. Do not drain.)
- Add the pasta in its water to the bowl with the wild rice mixture.
- Add the olive oil and salt and pepper to taste.
- Stir thoroughly and serve.

* To toast the pignola nuts, place them in a small non-stick pan over medium heat. Do not add oil. Shake or stir nuts until light brown on one or two sides. Do not toast them too darkly though, or the pignola will become very bitter.

Karen Frances Gray

STUFFED SHELLS FLORENTINE

Ingredients:

24 whole giant manicotti pasta shells
1 Tbs. vegetable oil
One 10-oz. pkg. frozen spinach-chopped
1 sm. onion, minced
2 Tbs. butter, melted

1 lb. cottage cheese
1 egg, beaten
1/2 tsp. salt
1/4 tsp. black pepper
30 oz. tomato sauce
1 cup mozzarella cheese, shredded

Steps:
- Cook the shells in boiling, salted water for 9 minutes. Drain.
- Gently toss the shells in oil. Set them aside.
- Thaw the spinach and drain, squeezing out all the water.
- Preheat the oven to 350°F.
- Saute the onion in butter until soft, then stir in the spinach. Remove this mixture to a bowl and add cottage cheese, egg, onion, salt and pepper.
- Fill each shell with the spinach-cheese mixture.
- Pour half of the sauce into a 9x13-inch baking dish.
- Arrange the stuffed shells in the dish and cover them with the remaining sauce.
- Bake for 30 minutes.
- After 30 minutes, sprinkle the shells with mozzarella cheese, and return them to the oven until the cheese is melted and bubbly (about 3 minutes).

Pat Bryant also submitted a "heart heathy" version of this recipe, in which the butter was replaced with a small amount of olive oil, the egg was replaced with 1/2 cup of Egg Beaters egg substitute and the mozzarella cheese was replaced with 1/4 cup of grated Parmesan cheese. Pat's recipe also used fat-free cottage cheese and added chopped mushrooms to the onion-spinach mixture during the sautéing process.

LINGUINE WITH SPINACH PESTO AND FETA

Ingredients:

1 lb. spaghetti, linguine, or thin spaghetti, uncooked
One 10-oz pkg. frozen spinach, thawed and well drained
2 Tbs. vegetable oil
1/4 cup Parmesan cheese, grated
2 Tbs. parsley, chopped

2 cloves garlic
1/2 tsp. salt
1/2 tsp. dried basil
2 Tbs. butter or margarine
1/3 cup water
4 oz. feta cheese, crumbled

Steps:
- Prepare pasta according to the package directions. Drain.
- In a blender or food processor, combine the spinach, oil, Parmesan cheese, parsley, garlic, salt and basil. Blend at medium speed or process until finely chopped.
- Melt margarine in water.
- With the blender or food processor running, gradually pour in the melted margarine mixture until blended.
- Toss the pasta with the blended spinach-basil mixture
- Sprinkle feta on top and serve.

ARMENIAN RICE AND NOODLE PILAF

Armenian pilafs often contain browned noodles, and there are many theories about this. Some historians say that, because rice came to Armenia long after wheat (rice arrived in the Middle Ages), and because rice was more expensive than wheat, wheat noodles were added to stretch the rice.

Ingredients:
1 1/2 cups crushed vermicelli
1 1/2 cups long-grain white rice
3 cups chicken stock
3/4 cups water
6 Tbs. unsalted butter
Salt to taste

Steps:
- Preheat the oven to 400°F.
- On a baking sheet, spread the vermicelli to make one layer. Toast it in the hot oven for five minutes, or until it is golden, them remove it from the oven.
- In a saucepan, combine the rice, chicken stock, water, butter, and salt. Bring to a boil, then lower the heat, cover the pan, and cook the rice for 20 minutes.
- Stir in the toasted noodles, cover, and continue cooking for five minutes. Remove the pan from the heat and let the pilaf rest for 10 minutes, covered.
- Fluff with a fork and serve at once.
Serves 6

Debbie McDermott

BROCCOLI-SAUSAGE PASTA

This flavorful, colorful main dish is ready in 30 minutes and only has 6 grams of fat per serving.

Ingredients:
1 lb. turkey kielbasa, cut into 1/4-inch slices
1 med. bunch broccoli florets
1/2 cup red onion, sliced
One 14.5-oz. can diced tomatoes, undrained
1 tsp. dried or 1 Tbs. fresh basil
1 tsp. dried or 1 Tbs. fresh parsley
1 tsp. sugar
3 cups rotini pasta, cooked

➤

Steps:
- Saute the sausage, broccoli and onion together for 5 to 6 minutes in a lightly oiled skillet.
- Add the rest of the ingredients, except for the pasta. Stir to combine.
- Cover and simmer for 10 minutes.
- Add the cooked pasta and heat through.
Serves 6

Debbie McDermott

PENNE RITA

This dish was developed during a Christmas holiday break. The colors of this dish—red and green—might well have made the name "Christmas Pasta."

Ingredients:

1 lb. penne pasta (or other similar type)
2 Tbs. olive oil
2 cloves garlic, sliced
Crushed red pepper flakes or 1 sm. dried chili pepper, with seeds removed

1 can artichoke hearts, drained and quartered
Pinch dried oregano
Pinch dried basil
1/2 lemon, juiced
2 Tbs. capers

Steps:
- Boil water and begin preparing the pasta.
- While it is cooking, saute the garlic and crushed chili pepper in a frying pan with oil (about 2 minutes over medium heat).
- Add the artichoke hearts and turn the heat to low.
- Add the oregano, basil and capers, then cover and simmer.
- Drain the pasta and put it into a bowl.
- Remove the cover on the frying pan and add the lemon juice. Stir once and pour the contents of the pan over the pasta.
- Toss the pasta.
- Add salt, pepper and grated cheese to taste.
Serves 3-4

Fred Spero

WILD RICE WITH MUSHROOMS AND ALMONDS

This recipe can be made early in the day and baked before serving. It's so tasty with chicken or pork. I sometimes add a handful of dried cranberries.

Ingredients:
1/4 cup butter
1 cup uncooked wild rice, washed
1/2 cup slivered almonds
2 Tbs. green onions, chopped
One 8-oz. can sliced mushrooms, drained
3 cups chicken broth

Steps:
- In an electric skillet or saute pan, melt the butter.
- Add the wild rice, slivered almonds, green onions and mushrooms.
- Stir until the almonds are golden (about 15 minutes)
- Pour the mixture into an ungreased 1 1/2-quart casserole dish.
- Stir in the chicken broth.
- Cover and bake in a preheated 350°F oven for 1 1/2 hours, or until liquid is absorbed.
Serves 6 to 8

Annie McTygue

VEGETABLE LASAGNA

I cook this casserole ahead of time and put it in the refrigerator. Just put it back in the oven to reheat. The top gets a light brown crust this way, which is good.

Ingredients for Cheese Sauce:
1/3 cup butter or margarine
1/2 cup flour
2 3/4 cup milk, divided
2 1/4 cups grated Parmesan cheese
3 Tbs. Dijon-style mustard
1/2 tsp. hot pepper sauce
1/4 tsp. salt

Ingredients for Vegetable Filling:
3 Tbs. vegetable oil
1/2 lb. fresh mushrooms, sliced
2 medium onions, chopped
4 cloves garlic, minced (optional)
2 cups coarsely chopped fresh carrots
9 lasagna noodles, cooked and drained
(Optional: dried tomatoes, soaked drained and cut up)

➤

Garnish:
2 hard-cooked eggs, sliced
2 mushrooms, sliced

Steps for Cheese Sauce:
- Melt the butter in a medium saucepan. Blend in the flour.
- Gradually add 2 1/2 cups of the milk, and cook over medium heat, stirring constantly until the sauce boils and thickens.
- Add 2 cups of the Parmesan cheese and cook until the mixture is smooth. Stir in the mustard, hot pepper sauce and salt.
- Set Cheese Sauce aside.

Steps for Vegetable Filling:
- Heat the oil in a large saucepan.
- Sauté the mushrooms, onions, and garlic until tender.
- Tear the spinach into bite-sized pieces. Add the spinach and carrots to the saucepan, and cook for two to three minutes until the spinach is tender.
- Drain the vegetables.
- Stir 1 1/2 cups of the Cheese Sauce into this vegetable mixture. Add the remaining 1/4 cup milk to the Cheese Sauce that is left in the pan.

To assemble the casserole:
- Butter a 13x9-inch baking dish and preheat the oven to 350°F.
- Pour half of the remaining Cheese Sauce into the casserole dish.
- Arrange three noodles over the sauce.
- Spread half of the Vegetable Filling over the noodles.
- Add 3 more noodles. Spread the remainder of the Vegetable Filling over the noodles. (At this point I have also added a layer of cottage cheese, which this recipe does not call for but is tasty.)
- Spoon the last of the Cheese Sauce over the noodles.
- Sprinkle the final 1/4 cup Parmesan cheese over top of the casserole.
- Bake in the oven for 25 minutes.
- Let stand for 10-15 minutes before serving.
- Before serving, add sliced eggs and mushrooms around the top of the casserole.

Clare Morash

GREEK SPAGHETTI WITH TOMATOES AND GARLIC

This is our favorite quick meal made with fresh tomatoes. True comfort food!

Ingredients:

2 tsp. olive oil
1 tsp. dried or 2 Tbs. fresh oregano
1 lg. clove garlic, minced
3 cups fresh tomatoes, diced
1/2 cup green onion, sliced
1/4 cup fresh parsley, chopped
2 Tbs. lemon juice
4 cups (8 oz.) cooked thin spaghetti, hot
1 cup (4 oz) feta cheese, crumbled
Freshly ground pepper
Lemon slices (optional)

Steps:
- Heat the oil.
- Add garlic and oregano and saute for one minute.
- Add the tomatoes, 1/3 cup green onion, 2 Tbs. of the parsley and all of the lemon juice. Cook for two minutes.
- Combine this mixture with the spaghetti and 3/4 cup of the feta cheese.
- Garnish with the lemon slices, plus the remaining parsley, green onion, and feta cheese.
Serves 4

Nancy Titcomb

SPAGHETTI-CHEESE BAKE

This is very easy to prepare and very delicious. It's a family favorite for all ages and can be easily reheated as leftovers.

Ingredients:

1 lb. thin spaghetti
2 to 3 Tbs. butter or margarine
24 oz. tomato sauce (1 lg. + 1 sm. or 3 sm. cans; I prefer DelMonte or Contadina brands)
Salt and pepper, to taste
8 to 12 oz. sharp Cheddar cheese, shredded

Steps:
- Cook the spaghetti al dente. Drain.
- Preheat the oven to 350°F.
- Combine the spaghetti with the butter or margarine, tomato sauce, salt and pepper.
- Add half the Cheddar cheese.

- Mix and put in a casserole dish.
- Sprinkle with the remaining cheese.
- Place in the oven 30-45 minutes before serving. The cheese on top should be well melted when this dish is finished cooking.
  Serves 8-10

Marion Vinecour

CHEESY SPAGHETTI

Ingredients:
1 lb. large sea-shell pasta
2 Tbs. butter
1 1/2 lbs. ground beef
1/2 cup onions, chopped
2 cups cottage cheese
1 very lg. jar spaghetti sauce (I prefer Prego)
1 cup or more mozzarella cheese, shredded

Steps:
- Cook the sea-shell pasta according to the package directions. Drain and toss pasta with the butter.
- Preheat the oven to 350°F.
- Brown the ground beef with the onions.
- In the bottom of an oblong baking dish, toss the cooked sea shells with the cottage cheese.
- Add the ground beef and the spaghetti sauce to the dish and mix everything well.
- Cover the dish and bake for one hour.
- After an hour, take the cover off and sprinkle the mozzarella cheese on top. Continue to bake until mozzarella is melted.

Karla Zimdars

> "The Greeks had just one word for 'economize.' Our New England grandmothers had twelve: 'Eat it up, use it up, make do, or do without.'"
>
> -Helen Adamson

"DIRTY" RICE

Ingredients:

2 Tbs. bacon fat or corn oil
2 onions, peeled and finely chopped
1 or 2 garlic cloves, peeled and minced
1 green pepper, cored, seeded and finely chopped
1 celery stalk, finely chopped
1 cup mushrooms, finely chopped
2 Tbs. fresh parsley, chopped

1/2 lb. chicken livers, diced
1/4 lb. ground or diced chicken giblets or ground lean pork
2 tsp. Worcestershire sauce
1/2 tsp. cayenne
Salt and black pepper
4 Tbs. water
1 1/2 cups long-grain rice

Steps:
- Heat the bacon fat or oil in a heavy pan. Add the onions, garlic, green pepper, celery, mushrooms and parsley. Cook all until lightly browned, stirring occasionally.
- Add the livers and giblets or pork. Cook until these are browned, mashing and stirring frequently.
- Stir in the Worcestershire sauce, cayenne, and salt and pepper to taste.
- Cover and cook over a low heat for 20 minutes, stirring from time to time. When necessary, add a spoonful or two of water.
- Meanwhile, cook the rice in boiling salted water until tender. Drain.
- Add the rice to the "dirty" mixture. Toss together and serve.
  Serves 4 to 6

Monique Galipeau

BAKED NOODLE-AND-CHEESE CASSEROLE

Ingredients:

1/2 pkg. (6 oz.) wide egg noodles
1 cup cottage cheese, large-curd kind
1 cup sour cream
1 garlic clove, minced or put through a press (optional)
3 Tbs. onion, grated

2 tsp. pimento, chopped (optional)
1/8 tsp. Tabasco sauce
3/4 tsp. Worcestershire sauce
1/4 tsp. salt
1/4 cup cheddar cheese, grated

Steps:
- Cook the egg noodles until tender in a large amount of boiling, salted water. Drain.
- Preheat the oven to 375°F.
- Combine the noodles with the cottage cheese, sour cream, garlic and other

➤

seasonings. (If mixed an hour or so before baking, the ingredients mingle nicely and are intensified.)
- Turn the mixture out into a buttered one-qt. casserole dish. Sprinkle the cheddar cheese over top.
- Bake in the oven for 25 minutes or until heated through. Cover while baking to keep this dish from drying out. (Baking a little longer seems to improve the flavors, however.)
Serves 6 to 8

Mimi McConnell

ORIENTAL NOODLES WITH HOT 'N SPICY PEANUT SAUCE

This recipe is very popular on buffet tables, since it is served at room temperature. Make the recipe a day in advance to really do justice to the flavors.

Ingredients:

1/4 cup smooth peanut butter
3 Tbs. sugar
1/4 cup soy sauce
1 tsp. red pepper flakes
1/16 tsp. ground red pepper
3 Tbs. sesame oil
3 Tbs. corn oil

1 lb Chinese noodles, vermicelli, angel hair or thin spaghetti, cooked according to package directions. (Break the pasta in half before cooking if not using Chinese noodles.)
Green onions, chopped
Red and green peppers, chopped
Sesame seeds or unsalted peanuts

Steps:
- In a small bowl, whisk the peanut butter, sugar, soy sauce, red pepper flakes, ground red pepper and oils.
- In a large salad bowl, place the drained pasta and toss it with the peanut sauce.
- Garnish the pasta with chopped green onions, red and green peppers, and sesame seeds or peanuts. If using sesame seeds to garnish, toast them in a pan at 350°F for five minutes before sprinkling over the noodles.
- Serves 4-6 as a main dish and 6-8 as a side dish

Marilyn Goldstein

FOUR-CHEESE CHICKEN FETTUCINE

Ingredients:

8 oz. fettucine
1 can cream-of-mushroom soup
One 8-oz pkg. cream cheese, cubed
One 4.5-oz. can sliced mushrooms
1 cup milk
1/2 cup butter or margarine
1/4 tsp. garlic powder

3/4 cup + 2 Tbs. Parmesan cheese, grated
1/2 cup mozzarella cheese, shredded
1/2 cup Swiss cheese, shredded
2 1/2 cups cooked chicken, cubed
1/2 cup seasoned bread crumbs
2 Tbs. butter, melted

Steps:
- Cook the fettucine according to the package directions.
- Meanwhile in a large kettle, combine the soup, cream cheese, mushrooms, milk, butter and garlic powder.
- Stir in the 3/4 cup Parmesan, and all of the mozzarella and Swiss cheeses. Cook and stir until melted.
- Add the chicken and heat through.
- Drain the fettucine and add it to the cheese sauce.
- Preheat the oven to 350°F.
- Transfer all to a shallow, greased, 2 1/2-quart baking dish.
- Combine the breadcrumbs, melted butter and remaining 2 tablespoons Parmesan, and sprinkle this mixture over the casserole.
- Cover the casserole dish and bake at for 25 minutes.
- Uncover and bake for five or 10 minutes longer, or until golden brown. Serves 6-8

Bettina Dinsmore

Bridge over Cape Cod Canal,
Connecting Buzzards Bay and Bourne, Mass.

R. R. Station, Sandwich, Mass.

Railroad Station, Sandwich Village

QUICK & EASY

201

N. PACKWOOD

Wholesale and Retail Dealer in

Carriages, Harness and Horse Furnishings

BOOTS, SHOES and GENTS' FURNISHING GOODS

ALL GOODS FIRST CLASS AND AT
REASONABLE PRICES

Jarves Street, - - - SANDWICH, MASS.

From the Bourne, Falmouth and Sandwich Business Directory, 1905

If a recipe cannot be written on the face of a 3"x5" card, off with its head.

—Helen Nearing, author and proponent of the voluntary simplicity movement

RUM-RAISIN CHEDDAR SPREAD

This is a wonderful spread for open-face party sandwiches.

Ingredients:
1 cup raisins
1/3 cup rum
8 oz. sharp Cheddar cheese
6 oz. cream cheese

Steps:
- Soak the raisins in rum for one hour or more.
- Process cheeses until smooth.
- Add raisins and rum to cheeses.

Norma Coleman

SHRIMP DIP

Serve with crackers.

Ingredients:
One 8-oz. carton sour cream
One 8-oz. pkg. cream cheese, softened
1 pkg. Italian salad dressing mix
One 4.5-oz. can shrimp, drained and finely chopped

Steps:
- Mix all ingredients.
- Chill.

ALMOND DELIGHT DIP

Serve this dip with apple slices that have been tossed with lemon juice.

Ingredients:
2 cartons vanilla low-fat yogurt (8 oz. each)
1/8 tsp. almond extract
2 Tbs. chopped toasted almonds

Steps:
- Combine yogurt and almond extract. Chill at least one hour.
- Sprinkle with chopped almonds.

BLEU-CHEESE WALNUT DIP

Serve with fresh fruit.

Ingredients:

4 oz. cream cheese softened
1/4 cup crumbled bleu cheese

One 12-oz. carton cottage cheese
2 Tbs. walnuts, finely chopped

Steps:
- Blend first three ingredients until smooth.
- Stir in walnuts.

MINI QUICHES

Ingredients:

1 can refrigerated buttermilk biscuit dough
1 cup Pepper Jack cheese, shredded

2 eggs
2 green onions with tops, finely chopped

Steps:
- Preheat oven to 375°F.
- Separate biscuit dough and divide each biscuit into three sections.
- Press each dough section into a lightly greased mini-muffin cup, stretching dough slightly to form a shell.
- Mix cheese, eggs and onions and spoon the mixture into the shells.
- Bake for 15 minutes or until filling is firm.

QUICK TORTILLA ROLLUPS

Ingredients:

One 8-oz. pkg. cream cheese, softened
1 tsp. taco seasoning

1/3 cup picante sauce
12 flour tortillas

Steps:
- Beat cream cheese until smooth.
- Add taco seasoning and picante sauce, and mix well.
- Spread mixture on each tortilla, and roll tortilla tightly.
- Place each rolled tortilla seam-side down in airtight container. Chill at least 2 hours. Slice each roll into 1-inch slices, forming a pinwheel.

HAM CRESCENT SNACKS

Ingredients:

1 can refrigerated crescent-roll dough
4 thin slices ham
2 tsp. mustard
1 cup Swiss cheese, shredded

Steps:
- Preheat oven to 375°F
- Unroll the crescent-roll dough into four long rectangles; press the perforations to seal.
- Place the ham slices on the dough rectangles.
- Spread the ham with mustard, and sprinkle it with cheese.
- Starting at the longest side, roll up the dough in jelly-roll fashion.
- Cut into half-inch slices. and place cut-side down on an ungreased cookie sheet.
- Bake for 15-20 minutes or until lightly browned.

CRAB APPETIZERS

Ingredients:

1/2 lb. Velveeta cheese
1/4 cup margarine
One 6-oz. can crab meat
1 pkg. garlic-flavored melba toast

Steps:
- Melt the cheese and margarine, and remove from the heat.
- Add the crab meat, and mix.
- Spoon onto the melba toast and broil until slightly browned.

TWIST STICKS

Ingredients:

1/2 cup sour cream
1/2 pkg. savory herb with garlic soup mix
1 pkg. refrigerated crescent-roll dough

Steps:
- Preheat oven to 375°F.
- Combine sour cream and soup mix.
- Spread out the crescent-roll dough into one long piece, pressing the seams together.
- Spread the mixture evenly onto the dough.
- Cut dough into 1-inch strips, and twist each strip loosely.
- Bake on an ungreased cookie sheet for 12-15 minutes.

WALDORF SALAD

Ingredients:

4 cups chopped apples
3/4 cup raisins
1/2 cup pecan pieces
1/2 cup mayonnaise

Steps:
- Combine ingredients.
- Refrigerate until ready to serve.

ICE-CREAM SALAD

Ingredients:

One 3-oz. package orange Jello
1 cup boiling water
1 pint vanilla ice cream, softened
1/2 cup pecans, chopped
One 8-oz. can crushed pineapple, drained

Steps:
- Dissolve Jello in boiling water.
- Mix in remaining ingredients and place in serving dish.
- Refrigerate until set.

MANDARIN SALAD WITH ORANGE-JUICE DRESSING

Ingredients:

2 tomatoes, peeled and sliced
Two 11-oz. cans mandarin oranges, drained
1/2 cup onion, thinly sliced
3 cups lettuce leaves, torn into bite-sized pieces
1/4 cup orange juice
2 tsp. red wine vinegar
1 Tbs. vegetable oil
2 tsp. honey

Steps:
- In a salad bowl, combine the four salad ingredients.
- In a small dish, mix the four dressing ingredients, and pour over the salad.

SPINACH SALAD

This salad is good served with poppy-seed dressing.

Ingredients:

1 lb. spinach, torn into bite sized pieces
1 med. red onion, thinly sliced

1 can mandarin oranges, drained
1/2 cup almonds, toasted

Steps:
- Combine ingredients.

SUPER SPINACH SALAD

Serve with an Italian or Ranch salad dressing.

Ingredients:

1 lb. spinach torn into bite sized pieces
8 oz. fresh mushrooms, sliced
8 slices bacon, fried and crumbled

Steps:
- Toss spinach, mushrooms and crumbled bacon together in a salad bowl.

CARROT SALAD

Serve on a crisp bed of lettuce.

Ingredients:

2 cups carrots, grated
1/2 cup raisins

One 8.75-oz. can pineapple tidbits, drained
1/3 cup mayonnaise

Steps:
- Combine ingredients.

> There was never an angel who wouldn't take off her wings and cook for the man she loved.
>
> —Unknown

SHRIMP AND RICE SALAD

Serve on a bed of crisp lettuce.

Ingredients:

2 cups rice, cooked
12 oz. shrimp, peeled and cooked
One 10-oz pkg. frozen peas and pearl onions, thawed
1/2 cup Italian salad dressing

Steps:
- Mix above ingredients.

PASTA SALAD

Serve with Caesar-salad dressing.

Ingredients:

One 16-oz. pkg elbow macaroni (cooked, rinsed and drained)
1 med. sweet red pepper, cut into strips
1 cup fresh mushrooms, sliced
1 cup broccoli flowerets

Steps:
- Combine ingredients and toss well. Chill.

SEAFOOD PASTA SALAD

Serve with an Italian or Ranch salad dressing.

Ingredients:

One 16-oz. pkg. vegetable rotini pasta (cooked, rinsed and drained)
One 6-oz. can pitted olives
One 10-oz. pkg. frozen chopped broccoli (thawed and drained)
One 8-oz. pkg. imitation crab meat

Steps:
- Combine ingredients.
- Toss and chill until ready to serve.

MARVELOUS MUSHROOMS

Ingredients:

1 lb. fresh mushrooms, stems removed
2 Tbs. vegetable oil
2 1/2 Tbs. chopped garlic
2 Tbs. soy sauce

Steps:
- Cut mushroom stems off.
- Heat oil in frying pan and add garlic. Cook garlic over medium-low heat for four to six minutes. Do not let garlic burn.
- Add mushrooms and cook two to three minutes.
- Add soy sauce. Toss and serve immediately.

SPICY POTATOES

Ingredients:

4 lg. baking potatoes
1/4 cup olive oil
1 pkg. onion-soup mix

Steps:
- Preheat oven to 375°F.
- Cut potatoes into bite-sized chunks or wedges.
- Toss potatoes in oil and soup mix to coat.
- Place on a baking sheet and bake for 45 minutes.

QUICK POTATO-CHEESE BAKE

Ingredients:

4 cups mashed potatoes
1/2 cup Parmesan cheese
2 eggs, slightly beaten
1/2 cup Cheddar cheese, grated

Steps:
- Preheat oven to 350°F.
- Combine potatoes, Parmesan cheese and eggs.
- Season to taste.
- Place in casserole dish and top with cheddar cheese.
- Bake for 25 minutes.

STUFFED BAKED SWEET POTATOES

Ingredients:
6 med. sweet potatoes
2 Tbs. margarine
One 8-oz. can crushed pineapple, drained
1/2 cup chopped pecans

Steps:
- Bake potatoes for 1 hour at 375°F.
- Cut a 1-inch wedge lengthwise from the top of each potato.
- Carefully scoop the pulp from the shells.
- Mix potato pulp, margarine and pineapple and beat until fluffy.
- Stuff back into potato shell and sprinkle the top with pecans.
- Bake for 12 minutes at 375°F.

FRIED GREEN TOMATOES

Ingredients:
6 lg. green tomatoes, cut into 1/4-inch slices
1 cup cornmeal
Salt and pepper
Vegetable oil

Steps:
- Dredge tomato slices in cornmeal and season with salt and pepper.
- Heat oil.
- Fry tomatoes over medium-high heat until browned, turning each slice once.

STIR-FRIED ZUCCHINI

Ingredients:
4 cups zucchini, sliced
1/4 cup margarine
2 Tbs. lemon pepper
Juice of one lemon

Steps:
- Saute the zucchini and lemon pepper in margarine. Cook for 10-15 minutes, stirring frequently.
- Add lemon juice.
- Stir and serve.

QUICK MEATBALLS

Ingredients:

2 lbs. lean ground beef
1/2 lb. sausage

One 6-oz. box Stove Top stuffing mix
3 eggs

Steps:
- Preheat oven to 350°F.
- Mix all ingredients and shape into balls.
- Place on a baking sheet and bake for 30 minutes.

BEEF AND CABBAGE ROLLS

Ingredients:

1 lb. ground beef
1 med. onion, chopped
1 cup sauerkraut, drained

3 pkgs. refrigerated crescent-roll dough

Steps:
- Preheat oven to 350°F.
- In a large skillet, brown beef and onions. Drain.
- Season to taste with salt and pepper.
- Add sauerkraut and cook until heated.
- Open crescent-roll dough, and crimp two triangles together to form rectangles.
- Place a small amount of meat mixture on each rectangle and roll up.
- Slice each roll into 2 or 3 rounds.
- Place on greased baking sheet, cut-side down.
- Bake for 10 minutes or until browned.

GARLIC CHICKEN

This dish is quick and easy, yet tasty. The chicken is so tender it falls right off the bones. My family loves it!

Ingredients:
6-8 pieces of chicken (I like the bone-in chicken, for flavor)
6 cloves garlic, crushed
1 cup white wine
1 pkg. Good Seasonings Herb and Garlic Salad Dressing

Steps:
- In a skillet, brown the chicken and garlic.
- Scrape everything into a crockpot and sprinkle Good Seasonings packet over the chicken. Pour wine over it all.
- Cook on high 4-5 hours or on low 6-8 hours.
- Serve juices over rice or noodles.
  Serves 6-8

Shani Luccketti

BROCCOLI CHICKEN

Ingredients:

6-8 boneless, skinless chicken breasts
Two 10-oz. pkgs. frozen broccoli
1 can nacho-cheese soup
1/4 cup cooking sherry

Steps:
- Preheat oven to 350°F.
- In a skillet, brown the chicken breasts and place in greased casserole.
- Mix broccoli, soup and sherry together. Pour over chicken.
- Bake uncovered for one hour.

CHICKEN SPINACH BAKE

Ingredients:

One 8-oz. pkg. fine egg noodles
One 9-oz. pkg. frozen creamed spinach, thawed
1 Tbs. vegetable oil
1 1/2 cups chicken, cooked and cubed

Steps:
- Preheat oven to 400°F.
- Cook noodles and drain.
- Coat 9x9 baking dish with cooking spray.
- Turn noodles into dish and stir in spinach and oil.
- Top with chicken and bake for 15 minutes.

HONEY-MUSTARD CHICKEN

Ingredients:

1/2 cup Miracle Whip salad dressing	1 Tbs. honey
2 Tbs. Dijon mustard	4 boneless, skinless chicken breasts

Steps:
- Combine salad dressing, mustard and honey. Brush chicken with 1/2 of mixture.
- Broil chicken on one side for 8 to 10 minutes. Turn chicken over.
- Baste with remaining mixture and broil for another 8 to 10 minutes.

ITALIAN CHICKEN

Serve with pasta.

Ingredients:

6-8 boneless, skinless chicken breasts	One 14-oz. jar spaghetti sauce with mushrooms
2 Tbs. vegetable oil	
1 cup onion, chopped	

Steps:
- Brown chicken in oil.
- Push the chicken to one side and sauté the onions until tender.
- Stir in the spaghetti sauce and cover the skillet.
- Simmer for 25 minutes or until chicken is tender.

PORK STIR FRY

Serve over rice.

Ingredients:

2 boneless pork loin chops, cut into 1/4-inch strips
One 14-oz. bag Oriental stir-fry vegetables with seasoning packet, frozen
1/4 cup water
1 Tbs. soy sauce
2 tsp. vegetable oil

Steps:
- Coat a large skillet with cooking spray.
- Heat to medium high and add the pork strips.
- Stir fry for three minutes or until no longer pink.
- Add the vegetables and cover, cooking for five minutes.
- Add water, vegetable seasoning packet, soy sauce and oil, then cook, stirring until the mixture is heated through.

OVEN-FRIED PORK CHOPS

Ingredients:

3 Tbs. margarine melted
1 egg plus 2 Tbs. water, beaten
1 cup cornbread-stuffing mix
4 pork chops

Steps:
- Preheat oven to 425°F.
- Place the margarine in a 13x9-inch baking pan.
- Dip pork chops into egg mixture, then in the stuffing mix to coat.
- Place the chops on top of the melted margarine.
- Bake for 20 minutes, then turn and bake 10-15 minutes more or until browned.

BUTTERMILK FRIED-FISH FILLETS

Ingredients:

2 lbs. skinless fish fillets
1 cup buttermilk
1 cup Bisquick baking mix
Cooking oil

Steps:
- Place the fish fillets in a shallow baking dish.
- Pour the buttermilk over the fish and let it soak for 30 minutes, turning once.

- Remove the soaked fish and roll each fillet in Bisquick, seasoning to taste with salt and pepper.
- Fry each fillet in hot oil for four to five minutes per side.

LEMON DILL FISH

Ingredients:

1 lb. fish fillets
1/2 cup Miracle Whip
2 Tbs. lemon juice
1 tsp. dill

Steps:
- Combine Miracle Whip, lemon juice and dill.
- Place the fish in a broiler pan and brush with the sauce.
- Broil for five to eight minutes, turn once and brush again with the sauce.
- Continue broiling for another five to eight minutes.

CAESAR'S FISH

Ingredients:

1 lb. flounder fillets
1/2 cup Caesar-salad dressing
1 cup round buttery crackers, crushed into crumbs
1/2 cup Cheddar cheese, shredded

Steps:
- Preheat oven to 400°F.
- Place the fillets in a lightly greased casserole dish.
- Drizzle the salad dressing over the fillets.
- Sprinkle the cracker crumbs over top of the fillets.
- Bake in the oven for 10 minutes.
- Top with cheese and bake for an additional five minutes or until fish flakes easily with fork.

SHRIMP MARINARA

Serve over rice.

Ingredients:

1 clove garlic, minced
1 Tbs. vegetable oil
One 28-oz. can Italian-style tomatoes
1 lb. frozen shrimp, shelled and deveined

Steps:
- Sauté the garlic in oil until it is tender.
- Add the tomatoes and cook until the sauce thickens and the tomatoes break up (about 20 minutes).
- Add the shrimp and cook for five more minutes.

MARINATED GRILLED SHRIMP

Ingredients:

2 Tbs. soy sauce
2 Tbs. vegetable oil
1 Tbs. honey
1 lb. large shrimp, peeled and deveined

Steps:
- Mix the soy sauce, oil and honey and pour it all over the shrimp. Marinate for at least one hour.
- Place the shrimp on skewers and grill or broil for four to five minutes until shrimp are cooked through and browned.

CRISPY BACON-WRAPPED OYSTERS

Ingredients:

One 12-oz. jar fresh oysters, drained
8 slices bacon, cut into thirds
2 Tbs. parsley
salt and pepper

Steps:
- Place one oyster on each piece of bacon.
- Sprinkle each oyster with parsley, salt and pepper, then wrap the bacon around the oyster and secure it with a toothpick.
- Place the broiler rack four inches from the heat and broil the oysters for eight minutes on one side.
- Turn and broil for five minutes on the other side.
- When done, the bacon will be crisp and the oysters will have curled.

GRILLED TUNA STEAK

Ingredients:

4 tuna steaks
1 cup Italian salad dressing
2 tsp. fresh-ground pepper
1 lemon

Steps:
- Place the tuna steaks in a casserole dish, and pour the dressing over them.
- Cover the tuna steaks and refrigerate them for one hour, turning once.
- Remove the fish from the marinade, and sprinkle pepper on both sides.
- Grill or broil tuna steaks for five minutes on each side.
- Squeeze lemon over tuna and serve.

NO-BAKE PINEAPPLE-LEMON PIE

Ingredients:

1 can frozen lemonade (6 oz.)
One 14-oz. can sweetened condensed milk
1 container Cool Whip (8 oz.)
One 15.25-oz. can crushed pineapple, drained
1 graham-cracker pie crust

Steps:
- Mix the first four ingredients and pour them into the graham-cracker crust.
- Freeze until ready to serve.

BLUEBERRY CREAM-CHEESE PIE

One 22-oz. can blueberry-pie filling
1 carton Cool Whip (8 oz.)
One 8-oz. pkg. cream cheese, softened
1 graham-cracker pie crust

Ingredients:
Steps:
- Place pie filling in graham-cracker crust.
- Combine softened cream cheese with Cool Whip and spread over pie filling.
- Chill for at least one hour before serving.

BUTTER-PECAN PIE

Ingredients:

1 1/2 cups butter-pecan ice cream, softened
Two 1.5-oz. English toffee-flavored candy bars, crushed
1 1/2 cups vanilla ice cream (softened)
1 graham-cracker crust

Steps:
- Spread butter-pecan ice cream in crust.
- Sprinkle with half of the crushed candy bar.
- Freeze.
- Spread the vanilla ice cream over top of crushed candy bar.
- Sprinkle with the remaining candy and freeze until ready to serve.

COOKIE-CRUST ICE-CREAM PIE

Ingredients:

1 roll of refrigerator chocolate-chip cookie dough
1 qt. chocolate ice cream, softened
One 12-oz. jar chocolate fudge sauce
One 8-oz. carton Cool Whip

Steps:
- Preheat oven to 375°F.
- Slice cookie dough 1/8-inch thick.
- Line the bottom and sides of a 9-inch pie pan with the cookie slices, overlapping the sides to make a scalloped edge.
- Bake for 10 minutes.
- Cool.
- Fill the cooled, cooked crust with the softened ice cream.
- Top the pie with syrup and frost it with cool whip. Freeze.
- Cut into wedges to serve.

STRAWBERRY-MALLOW PIE

Ingredients:

One 10-oz. pkg. frozen sweetened strawberries, thawed
20 lg. marshmallows
One 8-oz. carton Cool Whip
One pre-baked pie shell

Steps:
- Pour the juice from the strawberries in a pan, and heat slowly, adding marshmallows.
- Stir until the marshmallows are melted.
- Cool.
- Fold in the Cool Whip and strawberries. Mix well.
- Pour into the pie shell and refrigerate.

PEANUT-BUTTER PIE

Ingredients:

One 8-oz. pkg. cream cheese, softened
1 cup powdered sugar
1 cup crunchy peanut butter
One 8-oz. carton Cool Whip
1 graham-cracker crust

Steps:
- Cream the cream cheese.
- Add sugar and peanut butter, beat until smooth.
- Fold in the Cool Whip.
- Place mixture in the graham-cracker crust.
- Refrigerate or freeze.

GERMAN-CHOCOLATE PIE

Ingredients:

1 pkg. Baker's German sweet chocolate (4 oz)
1/3 cup milk
One 3-oz. pkg. cream cheese, softened
1 carton Cool Whip (8 oz.)
1 baked chocolate-crust pie shell

Steps:
- Heat chocolate and 2 Tbs. milk over low heat.
- Stir until melted. Remove from heat.
- Beat cream cheese, and add remaining milk to chocolate mixture. Beat until smooth. Fold Cool Whip into chocolate mixture and blend until smooth.
- Spoon into crust.
- Freeze about four hours before serving.

ORANGE DESSERT

Top with whipped cream.

Ingredients:

1 pkg. lemon Jell-O
1 cup boiling water

1 pint orange sherbet
1 sm. can mandarin oranges, drained

Steps:

- Dissolve the lemon Jell-o in the boiling water. Let stand a few moments to cool.
- Fold in the orange sherbet, and add the mandarin orange sections.
- Can be served in an hour.
  Serves 6-8

Mira Howell

EASY CHERRY COBBLER

This is something I started making years ago when my grandchildren came to visit. They loved it. Now they are grown, but they still expect it every time they come. It's so easy!

Ingredients:

1 can cherry pie pilling
1/2 box white cake mix

1 stick melted oleo margarine or butter
Nuts, chopped

Steps:

- Preheat oven to 350°F.
- Spread one can of cherry pie filling in a square pan (8-inch is just right, but you could use a 9-inch).
- Crumble the white cake mix on top and then cover with the melted margarine or butter.
- Top with chopped nuts.
- Bake for one hour.
  Serves 6-8

Jacqueline Jacobsen

TRIPLE FUDGE CAKE

Top with whipped cream, if you like.

Ingredients:
1 pkg. chocolate-pudding mix
2 cups milk
1 pkg. Devils Food Cake mix
1/2 cup semi-sweet chocolate chips

Steps:
- Preheat oven to 350°F.
- Cook the chocolate pudding in 2 cups of milk.
- Blend the cake mix into the hot pudding, beating by hand or mixer for two minutes.
- Pour all into a greased and floured 9x13-inch cake pan.
- Sprinkle the batter with chocolate chips.
- Bake for 35 minutes.

UGLY-DUCKLING CAKE WITH FROSTING

Ingredients for Ugly-Duckling Cake:
1 box yellow cake mix
One 17-oz. can fruit cocktail in syrup
1 cup coconut, flaked
2 eggs

Steps for Ugly-Duckling Cake:
- Preheat oven to 350°F.
- Blend all ingredients and beat with an electric mixer for two minutes at medium speed.
- Pour into a greased 9x13-inch cake pan.
- Bake for 45 minutes.

Ingredients for Ugly-Duckling Frosting:
1 cup brown sugar
1/4 cup evaporated milk
1 stick margarine
1 cup coconut, flaked

Steps for Ugly-Duckling Frosting:
- In a saucepan, combine the brown sugar, evaporated milk and margarine, and cook for five minutes over medium heat, stirring constantly.
- Remove mixture from the heat and stir in the coconut.
- Pour frosting over the cake.

ALMOND-BARK COOKIES

Ingredients:

One 24-oz. pkg. almond bark
1 cup peanut butter
8 cups Captain Crunch cereal
1 cup salted peanuts

Steps:
- Melt the almond bark.
- Add the peanut butter and mix.
- Remove mixture from the heat and stir in the cereal and peanuts.
- Drop by spoonfuls onto waxed paper.
- Cool.

ORANGE COCONUT BALLS

Ingredients:

3 cups vanilla wafers, finely crushed
2 cups flaked coconut
1 cup pecans, finely chopped
One 6-oz. can frozen orange juice concentrate, thawed

Steps:
- Combine all ingredients and shape into bite-sized balls.
- If desired, roll in additional crushed-wafer crumbs.
- Refrigerate in an airtight container.

PEANUT-BUTTER-CANDY COOKIES

Ingredients:

1/2 cup peanut butter
1/2 cup sugar
1/4 cup evaporated milk
2 1/2 cups cornflakes

Steps:
- Preheat oven to 375°F.
- Mix peanut butter, sugar and milk into a smooth cream.
- Stir in the Cornflakes until thoroughly blended.
- Drop by the teaspoon onto ungreased cookie sheets.
- Bake for six minutes or until evenly browned.

CHOCOLATE BITES

Ingredients:

One 6-oz. pkg. semi-sweet chocolate chips
1/2 cup peanut butter
1/2 cup margarine
8 cups Rice Chex cereal

Steps:
- Combine the first three ingredients in a saucepan and cook over low heat until the chocolate melts, stirring occasionally.
- Remove from the heat and stir.
- Pour over the cereal and stir to coat evenly.
- Spread on wax-paper-lined cookie sheets.
- Let cool for one hour.
- Break into bite-sized pieces.

CANDY TRIFLES

Ingredients:

One 12-oz. pkg. semi-sweet chocolate chips
1 cup Spanish peanuts
2 cups Chow Mein noodles

Steps:
- In a double boiler over hot water, melt the chocolate chips.
- Stir in the nuts and noodles until they are all well coated.
- Drop this mixture by the teaspoon onto waxed paper.
- Chill until firm.

CHOCOLATE-MARSHMALLOW MOUSSE

Ingredients:

One 7-oz. bar Hershey's milk chocolate
1 1/2 cups miniature marshmallows
1/3 cup milk
1 cup whipping cream, chilled

Steps:
- Break the chocolate bar into pieces.
- In a double boiler, melt the chocolate bar and marshmallows with the milk.
- Cool to room temperature.
- In a small mixing bowl, beat the whipping cream until stiff.
- Fold the whipped cream into the cooled chocolate mixture and pour it into dessert dishes. Cover and chill for one or two hours, until firm.

STRAWBERRY TRIFLE

Ingredients:

Two 3.4 oz. pkgs. instant vanilla pudding
4 cups milk
20 vanilla wafers
2 pints strawberries, hulled and sliced

Steps:
- Combine the pudding mix and milk, and beat well.
- Pour half of the pudding into a two-quart bowl or trifle dish.
- Top the pudding with the vanilla wafers, then sprinkle with strawberries, then top with the remaining half of the pudding.
- Cover and refrigerate for at least four hours, or up to 24 hours.

APPLE CRISP

Ingredients:

1/3 cup butter, softened
1 cup brown sugar
3/4 cup flour
4 cups tart apples, sliced

Steps:
- Preheat oven to 350°F.
- Mix butter, sugar and flour.
- Place apple slices in 8x8-inch pan.
- Sprinkle butter topping over apples.
- Bake for 1 hour.

SEAFOOD

Fisherman's House & Boats, Sandwich, Mass.

"Give a man a fish, and you feed him for a day,
Teach him to fish, and you feed him for a lifetime."

Chinese proverb

Cape Cod Fruit

225

CLAMBAKE ON CAPE COD.

THE WAKPEE CAMP
(WALK-PEE)
JOHN PERCIVAL, Proprietor
Boats to Let and Fishermen Accommodated
Situated on Shore of Wakpee Lake.
Good Beds, Good Food, Good Fishing
TELEPHONE COTUIT 31-32
SOUTH SANDWICH, MASS.

Advertisement in 1905 Bourne, Falmouth & Sandwich Directory

CLAM FRITTERS

This recipe is a favorite at summer family gatherings. Cooking it outside on a Coleman stove makes for an odor-free home.

Ingredients:

1/4 tsp. baking soda
1 pint chopped clams, drained
1/2 cup milk
2 eggs, well beaten
1 cup flour
1/2 tsp. salt
Vegetable oil, for deep frying

Steps:
- Add the baking soda to the clams.
- Mix the remaining ingredients in a separate bowl.
- Add the clams to the bowl of batter.
- Drop spoonfuls of clam batter into hot oil to deep fry.

Stan Lucas

HINT: *Freeze the clams if they are whole. Then, defrost them in the microwave and chop them when partially thawed. Drain completely once defrosted.*

SEA-CLAM PIE

Ingredients:

2 cups sea clams (or 2 cans clams), chopped
1 pkg. Ritz crackers, crushed
1 cup clam juice
Butter

Steps:
Preheat the oven to 350°F.
Mix all of the ingredients together.
Add dabs of butter.
Put into a regular pie plate and bake until the crust is brown.

FACT: *The part of the bay scallop that is eaten is the adductor muscle, which opens and closes the shell.*

CLAM SOUFFLÉ

This is one soufflé that will not fall! It may also be reheated.

Ingredients:

12 Saltines, crumbled
1 cup milk
2 eggs, well beaten
1 can minced clams
1/4 cup butter, melted
1 Tbs. onion, minced
1 Tbs. green pepper, minced
Salt and pepper

Steps:

- Preheat the oven to 350°F
- Pour the milk over the crumbled crackers and let stand for 20 minutes.
- Add the butter, clams with juice, eggs and seasonings.
- Pour into a greased casserole dish.
- Bake for 30 minutes.
  Serves 4

Nancy Carvalho

AMERICA'S LINGUINE WITH WHITE CLAM SAUCE

This is an old family recipe brought over from Italy. When I was born in 1912 in Italy, it was my father's dream to come to America. So I was named America. My family finally arrived in New York when I was seven, after many struggles and hardships. I have always been proud of my name.

Ingredients:

1 lb. linguine
4-5 garlic cloves, chopped
Pinch red-pepper flakes
4 Tbs. olive oil
1 doz. little-neck clams in shells
Handful fresh Italian parsley (flat-leafed parsley)

Steps:

- Cook the linguine, as directed on package, to be al dente.
- While the linguine is cooking, sauté the garlic and red-pepper flakes in the olive oil, in a saucepan, over medium heat for two or three minutes.
- Add the clams, cover and turn the heat down to simmer. The clams will open when done. Discard any that do not open.
- When the linguine is done, drain it and put it into a serving bowl. Ladle the clam sauce over the linguine, and place the clams on the pasta.
- Salt and pepper to taste.
  Serves 3 or 4

America Spero

> *"Throw a lucky man into the sea, and he will come up with a fish in his mouth."*
>
> —Arab proverb

LINGUINE AND MUSSELS

This recipe sounds complicated, but is actually very easy and fast.

Ingredients:

2 med. shallots, finely chopped (or one Vidalia onion)
2 Tbs. unsalted butter
1 lg. garlic clove, minced
1/2 red pepper, thinly sliced
1 lb. cultivated mussels, scrubbed

6 oz. dry linguine
3 Tbs. heavy cream
3/4 tsp. salt
1/4 tsp. pepper
3 Tbs. flat-leafed parsley, chopped

Steps:

- Cook the shallots in a heavy skillet in butter until soft (about five minutes).
- Add the garlic and red pepper, and cook, stirring occasionally, until the peppers are tender (about four minutes).
- Add the mussels and cook, covered, over moderate heat until they are just opened (about six minutes). Check periodically after four minutes, and transfer to a bowl as they open. Discard any mussels that are not opened after six minutes.
- While the mussels cook, cook the linguine according to package directions.
- Reserve 3/4 cup of pasta water, and then drain the pasta, reserving more water. Add the linguine to the skillet along with the cream, salt and pepper, and the reserved pasta water.
- Bring to a simmer and add the mussels.
- Toss the pasta carefully, adding more pasta water if necessary.
- Serve immediately topped with chopped parsley.

Barbara Walsh

BAKED FISH MOZZARELLA

Serve with salad and hot bread.

Ingredients:

2 lbs. thick flounder or sole fillets, rinsed and patted dry
2 cups mozzarella cheese, shredded (low-fat works fine)
1 lg. tomato, thinly sliced
1/2 tsp. dried oregano
Granulated garlic (or any kind of minced garlic)
Salt
Black pepper, freshly ground

Steps:
- Preheat the oven to 375°F.
- Butter a large baking dish and arrange the fillets in a single layer in the dish.
- Sprinkle the fish with the cheese.
- Layer the top of the fish with tomato, then sprinkle with oregano, garlic, salt and pepper.
- Bake until the fish is opaque, about 10 minutes and serve immediately.
- This dish also could be prepared earlier in the day and baked when needed. If you do this, allow the casserole to come to room temperature (about 20 minutes after removing it from the refrigerator) before baking.
Serves 6

Marilyn Goldstein

LEGAL SEA FOODS' FISH CAKES

Legal Sea Foods originated in Cambridge, MA over 50 years ago, and its 26 restaurants across seven states still serve these fish cakes day and night.

Ingredients:

5 Tbs. butter
1/3 cup scallions, chopped
1 Tbs. sour cream
8 oz. cooked fish (or more)
1/4 tsp. dry mustard
Salt and pepper
3 Tbs. parsley, chopped
1 2/3 cup mashed potatoes
1 egg, beaten
Dried bread crumbs
Oil, for frying

Steps:
- Heat 2 Tbs. of butter and sauté the scallions. Set aside.
- Combine the sour cream with the cooked fish.
- In a separate bowl, mix the dry mustard, salt, pepper, sautéed scallions, parsley, mashed potatoes, and egg together.

- Combine the mashed-potato mixture with the fish mixture, and form into eight cakes.
- Dip the cakes into breadcrumbs.
- Heat the remaining 3 Tbs. butter with a dash of oil, and sauté the cakes for three minutes on each side.
Makes 8 cakes

Norma Coleman

BAKED CREAMY COD, SPINACH AND EGG NOODLES

Ingredients:

3 Tbs. butter or margarine	One 8-oz. pkg. med. egg noodles, cooked and drained
3 Tbs. flour	
3 cups milk	Two 10-oz pkgs. chopped spinach, thawed and drained
1 Tbs. lemon juice	
1/2 tsp. salt	1 1/2 lbs. cod fillets
1/8 tsp. pepper	Paprika
1 1/2 cups sharp Cheddar cheese, shredded	

Steps:
- Preheat the oven to 375°F.
- Melt the butter. Blend in the flour, and add milk. Stir over medium heat until smooth and thickened (it will be a little on the thin side).
- Stir in the lemon juice, salt, pepper and 1 cup of the cheese.
- Combine the cooked noodles with half of the cheese sauce, and pour into a 2-qt. baking dish or 9- x 12-inch pan.
- Top the dish with the spinach, then arrange the fish on top of the spinach.
- Pour the remaining sauce over the fish, and sprinkle with the remaining cheese and paprika.
- Bake for 25 minutes, or until the fish is cooked.
Serves 6

Anne Quagge

ITALIAN CIOPPINO

This fish soup is a complete meal when served with a green salad and French bread.

Ingredients:

1 1/2 lbs. white-fleshed fish
1 cup onion, chopped
2 garlic cloves, minced
1 Tbs. oil
One 28-oz. can tomatoes, drained and mashed
One 8-oz. can tomato sauce
1/2 cup dry white wine or water
1 tsp. each of dried basil, thyme, marjoram and oregano
1 bay leaf
1/4 tsp. pepper
4 whole cloves (optional)
1 Tbs. parsley, minced

Steps:
- Cut the fish into 1/2-inch chunks, and set aside.
- In a large soup pot, sauté the onion and garlic in oil until tender.
- Add the tomatoes, tomato sauce, wine or water, and all seasonings except parsley.
- Let simmer for 20-30 minutes, stirring occasionally.
- Add the fish and cook until done, about 10 minutes.
- Add the parsley before serving.
  Yields 7 cups

LEMON-CRUMB TOPPED FISH BAKE

Ingredients:

Cooking spray or a drizzle of extra-virgin olive oil
1 1/2 lbs. haddock or cod fillets, rinsed and patted dry
A few pinches of coarse salt
Juice of half a lemon
1 Tbs. mayonnaise
1 tsp. Old Bay Seasoning
A few grinds of fresh black pepper
1/2 cup plain breadcrumbs
1 1/2 Tbs. butter, melted
A palmful of fresh parsley, chopped

Steps:
- Preheat the oven to 425°F.
- Spray a baking dish with cooking spray or wipe it with a little olive oil.
- Sprinkle the fish with a little coarse salt.
- Combine the lemon juice, 1 Tbs. mayonnaise, Old Bay Seasoning and black pepper, then spread over the fish fillets.
- Sprinkle the fish with the breadcrumbs, and drizzle them with the butter.
- Bake the fish for 20 minutes until it is opaque and flaky.
- Sprinkle with the parsley before serving.

Chris Evans

BAKED BLUEFISH

Ingredients:

2 Bluefish fillets, skinned
2 med. onions
2 limes
Salt and black pepper
Dried parsley
Garlic powder

Oregano
Sweet basil
Breadcrumbs
2-3 tomatoes, sliced
Butter or margarine

Steps:
- Preheat the oven to 350°F.
- Place fish fillets into a well buttered baking pan, skinned side down. Make three diagonal cuts into each fillet.
- Dice one onion and place the pieces of onion into the cuts in the fillets.
- Squeeze the juice of half a lime over each fillet.
- Sprinkle on salt, pepper, parsley, garlic powder, oregano and sweet basil.
- Cover the fillets with breadcrumbs.
- Dice the second onion and sprinkle the pieces over the fillets.
- Add the sliced tomatoes to the top of the fillets, and cover them with more breadcrumbs.
- Place 3 pats of butter or margarine on each fillet and, again, squeeze the juice of half a lime over each.
- Bake for 45 minutes to 1 hour, depending on the size of the fillets.
- Remove the pan from the oven and let it cool for 15 minutes before serving. Serves 2 to 4

Anne Quagge

EASY, CHEESY SEAFOOD SUPPER

Ingredients:

1 1/2 lbs. fish fillets
1 cup onions, sliced
2 Tbs. margarine, melted
One 11-oz. can condensed cheddar-cheese soup
1/4 cup water
One 16-oz. can whole small potatoes, drained and sliced
One 9-oz. pkg. frozen cut green beans, thawed
1/2 tsp. salt
1/4 tsp. pepper
1/4 tsp. dry mustard
1 cup American cheese, shredded
3/4 cup dry breadcrumbs, mixed with 2 Tbs. melted margarine

Steps:
- Cut the fish into 1 1/2-inch chunks and set aside.
- Cook the onion in the margarine until tender, but not brown.
- Preheat the oven to 350°F.
- To the onion, add the soup, water, potatoes, beans, salt, pepper and mustard. Mix well.
- Heat until bubbly.
- Fold in the fish chunks and half of the American cheese.
- Spoon the mixture into a shallow 1 1/2-qt. casserole dish.
- Sprinkle the remaining American cheese over top, then cover with breadcrumbs.
- Bake until hot and bubbly, about 25-30 minutes.
Serves 6

Anne Quagge

SEA CAPTAIN'S DINNER: COD WITH SALT PORK

This recipe came from an old sea captain of Salem, Massachusetts. He lived in a house across the road from the "House of the Seven Gables" made famous by Nathaniel Hawthorne. If you were recommended, the captain, with the help of his daughter, might condescend to cook you a dinner of fish he had caught that morning in Salem Harbor. It was always the same: cusk (ocean catfish), cut into chunks and broiled with a piece of salt pork atop each piece. When the salt pork had browned, the fish was done and transferred to hot plates. Melted butter was poured over the fish before serving.

Don Small, who ran an immaculate fish shop in Sagamore, Mass., sniffed at the word cusk. "Ocean catfish—looks like a drowned baby," he said. But at last inquiry, the Ipswich Fish Store was sending cusk to New York's specialty restaurants. Nowadays, I substitute thick pieces of cod, and imagine them as tasty as the old captain's fish dinner.

Ingredients:

Fresh thick end of cod - you'll need at least 1 to 2 inches square per person
Fresh piece of salt pork, sliced
Butter, salt and pepper to taste

Steps:
- Place a piece of salt pork on each square of fish
- Broil until salt pork is browned
- Serves 1 square inch per person

Shirley Cross

SEAFOOD-STUFFED SOLE-FILLET ROLL-UPS

This recipe is from Capt. Frank's Fish and Lobster Restaurant in New Bedford, MA.

Ingredients:

1/2 cup scallops, shrimp or lobster meat, finely chopped	Salt, pepper and garlic salt
1/3 cup salad oil	20 Ritz crackers (crushed)
1 Tbsp onion, minced	6 fillets of sole
1 Tbsp parsley, minced	Parmesan cheese, grated
	Lemon juice

Steps:
- Sauté the scallops (or shrimp or lobster) in oil with onion, parsley, and seasonings for one minute.
- Mix in the cracker crumbs.
- Spread the dressing evenly over each fillet and then sprinkle on the cheese. Add a few drops of lemon juice over the dressing.
- Preheated the oven to 350°F.
- Roll each fillet, jelly-roll fashion, and skewer it with toothpicks. (These may be cut after rolling, making 2 roll-ups each).
- Dot each roll-up with butter, and place it on a cookie sheet lined with foil.
- Cover roll-ups lightly with foil and bake for 10 minutes.
- Remove the foil and cook for another 10 minutes, or until the fish flakes easily when touched with a fork.
Serves 6

Jennie Zantuhos

EARL'S STRIPED BASS WITH GARLIC-MUSTARD SAUCE

This recipe is delicious with bluefish, too.

Ingredients:

2 lbs. striped bass fillets, skinned and boned
1/4 cup flour
1 tsp. salt
1/2 tsp. pepper
2 eggs, beaten
1 tsp. butter
3 Tbs. olive oil
1 stick butter
4 garlic cloves, crushed
1 Tbs. Dijon mustard
2 tsp. lemon juice
1/4 cup white wine

Steps:
- Preheat oven to 375°F.
- Cut fish into serving-size portions.
- Combine flour, salt and pepper in a shallow dish.
- Place the eggs into another shallow dish.
- Dip the fish in the beaten eggs and then dredge in the flour mixture.
- Melt the butter and add the olive oil, and heat.
- Add the fish fillets and sauté until golden brown on both sides.
- Place the fillets in the buttered baking dish, and bake for 10 minutes.
- Melt the butter and add the garlic, mustard, lemon juice and white wine. Whisk until blended and cook for two minutes over medium heat.
- Remove the fish from the oven, and top it with the sauce.
Serves 4-6

Earl Zinck

SALMON WITH SIZZLE

Serve with brown rice or rice pilaf, and green beans or asparagus spears.

Ingredients:

1/3 cup maple syrup
3 Tbs. apple-cider vinegar
1 Tbs. brown mustard
1 Tbs. soy sauce or Tamari
1 Tbs. cooking oil
1 clove garlic, chopped
1/2 tsp. pepper
1-lb. salmon fillet or 4 boneless

Steps:
- In a small bowl, mix all of the ingredients except the salmon, until well blended.
- Pour half of the mixture over the salmon fillets or steaks.

- Broil for eight minutes, pink side up, then turn the fish and broil for another six minutes. The fish should be flaky when pierced with a fork.
- Heat the remaining sauce lightly and pour over the cooked fish or serve alongside.

Serves 4

Debbie McDermot

MAPLE- AND MUSTARD-GLAZED SALMON

Maille mustard, from France, is the best one to use in this recipe. It has more grains than other mustards, and adheres better to the salmon. It can be found in any good grocery store.

Ingredients:

3 Tbs. Maille Old Style whole-grain Dijon mustard
3 Tbs. pure maple syrup
Four 2-inch pieces of salmon fillet (approx. 1/4 -1/3 lb. each)

Steps:

- Preheat oven to 400°F.
- Mix the mustard and syrup in a small bowl.
- Place the salmon pieces half an inch apart on a baking pan sprayed or brushed with vegetable oil. (HINT: Cover the pan with aluminum first, then spray. The glaze can then burn onto the pan without worry about clean up!)
- Spoon or spread the mustard-syrup mixture over the tops and sides of each piece of fish. It will drip.
- Bake for 20 minutes. The glaze will be semi-crispy, and the salmon will be moist.

Serves 4

Karyn Frances Gray

SALMON, ONIONS 'N SOY

This is a simple, quick, perfect dish and tastes great served over basmati rice..

Ingredients:

1 Tbs. extra-virgin olive oil
3 lg. Vidalia onions, halved and sliced
Salt and pepper to taste
Two 6-oz. pieces salmon fillet
1/4 cup soy sauce (reduced-salt version may be used)

Steps:
- Heat a large frying pan over medium heat, then add olive oil.
- When the oil is hot, add the onions, salt and pepper to taste. Sauté for eight to ten minutes until onions are soft.
- Place the salmon fillets over the onions.
- Add the soy sauce, then cover and cook for 12 minutes.
- Serve immediately
  Serves 2

NOTE: This recipe may be doubled, but do not use more than 1/4 cup soy sauce or it will be too salty. Increase the onions to five or six and use four 6-oz salmon fillets. Cook for 12 minutes.

Irma Moss

LIGHT SHRIMP ALFREDO

Serve over hot fettuccine noodles.

Ingredients:

1 1/3 cups skim milk
2 sm. garlic cloves, minced
2 tsp. flour
2 Tbs. fat-free cream cheese
1 cup dry Parmesan cheese, grated
1 Tbs. plus 2 tsp. butter-flavored powder
Cooked shrimp

Steps:
- In a medium saucepan, over high heat, whisk the milk, garlic, flour and cream cheese. Bring to a boil while whisking constantly.
- Reduce the heat and simmer for two minutes or until thickened.
- Add the Parmesan cheese and whisk until blended.
- Remove from heat and stir in the butter-flavored powder and the cooked shrimp.
  Serves 4

Nicole Amsel

SHRIMP SAUTÉED IN THE SHELL

Shrimp cooked in the shell gains flavor. Jumbo shrimp are easier to cut in half, and the meat is easier to remove from the shell. Serve this dish with napkins, because it's fun to pull the meat out of the shell using your fingers.

Ingredients:

1 lb. jumbo shrimp, raw in the shell
4 Tbs. butter
1/3 cup dry white wine
Few drops fresh lemon juice
Salt and pepper to taste

Steps:

- Lay the shrimp flat on a cutting board. Using a flat-bladed knife, cut the shrimp in half lengthwise.
- In a very large pan, over medium-low heat, melt half of the butter. When bubbly, sauté the shrimp, cut-side down. Avoid overcrowding.
- Sauté shrimp for two minutes on each side. Shells should be bright pink and curled, but the inside should be juicy.
- Place shrimp on a serving plate and keep them warm.
- Deglaze the pan with the wine. Stir over medium heat to dissolve sediment and evaporate the liquid.
- Stir in the lemon juice, and then swirl in the remaining two tablespoons of butter until it is melted and incorporated into a sauce.
- Season the sauce with salt and pepper, then spoon it over the shrimp. Serve at once.
  Serves 3

Judy Koenig

SHRIMP SCAMPI

Rose Leaman from the Holly Ridge Golf Club, Sandwich, MA says the dish is very popular with golfers and their guests. Spoon the shrimp scampi over hot cooked linguini, and serve grated Parmesan cheese on the side.

Ingredients:

1 lb. salted butter
1/4 cup garlic, chopped
2 Tbs. dry white wine
Juice from half a lemon
1 lb. med. raw shrimp, peeled and deveined

Steps:
- Melt the butter over low heat and sauté the garlic until it is tender but not brown.
- Add the white wine and lemon juice, and continue to cook for three or four minutes to "cook off" the wine.
- Add the raw shrimp and toss until the shrimp turns pink. Do not overcook!
Serves 4-6

Rose Leaman

DEVILED SHRIMP

Very tasty and easy to make

Ingredients:

1/2 cup (1 stick) unsalted butter, room temperature
4 anchovy fillets, drained and minced
2 lg. garlic cloves, pressed
1 1/2 tsp. Dijon mustard
1 1/2 tsp. Tabasco sauce
1 1/2 tsp. Worcestershire sauce
1/4 tsp. salt (optional)
24 uncooked jumbo/lg. shrimp, peeled and de-veined
1/4 cup fresh Italian parsley, minced

Steps:
- Using the back of a spoon, mash the first seven ingredients together in a small bowl.
- Preheat the broiler.
- Place the shrimp in a single layer in a large, broiler-proof baking dish.
- Smear the butter mixture over the shrimp.
- Broil without turning until cooked through (about five minutes).
- Sprinkle with parsley before serving.
Serves 8

Wendy Harte

LEMON-BUTTER SAUCE FOR SEAFOOD

Ingredients:

1/4 cup butter
2 Tbs. lemon juice
1 tsp. onion, minced
Dash of Tabasco sauce

Steps:
- Combine all ingredients and mix well.
  Yields 1/2 cup

Regina Murphy Silvia

THE PADDOCK'S POLENTA CRAB CAKES

The Paddock Restaurant in Hyannis, MA submitted this recipe.

Ingredients:

1/8 cup red pepper, diced
1/8 cup green pepper, diced
1/8 cup onion, diced
1 oz. butter
3/4 tsp. garlic
1/4 cup lobster stock
3/4 cup light cream
1/4 cup cornmeal
2 Tbs. Romano cheese
2 Tbs. Parmesan cheese
Red pepper flakes, to taste
1 1/4 lbs. dry crabmeat

Steps:
- Cook the pepper, onion and garlic in butter until the onions are transparent.
- Add the lobster stock and light cream. Bring to a slow boil.
- Slowly add the cornmeal, cheeses and red pepper flakes.
- Add the dry crabmeat to mixture off the heat.
- Let cool a bit, then scoop out 6-oz portions and roll in cornmeal.
- Use cookie cutter rounds to press the balls into a cake shape.
- Fry cakes in 1 tablespoon of butter. Serve with a garnish of parsley.
  Serves 4

FACT: Scallop shells have been found in the ruins at Pompeii, Italy.

CRAB-RANGOON WREATH

Ingredients:

Two 12-oz pkgs. cream cheese
One 16-oz pkg. frozen imitation crab (Seafood Salad mix)
2 tsp. horseradish
1/2 cup chives or scallions, chopped
1 cup sharp Cheddar cheese, shredded finely
2 pkgs. ready-to-bake croissant dough (do not use a low-fat version)

Steps:

- Defrost the imitation-crab mix. You will need this mixture to be somewhat wet, so squeeze out a bit of the water a little at a time over the sink.
- Chop the seafood finely.
- Place the seafood mixture into a large mixing bowl with the cream cheese.
- Add the chives or scallions, the Cheddar cheese and the horseradish to the mixture. Blend using a fork until the ingredients are all fairly well mixed together. This will be a stiff mixture, and if you do not mind getting a bit messy, it probably blends better using bare hands.
- Preheat the oven to 350°F.
- Get out a nonstick cookie sheet and begin opening packages of croissant rolls.
- Place the triangles of dough in a circle with the small edge of the triangle facing in, and the long point of the triangle facing out, overlapping the next piece of dough beside it. (Your final arrangement should look like the sun with a hollow center.)
- Start spooning the crab mixture onto the inner part of the circle. You will find that you will not use all of the mixture, but the rest can be consumed on wheat crackers while you are cooking.
- Begin taking the long points of your triangles of dough and folding them over the mixture. You will need to handle the dough a bit, pinching it together and making sure that the dough covers all of the seafood-cheese mixture.
- Bake the wreath for 20 minutes, browning the croissant dough, but taking care not to burn the bottom of your wreath.
- After allowing the wreath to cool for 10-15 minutes, you can slice and serve it while it is still warm, or wait a bit and serve it when cooler.

Lisa Marie Dunn

LOBSTER OR LANGASTINO CASSEROLE

Ingredients:

1 stick butter or margarine
1 sm. onion, finely chopped
2 stalks celery, finely chopped
1 sm. can mushrooms
1 can lobster meat or
1 pkg. langastinos
1/2 lb. shrimp or 1 can baby clams
Buttered breadcrumbs, to your liking

Steps:
- Preheat the oven to 350°F.
- Put the butter in a pan and sauté the onion and celery until soft.
- Add the mushrooms, lobster meat and shrimp or baby clams.
- Pour over buttered breadcrumbs in a casserole dish. Pour more crumbs over the top and bake for 20-30 minutes.
  Serves 4 to 6

Ann North

LOBSTER STOCK

Ingredients:

Shells and remains from 2 or more cooked lobsters (either steamed or boiled)
1 lg. onion, chopped
1 bottle dry white wine

Steps:
- In a 6-quart kettle or saucepan, combine the lobster shells, onion and wine. Mix, cover and simmer over low heat for 1 1/2 hours.
- Remove from the heat, strain the liquid into jars (discarding the shells) and freeze until ready for use.
  Makes about 1 quart.

John Carafoli

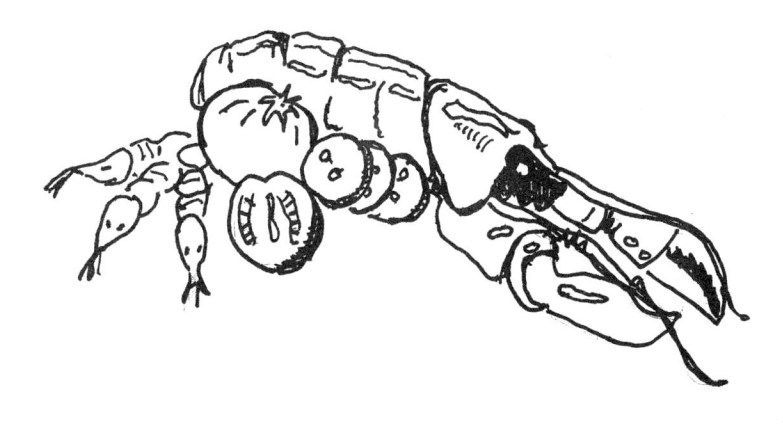

LOBSTER-AND-SCALLOP BUNDLE WITH CHARDONNAY CREAM SAUCE

Chef Argos Pilo from the Belfry Inne & Bistro of Sandwich, MA, submitted this recipe. To serve, put two ounces of cream sauce on a seven-inch plate and place the seafood bundle on top.

Ingredients for Lobster and Scallop Bundle:

1 bunch celery	1 oz. lobster meat
1 bunch scallions	1 oz. scallops
1/2 bunch leeks	2 sheets phyllo dough

Ingredients for Chardonnay Cream Sauce:

2 oz. Chardonnay wine	Pinch of lobster base
Shallots	Cornstarch
4 oz. heavy cream	Salt and pepper, to taste

Steps:
- Sweat the celery, scallions and leeks. Sauté them with butter and let them cool.
- Combine the vegetables with the lobster and scallops.
- Preheat the oven to 350°F.
- Take two sheets of phyllo dough, fold them in half and wrap the dough in a bag-type configuration. Place the mixture inside.
- Tie the bag with leek leaves that have been blanched in hot water for 30 seconds.
- Bake for 5 minutes.
- Prepare the Chardonnay cream sauce by reducing the wine with the shallots, then adding heavy cream and lobster base; reduce.
- To thicken, add a bit of cornstarch and let sit.
  Serves 1

Argos Pilo

LOBSTER CASSEROLE WITH LEMON-HERB TOPPING

Ingredients:

1/3 cup + 5 Tbs. butter	1 Tbs. fresh herbs, chopped (parsley, chives, tarragon, or whatever mixture of herbs that you like)
1/3 cup white wine or fish or chicken stock	
3/4 lb. lobster meat, cooked	Salt and pepper to taste
3 Tbs. onion, minced	1 cup fresh breadcrumbs
2 cloves garlic	1 1/2 Tbs. lemon rind, grated

Steps:
- Melt the 1/3 cup butter, and add the wine or stock.
- Mix in the lobster meat.
- Place the mixture in one layer in a shallow baking dish, and let it set for a few minutes to absorb the liquid. (It should be moist, not wet.)
- Preheat the oven to 375°F.
- Sauté the onion and garlic in the remaining five tablespoons of butter until soft.
- Mix the herbs, salt, pepper, breadcrumbs and grated lemon rind together. Add this mixture to the onions and garlic, and cook for a few minutes.
- Spread the mixture over the lobster; then bake for 15 minutes.

Peggy Dolan

LOBSTER CAKES

This looks like a lot of ingredients, but it goes together pretty quickly. I sometimes add sherry and lemon juice. Add or subtract seasonings according to your taste! These lobster cakes freeze well.

Ingredients:

1/4 cup onions, minced
1/4 cup green pepper, minced
1/2 Tbs. fresh ginger, minced
4 Tbs. oil
1 egg
3 Tbs. mayonnaise
1 1/2 tsp. dry mustard
3 Tbs. parsley, minced

3/4 tsp. Old Bay Seasoning
1 tsp. Worcestershire sauce
3 dashes Tabasco sauce
1/4 tsp. black pepper
1 lb. lobster meat, chopped
20 Saltine crackers, crushed
2 Tbs. butter

Steps:
- Sauté the onions, green pepper and ginger in two tablespoons of the oil. Set aside.
- Mix together the egg, mayonnaise, dry mustard, parsley, Old Bay Seasoning, Worcestershire sauce, Tabasco sauce and pepper.
- Add the lobster and 1/2 cup of the cracker crumbs to the mayonnaise mixture, and then add everything to the onions and peppers.
- Spread the remaining cracker crumbs on a plate.
- Measure out the lobster mixture in 1/3-cup measures and form into patties. (If the mixture is too soft, add more cracker crumbs.) Coat the patties with the remaining cracker crumbs.
- Melt the butter and the remaining two tablespoonse of the oil in a large skillet and sauté the cakes until golden brown (about one or two minutes on each side).

Peggy Dolan

LOBSTER CACCIATORE

Ingredients for the Sauce:

Olive oil
1 garlic clove, minced
One 28-oz can peeled, crushed tomatoes with puree
2 Tbs. fresh parsley, chopped
1 Tbs. fresh basil, chopped or 1 tsp. dried basil
1 tsp. fresh oregano, chopped or 1/4 tsp. dried oregano
1 bay leaf
1/2 tsp. fresh marjoram, chopped or 1/4 tsp. dried marjoram
1/4 to 1/2 tsp. or more of red crushed pepper

Steps:
- Pour enough olive oil into a medium saucepan to cover the bottom. Place the saucepan on medium-high heat, add the garlic and stir for 30 seconds. Do not brown.
- Blend in the tomatoes, parsley, basil, oregano, bay leaf, marjoram and red pepper. Simmer until the sauce is thickened, stirring occasionally for 30-35 minutes.
- Set aside.

Ingredients for the Lobster:

Olive oil
3 Tbs. clarified butter
1 garlic clove
Two 1 1/2 - 2 lb. whole, live, unshelled lobsters, cut into serving pieces*
2 Tbs. Cognac, warmed
1 cup dry white wine
Cooked pasta noodles of your choice

If you do not wish to deal with cutting up the lobster, have the fishmonger do it for you.

Steps:
- Pour enough olive oil into a 12-inch skillet to cover the bottom. Add the butter and melt over high heat.
- Add the garlic and cook until slightly brown. Discard garlic.
- Add the lobster pieces to the skillet and sear one minute on each side.
- Pour in the warmed Cognac and ignite it, shaking the pan gently until the flames subside. Stir in the sauce (made previously, above) and the wine.
- Reduce heat to low and simmer for 15-20 minutes, covered.
- Butter a heated serving platter or individual shallow bowls. Add the pasta noodles to each bowl, then top with the sauce and serve immediately. Serves 4-6

John Carafoli

BAKED SCALLOPS

Ingredients:

1 lb. scallops
1 egg, beaten with water
Saltine crackers, crushed into crumbs with a rolling pin
3/4 stick butter

Steps:
- In the morning, dip the scallops in the egg.
- Roll the scallops in the cracker crumbs.
- Grease a baking sheet, and, starting at the center of the sheet, place the scallops close together on it.
- Cover the scallops with wax paper and refrigerate.
- At dinnertime, preheat the oven to 375°F.
- Melt the butter and pour it over the scallops.
- Bake the scallops for 25-30 minutes or until browned.
Serves 4

Nancy Hallaren

SCALLOP CASSEROLE

This is a very easy recipe, and a company and family favorite.

Ingredients:

1/2 cup butter
1 1/2 cup cracker crumbs (I use Ritz or Town House)
1 pint scallops (if large, cut in half)
2/3 cup cream or milk
Salt and pepper

Steps:
- Preheat the oven to 400°F.
- Melt the butter and add the cracker crumbs.
- Put a layer of crumbs (about half) in a buttered casserole dish and cover with half of the scallops, half of the cream, and salt and pepper to taste. Repeat with another layer, covering with buttered crumbs.
- Bake until the crumbs are brown (around 30 minutes).

Barbara Walsh

ELAINE'S STUFFED BAY SCALLOPS

Karin, Marty, Judy and Elaine Tammi prepared this dish and served it at the Westport Rivers Vineyard and Winery's "Oysterfest" in Westport, MA, on October 4, 1998.

Ingredients:
1 stick butter or margarine
1 sm. onion, diced
1/3 cup white wine
1/2 tsp. Worcestershire sauce
2/3 to 1 cup breadcrumbs
1 lb bay scallops, cleaned and diced
18-20 cleaned scallop shells (2 to 3 inch)
2 Tbs. fresh parsley, chopped
2 Tbs. fresh cilantro, chopped

Steps:
- Melt the butter or margarine in a large frying pan over medium heat. Add the diced onion and sauté until transparent.
- Add the wine and Worcestershire sauce; mix well.
- Stir in the breadcrumbs and brown the mixture, adding more wine if necessary to get a stuffing-like consistency.
- Preheat the oven (or grill) to 375°F.
- Combine the scallops with the stuffing.
- Fill the scallop shells with the mixture and top with chopped parsley and cilantro.
- After the shells are stuffed, place in the oven or on the grill for eight to ten minutes, to heat until bubbly.
  Serves 4-6

VARIATION: Mushroom caps may be substituted for the scallop shells, if scallop shells cannot be found. In this case, remove the stems from the mushroom caps and stuff the caps with scallop stuffing. Proceed as above, then cook in a frying pan with butter over medium heat for 10 minutes.

Elaine Tammi

"The best recipe for bluefish? Turn it into lobster."

-Local fisherman,
baiting his lobster pot with bluefish scraps

KARIN'S SEARED SCALLOPS

The Tammis says this is one of their favorite recipes, and the favorite of most people that they've interviewed: chefs, scientists and scallopers. A side-dish suggestion is garlic mashed potatoes.

Ingredients:

1 lb. bay or sea scallops, cleaned and trimmed
Freshly ground pepper, to taste
4 Tbs. butter
2 Tbs. Italian parsley (or cilantro, chives, oregano, basil, according to your taste)
2 garlic cloves, chopped
1 lemon, cut in wedges

Steps:
- Sprinkle the scallops with pepper on both sides.
- Heat a large, 11-inch frying pan over medium-high heat for about one minute. Add the butter to the pan and melt it, swishing to coat the bottom of the pan. Continue to heat until the butter turns golden brown.
- Add the scallops to the pan but don't crowd them. The cooking time may vary between two to five minutes per side, depending on the size of the scallops. Turn the scallops with tongs, one at a time (this is important!). Turn only once, but caramelize them on both sides, forming a nice crust.
- When the scallops are seared, add the parsley and garlic, and stir it into the scallops.
- Garnish each serving with a lemon wedge.
  Serves 4

Karin and Elaine Tammi

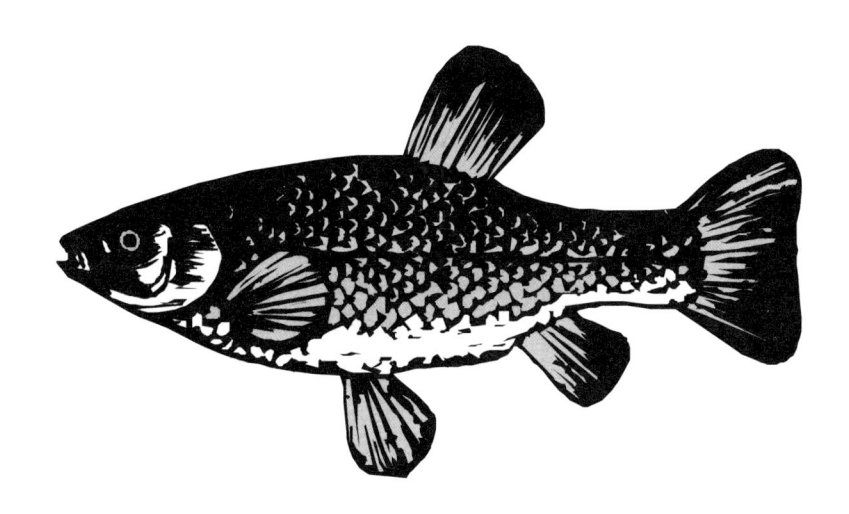

RON'S WORLD-FAMOUS OYSTER SOUP

Ingredients:

1 pint shucked oysters (previously frozen oysters work well, just separate the liquid into another container)
1 qt. half and half (or 1 pint of cream and 1 pint of milk)
1 celery stalk, washed and chopped finely
1 med. yellow onion, peeled and chunked
1/2 green pepper, chunked
2 lg. garlic cloves, chopped finely
1/4 cup parsley, chopped
2 Tbs. olive oil or vegetable oil
1 cup chicken stock
1/2 cup white wine
1 Tbs. white Worcestershire sauce (optional)
3 shakes Tabasco sauce (optional)
Freshly ground black pepper

Steps:

- Put the celery, green pepper and onion into a food processor and pulse until chopped.
- Combine the cream, milk and oyster liquid into another container and heat almost to a boil. (This will reduce the overall cooking time if it's hot when combined later.)
- Pour the oil into a large hot saucepan or frying pan, and put in the chopped veggies. Cook until they begin to soften, about five minutes, and then add the chopped garlic.
- Add the chicken stock and cook for five more minutes at low heat with the lid on.
- Add the cream mixture into the main pot, and bring it to a low boil. Add the chopped parsley. The mixture will curdle but don't worry-later blending will take care of that.
- Now add the oysters and simmer until the oyster edges begin to curl. Then simmer for five more minutes.
- After the oysters are cooked, pour in the wine and bring back to a boil. Turn off the heat and allow the soup to cool.
- Use pepper to your taste. The liquid is already salty, so be careful and don't use salt until you taste the soup.
- After the soup has cooled, puree it in a blender or food processor, or by using a hand-held submersible blender.
- Taste the soup, and then add the Worcestershire and Tabasco sauces. Use as much as you want, but don't overpower the taste of the oysters.
- You may want to add more wine, pepper or salt to taste at this point.

Ron Dolan

SCALLOPED OYSTERS

Ingredients:

1 pint oysters
1/3 cup cream
1/2 cup butter, melted
One box Uneeda Biscuit crackers, crushed
1/2 cup breadcrumbs
Paprika

Steps:
- Drain the oysters.
- Preheat the oven to 375°F.
- Mix the cream with the drained oysters.
- Add the melted butter to the cracker crumbs and breadcrumbs.
- In an 8- or 9-inch casserole dish, layer as follows:
    1 layer breadcrumbs
    1 layer oyster mixture
    1 layer cracker crumbs
- Sprinkle with paprika and bake for 25-30 minutes, until light brown on top.

Brenda Wood

OYSTER STIR-FRY

Serve over rice.

Ingredients:

1 Tbs. cornstarch
1 Tbs. water
1 1/2 Tbs. oil
1 garlic clove, minced
2 Tbs. green onion, chopped
1 Tbs. fresh ginger, peeled and minced
3/4 lb. oysters, shucked and drained
1/3 cup orange juice
2 Tbs. low-sodium soy sauce

Steps:
- Mix the cornstarch with the water in a small bowl, and set aside.
- Heat the oil in a wok or skillet.
- Add the garlic, onion and ginger, and stir-fry for approximately one minute.
- Add oysters, orange juice and soy sauce. Stir-fry for an additional 30 seconds.
- Add the cornstarch slurry, mix and cook until the sauce just starts to thicken, about one minute more.
- Serve immediately.
  Serves 4

Bruce T. Wood

PERRY FISH CHOWDER

The Perrys originally came from Sandwich, MA, and Ezra Perry married Dorothy Burgess. In 1781, the Perrys went to Nova Scotia and received land grants. My relatives in Nova Scotia like this recipe, which can be halved if you wish.

Ingredients:

2 lbs. haddock
1-2 sm. onions, chopped
4 potatoes, pared and cut fine
1/2 cup butter or margarine
1/2 tsp. dill

2 1/2 tsp. salt
1 sm. clove garlic, chopped
2 cups boiling water
2 cups light cream or milk

Steps:
- Preheat the oven to 375°F.
- Put all of the ingredients (except the cream or milk) into a large, deep casserole dish. Cover and bake for 1 hour.
- Remove from the oven, then stir in the cream or milk and stir. Serves 8

Francis A. Perry

East Sandwich Railroad Station. The trains brought passengers, freight, bulk foods, and the mail. The arrival of the train each day brought excitement to the rural seaside community.

253

WILLIAM M. RILEY
Blacksmith, Wheelwright and Horse Shoeing

Automobile Repairing and Supplies
A SPECIALTY
Depot Street,   -   -   North Falmouth, Mass.

1908 Directory of Sandwich shows the period of transition from horses to automobiles. Note Wright's ad: It is both a garage and a stable. There were 4 gasoline dealers: Joshua A. Hall 1911, Jerome Holway 1912, Mark Ellis 1913, and W.A. Winsor 1915.

N. H. WRIGHT
GARAGE
AND
BOARDING STABLE
Gasoline and Auto Oil for sale

Megansett Ave.   North Falmouth, Mass.

CHEESE ALE SOUP

Ingredients:

1 onion
Margarine
1/4 cup flour
1 qt. chicken stock
2 cups sharp Cheddar cheese
1 bottle Frank Jones Ale or Bass Ale

Steps:

- Sauté the onion in a small amount of margarine until transparent.
- Add the flour and cook for five minutes, being careful not to scorch bottom.
- Add one quart of chicken stock, swishing it into the mixture to avoid lumps
- Melt the Cheddar cheese in a microwave or over a double boiler, then add it to the soup, simmering for 20 minutes.
- Just prior to serving, add the ale
- If additional thickness is desired, make more roux (equal parts butter and flour, sautéed together) and temper it into the soup until the desired thickness is reached. To temper, simply add a small amount of the soup to the roux and mix until smooth. Keep adding small amounts of liquid and mixing until a thick, smooth mixture is achieved. Then add it to the soup. Yields 8 to 12 cups

Susi Lott

CARROT WITH FENNEL SOUP

People are always trying to guess what's in this soup! I often use less stock than described here, because I like mine thicker.

Ingredients:

1 Tbs. olive or canola oil
1 Spanish onion, coarsely chopped
1 1/2 to 2 lbs. carrots, peeled and sliced
8 cups chicken or vegetable stock
1 tsp. fennel seed

Steps:

Heat the oil over a low flame in a three-quart soup pot.
Add the onion and carrots, and cook, covered, until the vegetables are tender (15 to 20 minutes).
Add the stock and fennel seed, and bring to a boil. Reduce the heat to low and simmer for 20 more minutes.
Remove the solids and place the soup in a food processor or blender. Process till smooth, gradually adding the remaining broth.
Serves 6 to 8

Wynne Joyce

LAZY MAMA'S BORSCHT

Diced potatoes can be added to this soup for a complete meal. Also a traditional scoop of sour cream can be added instead of the egg and cream. Chicken or beef bouillon can be substituted for the pork meat, if desired.

Ingredients:
2 cups water
Onion salt and pepper, to taste
Two 15 1/2-oz. cans diced beets, undrained
2 pork chops, cut into bite-size pieces
1/4 cup vinegar
Celery salt, to taste
1 egg
2 Tbs. cream

Steps:
- In a pot, bring the water to a boil with the onion salt and pepper.
- Open the beets and add the beets and their liquid to the pot.
- Add the pork meat, and continue boiling.
- Add the vinegar and celery salt.
- Mix the egg with the cream, then combine this with a little of the hot stock until completely mixed. Add this to the pot.
- Heat to boiling, then serve
  Serves 2 to 4

"Nano" and Judy Lesiak

PARSNIP SOUP

This is an old New Hampshire recipe that my grandmother used to make. It's awfully good!

Ingredients
Four 1/4-inch slices salt pork
1 medium onion, peeled and chopped
2 cups boiling water
1 1/2 cups parsnips, peeled and diced
2 med. potatoes, peeled and diced
1 tsp. salt
Pinch of black pepper
1/4 tsp. ground mace
4 cups milk, scalded
1 Tbs. butter

Steps:
- In a stockpot, fry the salt pork until golden brown.
- Add the onion, and continue cooking for five minutes longer. Pour off the fat.
- Add the boiling water, parsnips, potatoes, salt, pepper, and mace. Simmer

until very tender (about 30 minutes).
- Add the scalded milk and butter.
- Heat until very hot, but do not boil.
Serves 6

Barbara Lucas

CHICKEN AND VEGETABLE STEW

Serve this stew in wide soup bowls with biscuits or crackers.

Ingredients:

1 lb. skinless, boneless chicken breasts	1 tsp. dried tarragon or 2 tsp. fresh, minced
2 cups light chicken broth	1/2 lb. cut green beans
8 sm. thin-skinned potatoes, scrubbed	1 tsp. salad oil
2 or 3 carrots, peeled and sliced	2 Tbs. cornstarch
	1/4 cup water
Four 1-inch wide shallots, peeled and cut in half, lengthwise	1 cup cherry tomatoes, cut in half
	Salt and pepper, to taste.

Steps:
- Rinse the chicken, and cut it into one-inch chunks.
- In a stockpot, stir the chicken pieces in oil until lightly browned (about eight minutes). Transfer chicken to a bowl and set aside.
- To the stockpot, add the broth, potatoes, carrots, shallots, and tarragon. Cover and simmer for about five minutes.
- Add the browned chicken and green beans to the pot. Cover and simmer until the chicken is white in the middle and the potatoes are tender (about eight to 10 minutes).
- In a small bowl, mix the cornstarch with the water until smooth.
- Turn the heat on high and stir in the cornstarch mixture. Continue cooking until the stew begins to boil.
- Add the tomatoes and salt and pepper, and heat for one to two minutes longer.
Serves 4 to 6

Pat Bryant

LOW-FAT CORN CHOWDER

This is good with any left-over fish added, too. Serve with milk crackers.

Ingredients

Kernels from 2 ears of fresh corn
2 med. potatoes, diced small
2 lg. carrots, peeled and diced small
1 med. onion diced small
2 1/2 cups hot water

Salt and black pepper, to taste
1/2 tsp. ground nutmeg
1 qt. 1% milk
1 med. firm tomato, chopped
1 Tbs. lite margarine

Steps:
- Add the vegetables to the hot water, and parboil until the vegetables are fork tender but still firm.
- Add the salt, pepper, and nutmeg.
- Add the milk and heat until bubbles form around the edges, but the soup doesn't boil.
- Before serving add the tomato and margarine, melted on top.
Serves 4

Barbara Lucas

ONION, HAM AND CHEESE CHOWDER

A very satisfactory, comforting chowder that may be served as a main dish with warm rolls.

Ingredients

2 cups potatoes, peeled and cubed
1/2 cup boiling water
1 cup onion, chopped
3 Tbs. butter
3 Tbs. flour

Dash black pepper
3 cups milk
1 1/2 cups sharp Cheddar cheese, shredded
1 1/2 cups chopped ham

Steps:
- Cook potatoes in boiling water until tender, about 10 minutes.
- Drain the potatoes, reserving the liquid. Add enough liquid to make one cup.
- In a pan, cook the onion in butter until tender, but not brown.
- Blend in the flour and black pepper.
- Add the milk and the potato water; stir and cook until mixture thickens and bubbles.
- Add the chopped ham and cheese, stirring until the cheese melts.
- Let the chowder sit for a few minutes before serving.
Serves 4

Judy Koenig

SIMPLE CHICKEN-NOODLE SOUP

This is a "comfort" kind of soup on a dreary day. It's easy to make and freeze, and lasts, frozen for about three months.

Ingredients

8 cups chicken stock
1 cup cooked chicken, minced
2 carrots, peeled and cut fine
2 stalks celery, minced
1 cup egg noodles or small pasta
1/2 onion, cut fine (optional)

Steps:
- Bring the chicken stock, chicken, carrots, celery, noodles or pasta, and onion to a boil.
- Simmer for about 20 minutes, or until pasta is done.
- Serve hot.
  Serves 4 to 6

Pat Bryant

LIGHT TOMATO-BASIL SOUP

This is a light version of traditional Tomato-Basil Soup. It's basically fat-free with reduced sodium. This recipe can be changed to suit individual tastes.

Ingredients:

2 tsp. olive oil
3 garlic cloves, minced
3 cups fat-free less-sodium chicken broth
3/4 tsp. salt (or less)
Three 14.5-oz cans no-salt-added diced tomatoes, undrained
2 cups fresh basil leaves, thinly sliced

Steps:
- Heat the oil in a large saucepan over medium heat. Add the garlic. Cook and stir for about 30 seconds.
- Stir in the broth, salt and tomatoes, and bring to a boil.
- Reduce the heat and simmer for 20 minutes.
- Stir in the sliced basil leaves.
- Place half the soup in a blender and process till smooth.
- Repeat the procedure with the remaining soup.
- Ladle hot soup into bowls and garnish with whole basil leaves, if desired.
  Serves 4 to 5

Pat Bryant

CREAM OF BROCCOLI SOUP

This soup can also be made using zucchini or yellow summer squash.

Ingredients:

2 stalks broccoli, cut up
2 potatoes, peeled, thinly sliced
4 Tbs. butter
1 med. onion, chopped
4 Tbs. flour

2 cups warm chicken broth
2 cups warm milk
1/2 cup heavy cream
Salt and pepper to taste

Steps:
- Cook the broccoli and potatoes until they are soft. Drain and set aside.
- In a large pan, heat the butter. Add the onions and flour and cook for three minutes.
- Add the broth and milk to the butter mixture, and heat to simmer.
- In a food processor, put the broccoli, potatoes, half the broth mixture and puree.
- Return to pan and add the remaining broth mix, heavy cream, and salt and pepper.

Norma Coleman

PORTUGUESE KALE SOUP

There are many variations of Kale Soup. Other vegetables may be added, depending on individual tastes.

Ingredients:

1 cup pea beans
1 lg. onion, cut in pieces
1 lb. chorizo sausage (or kielbasa, low-fat, mild), cut into small pieces
1 lb. kale, broken in pieces

1 Tbs. salt
1/2 tsp. pepper
1 Tbs. vinegar
11 cups water
2 cups potatoes, cubed

Steps:
- Soak the picked-over beans overnight in cold water.
- Drain the beans, and place them in a pot.
- Add to the pot the onion, sausage, kale, salt, pepper, vinegar, and 10 cups of the water.
- Bring to a boil, reduce heat, and cook gently for two to three hours, until the beans are tender.
- Add the potatoes and the remaining 1 cup of water. Continue cooking until the potatoes are tender.
Serves 6

Nancy Titcomb

TORTELLINI SOUP

Keep these ingredients either in your freezer or on a shelf, and you will always have a hearty last-minute meal on hand!

Ingredients:

2 cloves garlic, crushed
1 Tbs. butter or margarine
Two 13-oz. cans chicken or beef broth
One 8-oz. pkg. fresh or frozen cheese tortellini
One 10-oz. pkg. fresh or frozen spinach, thawed and drained
One 16-oz. can stewed tomatoes, undrained and coarsely chopped
Grated Parmesan cheese

Steps:

- In a large pan, over medium heat, cook the garlic in the butter for two to three minutes.
- Add the broth and tortellini, and bring to a boil.
- Reduce the heat and simmer for 10 minutes.
- Add the spinach and tomatoes, and simmer for five minutes.
- Serve topped with grated cheese.
  Serves 4 to 6

Carolyn Nelson

COLD CUCUMBER SOUP

Serve cold with chopped chives.

Ingredients:

1 med. onion, chopped
1 med. cucumber, peeled and cubed
3/4 cup chicken broth
1 can creamed chicken soup
1 cup sour cream
6 dashes Worcestershire sauce
6 dashes Tabasco sauce
1/8 tsp. celery salt
1/8 tsp. curry

Steps:

- Put all but the seasonings in a blender and blend until smooth.
- Add the seasonings and blend again.
- Chill for two hours before serving.

Norma Coleman

CURRIED BUTTERNUT-SQUASH SOUP

This is our favorite autumn soup!

Ingredients:

2 to 4 Tbs. butter
2 cups onions, finely chopped
4 to 5 tsp. curry powder
3 cups chicken stock
2 med. butternut squash (about 3 lbs.), peeled, seeded and cubed
2 apples, cored and chopped
1 cup apple juice
Salt and pepper to taste
1 Granny Smith apple, shredded, peeled

Steps:
- In a large pot, melt the butter. Add the chopped onions and curry powder, and cook over low heat until the onions are tender.
- Pour stock into the pan. Add the squash and the apples, and bring to a boil. Reduce heat and simmer until squash and apples are tender (about 25 minutes).
- Strain the soup, reserving the liquid, and transfer the solids to a food processor or blender. Add a cup of stock and process till smooth.
- Return to the pot, and add the apple juice and additional cooking liquid (about 2 cups) until the soup is of the desired consistency.
- Season to taste, then simmer briefly.
- Serve with a shredded-apple garnish.
Serves 4 to 6

Carolyn Nelson

CAULIFLOWER CHEESE SOUP

Very good!

Ingredients

1/4 cup butter
1 onion, chopped
2 cups cauliflower florets
1 potato, thinly sliced
1 1/4 cups chicken stock
1 1/4 cups milk
1/2 cup Cheddar cheese, divided
Salt and pepper to taste
1/4 cup light cream
1 Tbs. parsley, chopped

Steps:
- Melt the butter in a kettle and sauté the onion until soft (about five minutes).
- Add the cauliflower and potato slices. Cover and cook for 10 minutes.
- Stir in the stock and bring to a boil. Reduce heat and simmer for 25-30 minutes, until vegetables are very soft.

- Puree in a blender or food processor. Return to the pot, and, off the heat, stir in the milk.
- Heat the puree gently, and stir in half of the shredded cheese. Season with salt and pepper.
- Pour the soup into soup bowls, and swirl a tablespoon of cream into each bowl.
- Sprinkle the rest of the shredded cheese on top of each serving, and garnish with a little parsley on top.

Serves 4

Monique Galipeau

NEW ENGLAND CLAM CHOWDER

This chowder is served at the Christmas Craft Fair and other events at Green Briar Nature Center.

Ingredients:

1/2 lb. onions, chopped
1/2 cup butter
5 lbs. potatoes, peeled and chopped
One 51-oz. can clam juice
One 51-oz. can chopped sea clams, drained, liquid reserved
3 cans evaporated milk
1/3 cup flour

Steps:

- Sauté the onions in butter. Add the potatoes, mix well and cook in a large kettle or soup pot until the onions are tender.
- Add the clam juice; cover and simmer about 15 minutes until the potatoes are tender.
- Add the clams and cook until the clams are well heated.
- Add the milk, but do not boil.
- If a thicker chowder is preferred, mix the flour with a small amount of cool milk before adding it to the chowder.

NOTE: Once the chowder is cooked, do not cover it until it is cold. Reheat it when the crowd arrives.

Serves a crowd

Pam Anderson

BEEF AND BARLEY SOUP

Not many people use barley anymore, but I like the chewy texture it adds to soup.

Ingredients:

2 Tbs olive oil
1 lb. beef stew meat, cut into tiny pieces
10 cups beef stock
1/2 cup barley
2 carrots, thinly sliced
2 turnips, peeled and chopped
2 stalks celery, chopped
1 tsp. salt

Steps:
- Heat the oil in a large stockpot over medium high heat.
- Add the beef and cook until browned.
- Add the stock, barley, carrots, turnips, celery and salt, and bring the mixture to a boil.
- Reduce the heat to low and simmer for one hour until the barley is done and the beef is tender.
Serves 6-8

Sandra Rudloff

EASY FISH STEW

This stew has relatively low calories and less salt than most recipes.

Ingredients:

1 Tbs. olive oil
1 cup onion, chopped
1 cup green pepper, chopped
1/2 cup celery, diced
1 tsp. chili powder
2 cups water
1 1/2 cups frozen corn, thawed
1 Tbs. Worcestershire sauce
One 14.5-oz can no-salt-added diced tomatoes, undrained
1 sm. can no-salt-added tomato sauce
1 lb. cod or other white fish fillets, cut into bite-size pieces
1/4 cup fresh parsley, minced
Salt and pepper, to taste

Steps:
- Heat the olive oil in large saucepan over medium-high heat.
- Add the onion, pepper, celery, and chili powder, and sauté for three minutes, or until tender.
- Stir in the water, corn, Worcestershire sauce, diced tomatoes and tomato sauce, and cook for 10 minutes.
- Add the fish. Cook for three to five minutes, or until the fish is done.
- Stir in the parsley.
Serves 4-6

Linda West Eckhardt

POTATO LEEK SOUP

Ingredients:

1/4 cup butter
2 lbs leeks (white portions only)
6 cups chicken or vegetable stock
2 lbs. russet potatoes, cubed

1/4 cup chopped fresh chives
1/2 tsp. onion powder
Salt and pepper to taste

Steps:
- Cut the leeks in half lengthwise and carefully wash; slice 1/2 inch crosswise.
- In a large saucepan, melt the butter over medium heat. Add the leeks and sauté just until they begin to soften, 3-5 minutes.
- Cut the potatoes into bite-size pieces. Add the stock and potatoes, bring to a boil, reduce heat to low and simmer until the potatoes are tender, about 20 minutes.
- Season to taste with onion powder, salt and pepper.
- Ladle into bowls and garnish with chives.
Serves 8

Avis Clay

Celebrity Soup Facts from Wyler's (H.J. Heinz Co.):

- *John Fitzgerald Kennedy almost always had soup and a sandwich for lunch.*

- *Elvis Presley often enjoyed potato-cheese soup with French-fried onion rings on top.*

- *George Washington often dined on vegetable soup with fried bread.*

CARROT, SWEET POTATO AND GINGER SOUP

Traditional during the holidays, this soup is low in fat but tastes "rich and creamy."

Ingredients:

3 sweet potatoes
1 onion, sliced
1 tsp. garlic, minced
vegetable oil
3 lg. carrots, sliced
2-3 vegetable-bouillon cubes
2 qts. Water
1/2 Tbs. fresh or powdered ginger (adjust to your taste)
Zest and juice of an orange (adjust to your taste)
Salt and pepper

Steps:
- Bake the sweet potatoes at 350°F degrees for 40 minutes. Cool, peel, and cut them into large pieces.
- Cook the onions and garlic in oil until soft.
- Cook the carrots until tender.
- Dissolve the bouillon cubes in the water and add the sweet potato pieces, sautéed onions and garlic, cooked carrots and ginger.
- Simmer for 10 minutes.
- Puree in a blender, adding the orange zest and juice, as well as the seasonings.
- Adjust thickness as needed.
  Serves 6-8

Charlene Sendo-Mans

FISH CHOWDER

This is even better the next day!

Ingredients:

1 onion, chopped
4 Tbs. margarine
3 lg. potatoes, pared/sliced
2 tsp. salt
1/2 tsp. basil
1/4 tsp. pepper
2 cups water
1 lb. cubed fish fillets
One 14- or 15-oz. can cream-style corn
One 14- or 15-oz. can evaporated milk
One 14- or 15-oz. can filled with homogenized milk

Steps:
- Saute the onions in the margarine until soft
- Add the potatoes, salt, basil, pepper and water. Cover and simmer for 15

minutes
- Place the fish on top; cover, and simmer for five minutes
- Stir in the creamed corn and the two kinds of milk.
- Cover and heat just to boiling (but do not boil!).

Nancy Hallaren

SEAFOOD GUMBO STEW

My mother-in-law used to make this (in very large batches) as a hospital volunteer in Venice, Florida. She used all fresh seafood, of course. The dish was such a hit with the visitors at the hospital, that local restaurants complained she was taking away their business! This stew is low-fat and freezes well. Serve it over hot cooked rice, or with baked corn bread on the side.

Ingredients

3 Tbs. butter or margarine
2 cups green pepper, chopped
1 cup celery, diced
2 lg. onions, chopped
3 garlic cloves, minced
2 Tbs. flour
One 24- to 28-oz can tomatoes with juice, diced or whole, chopped
1 lg. can tomato sauce
1 cup chicken bouillon
2-3 cups frozen okra, cut into 1/2-inch pieces.
2 bay leaves
1 tsp. basil, chopped
1/2 tsp. ground nutmeg
1/4 tsp. ground hot red pepper (or adjusted to taste)
1 lb. med. shrimp, peeled and deveined
One or two 6-oz. cans crabmeat (any fresh firm white fish can also be used along with or in place of the crabmeat)

Steps:
- Melt the butter or margarine in a large pot, and add the pepper, celery, onions, and garlic. Sauté until soft.
- Add the flour and stir until the vegetables are coated.
- Add the tomatoes, tomato sauce, bouillon, okra, bay leaves, basil, nutmeg and red pepper.
- Bring to a boil and simmer, covered, 15-20 minutes.
- Add the shrimp, crabmeat and/or white fish to pot. Simmer, covered until the shrimp turns pink and the stew is hot.
- Discard the bay leaves before serving.
Serves 6-10

Irene Bryant

FRIENDLY FISH STEW

I make this for my summer guests on the occasion of those rainy Cape Cod afternoons when playing cards and telling stories are the events of the day! It's a quick, effortless and heartwarming stew.

Ingredients:

1 Tbs. olive oil
3 med. carrots, cut into a 1/2-inch dice
2 celery stalks, cut into 1/4-inch thick slices
1 bunch green onions, cut into 1/2-inch pieces
1 1/2 med. red potatoes, cut into a 1-inch dice
1 tsp. salt
1/4 tsp. coarsely ground black pepper

1/2 tsp. dried thyme
1/2 cup dry white wine
One 8-oz. bottle clam juice
2 cups water
2 lbs. scrod fillet, cut into 1-inch chunks
1 cup frozen peas
1/2 cup loosely packed fresh parsley leaves, chopped
1/4 cup heavy cream

Steps:

- In a nonstick 5-qt. Dutch oven or saucepot, heat the oil over medium heat until hot.
- Add the carrots and celery, and cook for six minutes or until vegetables are lightly browned, stirring occasionally.
- Stir in the green onions, potatoes, salt, pepper and thyme; cook for two minutes longer.
- Add the wine, clam juice and water, and heat to boiling. Reduce the heat to low; cover and simmer for 10 minutes.
- Add the fish and frozen peas; cover and simmer for five minutes longer, or until the vegetables are tender and the fish is opaque throughout.
- Stir in the parsley and cream.
- Heat through.
  Serves 4-6

Jeanne Cantwell

SCALLOP AND CORN CHOWDER

Serve with salt and freshly ground pepper and Westminster Oyster Crackers.

Ingredients:

- 2 cups potatoes, peeled and diced
- 2-3 Tbs. butter
- 1 cup leeks or onions, clean and diced
- 1 cup celery, chopped
- 2 cups water
- 2 1/2 cups half and half, evaporated milk or cream
- 1 1/2 cups fresh corn kernels
- 1 lb. bay scallops (or 1/2 lb. sea scallops, trimmed and chopped)

Steps:

- Place the potatoes in a bowl and cover them with water.
- In a large pan, melt the butter over medium heat. Add the leeks and celery, and cook until transparent.
- Drain the potatoes and add them to the pan, along with 2 cups of water. Cook until the potatoes are done (about 10 minutes).
- Meanwhile, warm the half and half in a separate pan over low heat, stirring occasionally.
- When the potatoes are done, stir in the corn and scallops.
- Cook the chowder for one or two minutes before mixing it with the warm half and half. Heat for three or four minutes.

Note: Onions can be used in place of the leeks, but the flavor won't be as good. Also, evaporated milk can be substituted for the half and half.

Serves 4-6

Karin Tammi

> *"Soup is sensitive. You don't catch steak hanging around when you're poor and sick, do you?"*
>
> —Judith Martin (Miss Manners)

ITALIAN CHICKEN-LENTIL SOUP

Ingredients:

1 Tbs. vegetable oil
1 lb. boneless, skinless chicken breast, cut into 1-inch pieces
1 med. onion, chopped (1/2 cup)
2 med. yellow squash, diced (2 cups)
4 med. carrots, thinly sliced (2 cups)
1 cup mushrooms
1 cup dried lentils, sorted and rinsed
1/4 cup chopped fresh or 1 Tbs. dried basil leaves
4 1/2 cups chicken broth
1/2 tsp. salt
1/4 tsp. pepper
One 28-oz. can Italian pear-shaped tomatoes, drained
Grated Parmesan cheese

Steps:

- Heat the oil in a Dutch oven over medium-high heat.
- Cook the chicken and onion in oil for 10-12 minutes, stirring occasionally, until the chicken is no longer pink in the center.
- Stir in the remaining ingredients except for the cheese. Break up the tomatoes.
- Heat to boiling, stirring occasionally, then reduce heat to medium-low.
- Cover and cook for 30-45 minutes, or until the lentils are tender.
- Serve with Parmesan cheese.

Mary Williams

CHICKEN-AND-BEEF STOCK

My Grandmother Carafoli used to make this stock when she was cooking chicken and beef for our Sunday dinner. Later, as a first course, she'd cook her homemade tortellini or fresh pasta in the broth. I still make this nourishing soup when I feel a cold coming on! The added beef gives the stock a richness not possible with chicken alone, but does not overwhelm the chicken. You need a real stewing hen (sometimes called a fowl) to stand up to the long cooking and give a good chicken flavor. Serve the sliced boiled beef and fowl as a supper dish along with condiments, such as sweet-pepper relish and mustard, and accompanied by a salad of bitter greens, a large loaf of good Italian bread (warmed) and a wonderful bottle of red wine.

Ingredients:

One whole 6-8 lb. stewing hen,* neck and innards removed and reserved.
2-3 lbs. beef chuck, in one piece with bone in, if possible
3 lg. onions, peeled and left whole
3 lg. carrots, peeled and cut into 2-3 pieces each
4 lg. celery stalks cut into 2-3 pieces each
6 parsley sprigs
2 bay leaves
6-8 white peppercorns
5-7 qts. cold water

Steps:
- Rinse the chicken and the beef under cold running water and wrap them separately in cheesecloth. Place them in a large stockpot or Dutch oven along with all the other ingredients.
- Add the neck, giblets and (if desired) the liver.
- Add the water, making sure it is enough to cover the ingredients. Bring to a boil.
- Immediately reduce the heat to very low, and skim any foam that rises to the surface. If this step is not done, the broth will become bitter.
- During the first half hour of cooking, check frequently and adjust the heat to prevent vigorous boiling, which causes the ingredients to disintegrate and make the soup "muddy".
- Cook the soup, partly covered, at barely a simmer for at least five or six hours.
- Remove the chicken and the meat.
- Strain the stock through a fine-mesh sieve or a colander lined with cheesecloth.
- Let the stock cool to room temperature.
- Refrigerate, covered, until the congealed fat can be lifted off. You can freeze the stock in pint or quart containers for future use, if desired.
Makes 4-6 quarts

* Fowl are available fresh or frozen in the meat department of your local supermarket. If they do not have one they can order one for you. If this recipe seems too much, it may be scaled down. Just have your butcher cut the hen in half, wrap it up and freeze it to use another time.

Note: I have not listed salt among the ingredients, because it should not be added until you are preparing the dish to be served.

John Carafoli

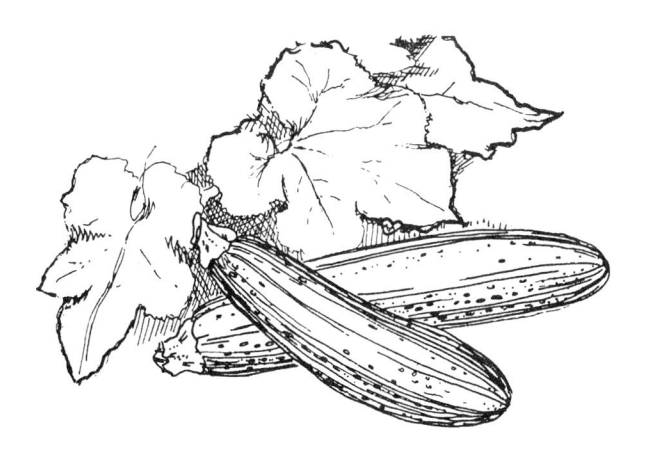

GARLIC SOUP

Here is a thrifty way of using good leftover bread.

Ingredients:

Half a long loaf of robust-textured Italian bread (use about 6-8 inches of the loaf), cut into 1 inch chunks
1/4 cup olive oil
4-6 garlic cloves, chopped

6 cups homemade chicken stock, heated
Salt and pepper to taste
Parmesan cheese (about 1 Tbs. per person, freshly grated)

Steps:
- Let the bread dry out at room temperature until it is rock hard.
- Heat the oil in a deep heavy skillet over medium heat. It should be hot.
- Add the bread and brown it in the hot oil, turning frequently until lightly browned on both sides. Add the garlic and cook, stirring occasionally until just lightly browned, but not burnt.
- Pour the broth over the bread and garlic, and bring to a boil over medium heat.
- Reduce the heat and let it simmer until the bread falls apart (about 10-15 minutes).
- Season to taste with salt and pepper, and top with the freshly grated cheese when serving.
  Serves 6

John Carafoli

GAZPACHO

You can triple this easy recipe for a crowd, and blend it in batches.

Ingredients:

1 clove garlic
1/2 sm. onion
1 sm. green pepper, seeded and sliced
3 ripe tomatoes, peeled and quartered
1 lg. cucumber, peeled and sliced

1/4 tsp. black pepper, freshly ground
1/2 tsp. fresh basil
1 tsp. salt
2 Tbs. olive oil
3 Tbs. wine vinegar
1/2 cup chicken broth, chilled

Steps:
- Place all ingredients in a blender and blend well until mixed but not smooth.
- Chill until serving time. Serve chilled.
  Serves 6

Mimi McConnell

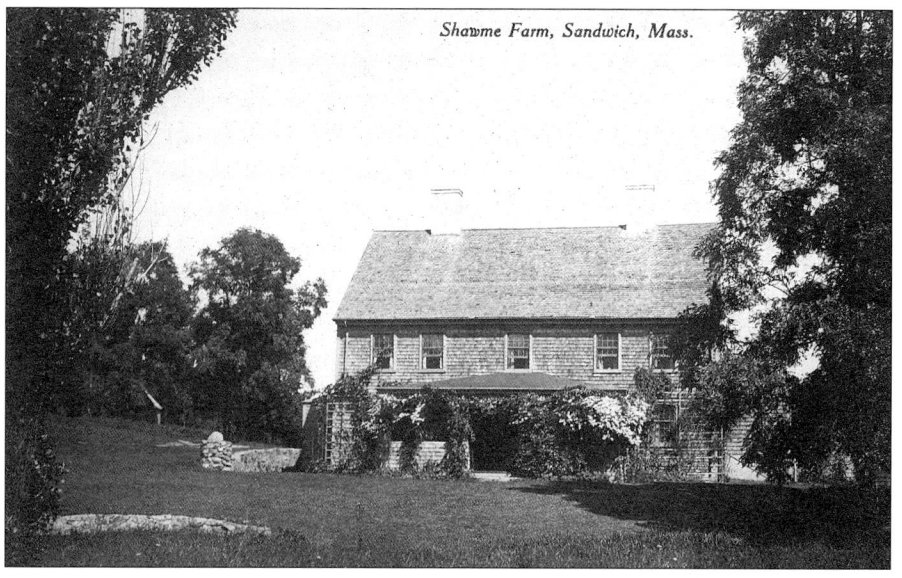

Shawme Farm, Sandwich, Mass.

SALADS

Shawme Farm was the home of Daniel Wing, dating about the 1690s and now the office of Heritage Museums and Gardens. It was owned in this view of 1908 by F. Edwin Elwell, a noted sculptor from the Metropolitan Museum of Art in New York. He used an adjacent barn as a studio for sculpture studies, and in it created the statue of the Dickens figure"Little Nell". This statue won a prize at the 1892 World's Fair in Chicago. Mr. Elwell brought many distinguished visitors to Sandwich, and was the one who suggested the Parade of Lighted Boats for the Town's 250th Celebration in 1889, based on a Venetian Boat Parade he had seen.

"Little Nell"

273

Old Mr. Toad Illustration by Harrison Cady

"The Adventures of Old Mr. Toad" was written by children's author Thornton W. Burgess. Burgess's career as a writer of animal and natural history stories developed out of a love of the woods, meadows, and ponds around his boyhood home in Sandwich, Massachusetts, on Cape Cod where he was born in 1874. He introduced Peter Rabbit and his animal friends in his first book, "Old Mother West Wind" in 1910.

LAYERED SALAD

Ingredients:

1/2 head Iceberg lettuce, thinly sliced and chopped
1 sm. red onion, diced
2 cups frozen peas
2 cups fresh broccoli florets, coarsely chopped
3 hard-boiled eggs, chopped
8 strips cooked bacon, crumbled
1 1/2 cups Swiss cheese, shredded
1 lg. bottle Hidden Valley Ranch salad dressing

Steps:

- In a large serving bowl, layer as follows
  Shredded lettuce   Diced onions
  Frozen peas   Broccoli
  Chopped eggs   Crumbled bacon
  Swiss cheese
- Pour the Ranch salad dressing over the top of the salad so it is completely covered.
- Cover with plastic wrap and refrigerate overnight.
- Just before serving, toss the salad well. Add more salad dressing, if desired.

Mary Scalera

FOUR-BEAN SALAD

Ingredients:

1/2 cup sugar
1/2 cup canola, vegetable or olive oil
1/2 cup wine vinegar
1 tsp. salt
Dash black pepper
1 can or 1 pkg. frozen green beans
1 can or 1 pkg. frozen yellow beans
1 can or 1 pkg. frozen lima beans
1 can kidney beans
1 red onion, cut or sliced as you prefer
1 green pepper, cut as you prefer

Steps:

- Combine the sugar, oil, vinegar, salt and pepper.
- If using frozen beans, cook the beans until al dente, then drain.
- Pour the dressing over all the vegetables and marinate for at least four hours.

Mimi McConnell

CHICKEN SALAD DELUXE

Ingredients:

4 Tbs. orange-juice concentrate
1 cup red seedless grapes
1 cup green seedless grapes
2 Braeburn apples, chopped into small pieces
3 cups white-meat chicken
1/4 cup Hellmann's mayonnaise

Steps:
- Marinate the grapes and apples in the orange-juice concentrate for an hour in the refrigerator, covered.
- When ready to serve, mix the chicken, marinated fruit and mayonnaise together. Keep the mixture on the dry side.
- Season to taste.

Mary Davidson

CRANBERRY SPINACH SALAD

Ingredients:

3/4 cup blanched slivered almonds
1 Tbs. butter
1 lb. spinach, rinsed, dried and torn into bite-sized pieces
1 cup dried cranberries
2 Tbs. sesame seeds, toasted
1 Tbs. poppy seeds
1/2 cup sugar
2 tsp. minced onion
1/4 tsp. paprika
1/4 cup white-wine vinegar
1/4 cup cider vinegar
1/2 cup vegetable oil

Steps:
- Sauté the almonds in butter until lightly toasted. Cool.
- In a large bowl, toss the spinach with the toasted almonds and cranberries.
- In a medium bowl, whisk the sesame seeds, poppy seeds, sugar, onion, paprika, and white wine and cider vinegars together with the vegetable oil.
- Toss the salad with the dressing just before serving.

Jamie Hensley

> *Garden tip: Plant nasturtiums amongst your radishes. They deter pests, and radishes love them.*

FOREST PASTA SALAD WITH HERB DRESSING

This is a low-salt recipe. Season it to your own taste.

Ingredients for Pasta Salad:

1 cup broccoli florets
1 cup carrots, sliced OR baby carrots, cut into chunks
1 cup zucchini, sliced
12 oz. rainbow-mix rotini noodles
1/2 cup red onion, chopped
2 cloves garlic, chopped
1 Tbs. butter or margarine
1 cup green pepper, cut into 1/2-inch strips
1/2 cup mushrooms
Cherry tomatoes
2 Tbs. parsley, chopped

Ingredients for Herb Dressing:

1/2 cup lemon juice
1 tsp. sugar
2 Tbs. Parmesan cheese, grated
2 Tbs. fresh basil, minced or 2 tsp. dried basil
2 Tbs. olive oil
1 clove garlic, minced

Steps:

- Steam broccoli, carrots and zuchini until crisp and tender.
- Cook rotini according to package directions. Drain and place in a large bowl.
- Sauté onions and garlic in melted butter or margarine until onions are translucent.
- Add green pepper and mushrooms and cook for one minute.
- Combine ingredients for Herb Dressing (above) in a mixing bowl, and stir well.
- Add the steamed vegetables, onion mixture and dressing to the pasta in the bowl. Toss gently.
- Refrigerate for two hours, or until dressing is absorbed.
- Add cherry tomatoes and chopped parsley, and toss salad again before serving.

Pat Bryant

FRUIT SALAD WITH YOGURT DRESSING

This fruit recipe is very versatile. Try different kinds of fruit and yogurt for different flavors.

Ingredients for Fruit Salad:

1 med. peach, pitted and sliced
1 med. nectarine, pitted and sliced
1 cup cantaloupe, cut into chunks or balled
1 pint strawberries, hulled and halved
1 cup fresh pineapple, cut into chunks

Ingredients for Yogurt Dressing:

One 8-oz. carton Pina Colada-flavor low-fat yogurt
1 cup non-dairy whipped topping
2 tsp. fresh lime juice

Steps:
- Combine the fruits and refrigerate until ready to serve.
- Mix the ingredients for the Yogurt Dressing until well blended. Chill.
- When ready to serve, spoon Yogurt Dressing over the fruit.

Barbara Wilson
Pat Bryant also submitted this recipe.

GREEN BEAN AND HAZELNUT SALAD WITH HERB-MUSTARD DRESSING

Ingredients:

1/3 cup salad oil
1//2 cup vinegar
2 tsp. sugar
1/4 tsp. salt
1/4 tsp. dried basil
1 tsp. Dijon mustard
1 pound fresh or frozen green beans, blanched and drained
2 cups cherry tomatoes cut in half
1 cup hazelnuts (filberts), toasted

Steps:
- In a large bowl, combine the first six ingredients.
- Toss the green beans in the dressing until they are well covered.
- Just before serving, stir in the tomatoes and hazelnuts.
  Serves 8

Regina Murphy Silvia

MUFFALETTA OLIVE SALAD

Ingredients:

3 lg. garlic cloves, crushed
1 cup pimento-stuffed green olives
1 cup black olives, pitted and chopped
1/2 cup roasted sweet red peppers, cut into chunks
1 cup olive oil
3 Tbs. fresh parsley, chopped
2 Tbs. white-wine vinegar
1 lg. round loaf freshly baked Italian bread
1/3 lb. salami, sliced thin
1/2 lb. provolone cheese, sliced thin
1/2 lb. mild cheese
1/3 lb. mortadella OR prosciutto OR ham, sliced thin

Steps:
- Combine the first seven ingredients in a large bowl to create an olive salad.
- Cut the bread in half horizontally. Scoop out some of the center and drizzle oil from the olive salad on both halves of the bread.
- On the bottom half of the bread, layer the meats and cheeses.
- Cover the meats and cheeses generously with the olive salad.
- Top all with other half of the bread loaf.
- Serve in pie-shaped wedges.

Mary Williams

ORIENTAL NOODLE SALAD

Makes a very large salad.

Ingredients:

1/2 cup margarine
2 pkgs. dried Ramen noodles, crushed (reserve the included flavoring packets)
1 sm. bottle sesame seeds
One 4-oz. pkg. slivered almonds
1/2 cup of sugar
3/4 cup vegetable oil
1/4 cup cider vinegar
2 Tbs. soy sauce
1 lg. Chinese cabbage (Bok Choy), chopped

Steps:
- In a frying pan, melt 1/2 cup margarine. Add the flavoring packets from the Ramen noodles.
- Add the sesame seeds, slivered almonds and the crushed Ramen noodles. Set aside when browned.
- Combine the sugar, oil, cider vinegar and soy sauce in a small saucepan and heat until the sugar is dissolved. Set the dressing aside to cool.
- Combine the cabbage, noodle mixture and dressing just before serving.

Cathy Shedowitz

GREEK ORZO SALAD

Ingredients:

1 box orzo pasta
One 7-oz. jar sun-dried tomatoes in oil or 1 pkg. dried tomatoes, finely chopped
1/2 can black olives, cut into fourths
1 red onion, finely chopped
1/2 bunch scallions, finely chopped
1/2 bunch fresh parsley, finely chopped
1 pkg. feta cheese, crumbled
Salt and pepper to taste
Bottled Greek-Salad dressing (vinaigrette style)

Steps:
- Cook the orzo according to the directions on the box. Do not drain.
- Chill the pasta in its water in the refrigerator, mixing with a tiny bit of oil to prevent sticking.
- Mix all ingredients with the bottled Greek dressing.
- Add feta cheese and salt and pepper to taste.

Mary Regan

MOM'S FRENCH DRESSING

Ingredients:

1 tsp. dry mustard
1 tsp. paprika
1 tsp. salt
1 tsp. celery seed
1 Tbs. onion, grated
1/2 cup cider vinegar
1/3 cup sugar
1 cup salad oil

Steps:
Put all the ingredients in a jar with a cover. Shake well.

Sarah Salois

OUT-OF-SIGHT COLE SLAW

Ingredients:

2 Tbs. sugar
2 Tbs. boiling water
2 Tbs. butter
3 Tbs. vinegar
2 eggs
1/2 tsp. mustard
2/3 tsp. white pepper
1 tsp. salt
4 cups cabbage, shredded

Steps:
- Mix all ingredients together in a large pot, and simmer to wilt the cabbage. Do not boil!
- Remove from the heat and cool.

PASTA PRIMAVERA SALAD

This recipe can be made up to 24 hours in advance.

Ingredients:

1 lb. spinach fetuccine
1 lb. egg fetuccine
1 cup olive oil
1 cup red onion, diced
1 lb. pea pods, strung

3 red peppers, sliced in strips
1 bunch scallions, diced
1 cup raspberry vinegar
1 cup Parmesan cheese, grated
1 pint cherry tomatoes, cut in half

Steps:
- Cook the fettucine until al dente.
- Cool pasta slightly, and mix with the diced onions and olive oil.
- Add the vegetables, vinegar and cheese. Toss together.

RICE SALAD

Ingredients:

1 cup green peas
1 cup celery, sliced
1 cup rice
2 Tbs. bottled French dressing
6 Tbs. mayonnaise

1 Tbs. onion, minced
1/2 tsp. curry powder
1/2 tsp. salt
Dash black pepper
1/2 tsp. prepared mustard

Steps:
- Refrigerate the peas and celery together.
- While the peas and celery are chilling, cook the rice according to the package directions. Drain.
- While the rice is still warm, mix the rice and French dressing together. Let cool.
- Mix the rice mixture with the chilled celery and peas.
- Add the rest of the ingredients and mix well.
- Chill before serving.

Jean Stott

SEA-FOAM SALAD

Ingredients:

6 oz. cream cheese
2 Tbs. milk
One large can pears, drained and mashed with a fork (reserve all pear juice)

One 3-oz. pkg. lime Jell-o
1 cup Cool whip or whipped cream

Steps:
- Soften the cream cheese by mashing it with the milk. Set aside.
- Take the reserved pear juice from the canned pears and add enough water to make one cup of juice total. Pour this juice into a saucepan and bring it to a boil.
- Pour the hot pear juice over the lime gelatin, and stir until the gelatin is dissolved.
- While the Jell-o mixture is still hot, pour it over the cream-cheese mixture.
- When the cream-cheese/Jell-o mixture is cooled and thickened, add the pears. Mix well.
- Gently fold in the Cool Whip or whipped cream until no cream shows.
- Pour all into a lightly oiled mold and chill until set.
- Loosen the sides of the salad with a knife and unmold.

Grace Grainger

STRAWBERRY CASHEW SALAD WITH POPPY-SEED DRESSING

Strawberry-Cashew Salad Ingredients:

2 heads Romaine lettuce
1/4 cup red onion, finely chopped

1 pint fresh ripe strawberries, sliced
1/4 to 1/2 cup cashew nuts, sliced

Poppy-Seed Dressing Ingredients:

1/3 cup sugar
1/2 cup mayonnaise
1/4 cup milk

2 Tbs. vinegar
2 Tbs. poppy seeds

Steps:
- Mix dressing ingredients (above) together.
- Just before serving, toss salad ingredients together.
- Pour a small amount of dressing over the salad and toss. Put the rest of the dressing in a pitcher for those who want more on their salad.

Wynne Joyce

SPAGHETTI CAESAR SALAD

You can add cut-up cooked chicken to this recipe to make Chicken Spaghetti Caesar Salad.

Ingredients:

16 oz. thin spaghetti
1 garlic clove, lightly crushed
1 egg yolk
1/4 cup olive oil
1/4 cup vegetable oil
1/4 cup lemon juice
2 tsp. anchovy paste
1/2 tsp salt
1/2 tsp. pepper
1/4 tsp sugar
1 sm. bunch romaine lettuce
1 cup herb-flavored croutons
1/2 cup Parmesan cheese, grated

Steps:

- Rub a deep serving bowl with a clove of garlic.
- Add egg yolk to the serving bowl, and mix lightly with a fork.
- Cook the pasta al dente, and drain. Rinse with cold water, then drain again thoroughly.
- Add the pasta to the egg yolk in the bowl and toss.
- Make a dressing by blending the next seven ingredients. Pour the dressing over the pasta.
- Add the lettuce and 1/4 cup of the Parmesan cheese. Toss.
- Top with the croutons and the remaining 1/4 cup of the Parmesan cheese. Toss lightly.
Makes 8-10 servings

Pat Maguire

SUN-DRIED TOMATO AND ARTICHOKE PASTA SALAD

You can sprinkle this salad with crumbled feta cheese before serving. The dish doubles easily.

Ingredients:

1 lb. gemelli, cavatappi or other short, twisted pasta
2 Tbs. olive oil
1 large red onion, chopped
2 cloves garlic, finely chopped
3/4 cup sun-dried tomatoes packed in oil, chopped, with 2 Tbs. of the oil reserved

One 14-oz. can artichoke hearts, drained, rinsed and quartered
1 Tbs. capers
1 Tbs. balsamic vinegar
Pinch of cayenne pepper
1/4 cup fresh basil, chopped
Salt and pepper, to taste

Steps:

- In a large pot, cook the pasta for six to eight minutes, or until it is al dente. Drain.
- In the same pot, heat the oil and cook the onion over medium heat, stirring often, for eight minutes, or until it softens.
- Add the garlic and cook for one minute more. Remove the pan from the heat.
- Add the sun-dried tomatoes and 2 Tbs. of their oil, the artichokes, capers, vinegar, cayenne pepper and fresh basil.
- Return the pasta to the pot and stir gently. Add the salt and pepper.
- Let pasta cool to room temperature before serving.
  Serves 8

Mary Ellen Pierce

---

*"My garden will never make me famous,
I'm a horticultural ignoramus,
I can't tell a stringbean from a soybean,
Or even a girl bean from a boy bean."*

-Ogden Nash, poet

VEGETABLES

Sydney Clark (on the right) selling vegetables at Crowell Road, Sagamore Beach in 1912. Raising and selling vegetables was his summer job during his college years. In the 1920s he became a nationally known author of many books of foreign travel, but always returned to his Cape Cod home.

Photo: Jackie Jacobsen, his daughter

SAGAMORE BEACH

Towns of Bourne and Sandwich, Sixty Miles from Boston

The Ideal Summer Resort for Family Life

CAREFULLY RESTRICTED!   EXCELLENCE WITHOUT EXTRAVAGANCE!

The "SAGAMORE IDEA" means Sabbath Observance; it means no intoxicating liquors; it means no dance hall; it means roomy artistic cottages; it means good sanitation; it means pure water from Sagamore Spring; it means all kinds of healthful recreations.

Salt and fresh water bathing, boating in ocean or lake, fishing in bay, brook or lake. Four tennis courts, double croquet grounds, base ball, quoits, tether ball, child's play tent, Arts and Crafts Shop, etc.

350 Seashore Lots for Sale $100 to $1000
10 Furnished Cottages to Rent $100 to $450
2 New Hotels   "Bradford Arms" and "Sagamore Lodge"

SAGAMORE BEACH CO.   88 Tremont St., Boston, Mass.
H. N. Lathrop, Gen'l Manager.

June 15 to Sept. 15, Sagamore Beach, Mass.

1908 Advertisement

Sagamore Highlands from Main Road

Sagamore Highlands, Cape Cod

286

ITALIAN MUSHROOMS

This recipe was passed on to me by an Italian friend, and I have since added the olives. This is better made the day before served. It also freezes well.

Ingredients:
Olive oil
6-8 cloves garlic, peeled
Three 8-oz. pkgs. fresh mushrooms with stems
Three 8-oz. pkgs. fresh mushrooms, sliced
Three 15-oz. cans Italian-style tomato sauce
Three 6-oz. cans tomato paste
Four to six 3-oz. cans sliced olives (optional)

Steps:
- In a large saucepan, put enough olive oil to generously cover the entire bottom of the pan. Place the whole garlic cloves in pan and fry until they are brown. Remove the cloves from the pan and discard.
- Add all of the mushrooms to the hot olive oil and allow the mixture to cool until the liquid is reduced to half.
- Stir in the tomato paste and, if desired, the olives.
- Let simmer for two to three hours, stirring occasionally.
- Serves 12 generously

Jack Mondin

CHEESY CARROT CASSEROLE

Ingredients:
Desired amount of carrots
1 to 2 Tbs. butter
1 onion
1 to 2 Tbs. flour
1 to 2 cups milk
Cheddar cheese, grated
Buttered Corn Flake crumbs

Steps:
- Cook your desired amount of carrots.
- Preheat oven to 300°F.
- In a saucepan, slowly heat the butter and onion until the onions are transparent.
- Add the flour, milk and cheese, and simmer until thickened.
- Pour creamy mixture over the carrots in a buttered dish.
- Spread buttered cornflake crumbs over all.
- Heat through in the oven for about 30 minutes.

Lynn and Jenna Cornell

CREAMED BROCCOLI WITH CRUNCH-AND-CRUMBS TOPPING

Ingredients for Creamed Broccoli:

Two 10-oz. pkgs. frozen chopped broccoli
4 Tbs. butter
4 Tbs. flour
2 chicken-bouillon cubes
2 cups milk

Ingredients for Topping:

2 cups seasoned stuffing mix
2/3 cup water
2 Tbs. butter
2/3 cup walnuts, chopped

Steps:
- Cook the broccoli according to the package directions. Drain and set aside.
- Preheat the oven to 350°F.
- Melt the butter. Add flour and mix. Add bouillon cubes and milk.
- Cook until the sauce thickens.
- Grease a 2-qt. baking dish and place the cooked broccoli in it. Pour the sauce over top.
- To make the Topping, combine the stuffing mix with the butter, water and walnuts.
- Place the Topping mixture on top of the sauce in the baking dish, and bake in the oven for 20 to 30 minutes.
- Serves 6 to 8 people

Mae Foster

MUSTARD SAUCE

This would be a great addition to one of Green Briar Nature Center's Ham and Bean suppers!

Ingredients:

4 heaping Tbs. mustard powder
5 level Tbs. flour
1 pint all-purpose cream
1 cup sugar
2 egg yolks
1 cup cider vinegar

Steps:
- Mix everything (except the cider vinegar) together in a double boiler.
- Cook over boiling water, stirring frequently until the mixture is smooth and thickened. Add 1 cup cider vinegar and cook a while longer.
- Fill and cover jars.
- Refrigerate when cool. Keeps indefinitely.

Rosemary J. Morse (granddaughter of Thornton W. Burgess)

CREAMY SQUASH 'N' TOMATO CASSEROLE AU GRATIN

Ingredients:

2 med. butternut squash (about 3 lbs.), peeled, halved, seeded and sliced crosswise about 1/16-inch thick
Salt and freshly ground black pepper
4 med. Idaho potatoes (about 1 1/2 lbs.), peeled and sliced 1/16-inch thick
5 med. tomatoes, peeled and thinly sliced crosswise

3 1/2 cups heavy cream
1 Tbs. garlic, finely chopped
1 tsp. thyme, finely chopped
1/2 tsp. nutmeg, freshly grated
1 1/2 cups fresh bread crumbs
1/4 cup Parmesan cheese, freshly grated
2 Tbs. parsley, finely chopped
1 Tbs. chives, finely chopped

Steps:
- Preheat the oven to 350°F.
- Butter a 14x10x2-inch baking dish (4 qt.).
- Layer half of the butternut-squash slices in the baking dish, overlapping them slightly; season with salt and pepper.
- Cover with half of the potato slices, overlapping them slightly; season with salt and pepper.
- Top with half of the tomato slices and season with salt and pepper.
- Repeat the layering process, seasoning as you go.
- In a medium saucepan, combine the cream, garlic, thyme and nutmeg. Bring to a boil over moderate heat.
- Pour the cream mixture evenly over the vegetables.
- Cover with foil and bake in the oven for about 45 minutes, or until the vegetables are tender when pierced with a knife.
- Meanwhile, in a small bowl, combine the breadcrumbs, Parmesan cheese, parsley and chives. Sprinkle the resulting crumbs evenly over the vegetables.
- Increase the oven temperature to 400°F and bake the casserole, uncovered, for 20-25 minutes or until the crust is golden brown.
- Let this dish rest for 10 minutes before serving.

- *Tip:* You can make this casserole ahead of time and refrigerate it overnight. Simply rewarm, covered, in a 300°F oven for 45 minutes. Uncover and bake until the top is crisp.
Serves 10

Kathy Leonard

APPLE-STUFFED ACORN SQUASH

This recipe is easy and fast to prepare, although it takes a while to bake. Cook this one dish in place of preparing a starch and a vegetable.

Ingredients:

2 med. acorn squash
1 lg. red apple, diced
2 Tbs. walnuts, chopped
2 Tbs. dark brown sugar
1/4 tsp. cinnamon
1 Tbs. butter, melted

Steps:
- Preheat the oven to 350°F.
- Cut the acorn squash in half lengthwise, and scoop out the seeds.
- Bake both squash halves for 30 minutes.
- While the squash is baking, mix the apple, walnuts, sugar, cinnamon and butter in a small bowl.
- When 30 minutes have passed, spoon the apple mixture into the partially baked squash halves and return them to the oven.
- Bake for 30 minutes longer, or until the squash pulp is tender.
- Serves 4

Pat Bryant

CRUNCHY PECAN SQUASH

Ingredients:

1 med. squash, cooked and mashed OR two 12-oz pkgs frozen butternut squash
2 Tbs. brown sugar
1 tsp. salt
1/2 tsp. nutmeg
1/3 cup butter, melted
1/3 cup evaporated milk
2 Tbs. corn syrup OR maple syrup
1/4 tsp. pepper
1/2 cup pecans or walnuts, coarsely broken

Steps:
- Preheat the oven to 375°F.
- Combine the squash, butter, milk, brown sugar, salt, pepper and nutmeg.
- Turn the mixture into a greased 1 1/2-qt. casserole dish.
- In a small bowl, combine the pecans with the syrup, and sprinkle this over the squash.
- Bake for 30 minutes.
- Serves 4-6

Jennie Zantuhos

ONION PIE

This was my grandmother's recipe, which she always made on holidays. It is good year round, though! This dish can be served hot or cold.

Ingredients:
6-8 onions, sliced thin
6 eggs, beaten
1 cup fresh breadcrumbs
1/2 cup Parmesan cheese, grated
1/2 cup fresh parsley, chopped
Oil

Steps:
- Preheat the oven to 375°F.
- Fry onions in oil until soft. Do not let them brown. Drain well.
- Beat the eggs. Add breadcrumbs, cheese, parsley and the drained onions. Mix well.
- Put the resulting mixture in a 10-inch pie plate or a 9-inch square pan.
- Bake in the oven until a knife inserted into the center comes out clean (30-45 minutes).
- Serves 9

Mary West

MAPLE-GLAZED ONIONS

Ingredients:
2 Tbs. butter
1 lb. sm. white onions, parboiled
3 Tbs. maple syrup
1/3 cup chicken or beef stock

Steps:
- Melt the butter in a non-stick pan over moderately high heat. Add the peeled onions, stirring to coat each one.
- Add the maple syrup, and continue cooking until the onions are coated and a little sticky.
- Add the stock, and cook uncovered for 10 minutes, or until the stock has evaporated.
- Serves 4

Jackie Jacobson

SUMMER-SQUASH CASSEROLE

Ingredients:

2 lbs. (6 cups) summer squash, sliced
1/4 cup onions, chopped
1 can cream-of-chicken soup
1 cup sour cream
1 cup carrot, shredded
One 8-oz. pkg. herb stuffing
1/2 cup butter or margarine, melted

Steps:
- In a saucepan, cook squash and onion in boiling water for five minutes. Drain.
- Preheat the oven to 350°F.
- In a bowl, combine the cream of chicken soup and sour cream. Stir in the shredded carrots and then fold in the drained squash and onions.
- In another bowl, combine the stuffing mix and butter.
- Spread half of the stuffing mixture in the bottom of 12x7x2-inch baking dish.
- Spoon the vegetable mixture on top of the stuffing in the dish.
- Sprinkle the remaining half of the stuffing mixture over top of the vegetables.
- Bake for 30 minutes or until heated through.
  Serves 6

Pauline Laughrea

CORN PUDDING

Excellent summer fare. Serve with grilled anything and a salad. This dish may be assembled and refrigerated until you're ready to cook.

Ingredients

2 Tbs. flour
2 Tbs. sugar
1 tsp. salt
2 cups cream
3 eggs, slightly beaten
2 cups corn (the shaved kernels and milk from 6-8 freshly picked "butter and sugar" corn makes this especially good)
2 Tbs. melted butter

Steps:
- Combine all of the dry ingredients.
- Beat in the cream until smooth.
- Add the eggs.
- Add the corn and melted butter.
- Pour the batter into a buttered 11x7x2-inch casserole dish.
- Bake at 325°F for 30-40 minutes, until golden brown on top.

Rosemary J. Morse (granddaughter of Thornton W. Burgess)

ROASTED SUMMER SQUASH

Ingredients:

2 zucchini squash, stems removed and cut into 1 to 1 1/2-inch chunks
2 yellow squash, stems removed and cut into 1 to 1 1/2-inch chunks
1 red pepper, cut into 1 to 1 1/2-inch pieces
6 to 8 cloves of blanched garlic*, optional
2 Tbs. light olive oil
Salt and black pepper, freshly ground
12 large basil leaves, thinly sliced
1 Tbs. balsamic vinegar or fresh lemon juice
2 Tbs. pine nuts, toasted

*To blanch the garlic, peel the garlic cloves, drop them into a pan of boiling water, cook at a rapid boil for five minutes, then drain.

Steps:
- Preheat the oven to 500°F.
- Place the squash, pepper and garlic on a baking sheet.
- Drizzle the oil over the vegetables, sprinkle them with salt and pepper, and turn them in the oil until they are lightly coated.
- Spread the oiled and seasoned vegetables out across the baking sheet and roast in the oven for 10 minutes.
- Remove the vegetables and let them cool slightly.
- Place the vegetables in a bowl, add the basil and toss with the vinegar or lemon juice. Sprinkle the top with the toasted pine nuts and serve.

Mardi Mauney

ASPARAGUS WITH LEMON-TARRAGON BUTTER

Ingredients:

2 Tbs. butter or margarine
1 tsp. fresh tarragon, chopped
1/2 tsp. lemon peel, grated
1 bunch fresh asparagus

Steps:
- In a small saucepan, melt the butter or margarine.
- Stir in the tarragon and lemon zest and simmer for two minutes over low heat.
- Cook the asparagus briefly in a large shallow pan of boiling water.
- After draining, pour the lemon-tarragon butter over the warm asparagus spears.
- Serves 4

Pat Maguire

SPICED SWEET-POTATO CASSEROLE

You can make this recipe ahead of time, in its casserole dish, and store it in the refrigerator for up to 24 hours.

Ingredients:

3 lbs. sweet potatoes, scrubbed and pierced
1/3 cup dark brown sugar, packed
2 Tbs. butter
2 Tbs. orange-juice concentrate

1 1/2 tsp. cinnamon
1/2 tsp. salt
1/2 tsp. nutmeg
2 lg. eggs
1/4 cup pecans, chopped (optional)

Steps:

- Bake the sweet potatoes in a 350°F oven for one hour, or until they are tender. Leave the oven on for later when the sweet potatoes are done baking.
- When baked, cut each potato in half lengthwise and scoop out the pulp into a large bowl. Discard the skins.
- To the sweet-potato flesh, add the sugar, butter, orange-juice concentrate, cinnamon, salt and nutmeg. Beat with a mixer at low speed, or by hand, until all ingredients are combined.
- Add eggs and beat until smooth.
- Spoon the mixture into a 1 1/2-qt. baking dish. Sprinkle with pecans if desired.
- Bake in the oven for 45 minutes or until thoroughly heated.
- Serves 4 to 8

Pat Bryant.

PARTY POTATOES

These potatoes are supposed to serve 10 to 12 people, but they really only serve six to eight people, because "seconds" almost ALWAYS follow the first servings!

Ingredients:

10-12 med. potatoes, cooked and drained well
1 cup sour cream
6 oz. cream cheese
1 tsp. onion salt
1 tsp. garlic salt

1 tsp. garlic powder
1 tsp. seasoned salt
1/4 tsp. seasoned pepper
1 Tbs. chives
Parmesan cheese for sprinkling

Steps:
- Mix the cooked potatoes, sour cream, cream cheese and seasonings together, then sprinkle with Parmesan cheese.
- Put the mixture into a 13x9-inch casserole dish, and refrigerate for at least one day. (It can be kept like this for two weeks if you leave off the Parmesan cheese.)
- Turn the oven to 350°F and, when hot, bake covered for 30-45 minutes. Remove the cover part way through the cooking. Do NOT add milk to the potatoes!

Barbara Driscoll

ORANGE-GLAZED SWEET POTATOES

Ingredients:

2/3 cup sugar
1 Tbs. cornstarch
1 tsp. salt
1/2 tsp. orange peel, grated

1 cup orange juice
2 Tbs. butter
2 lbs. or 6 med. sweet potatoes, cut in slices

Steps:
- Preheat the oven to 400°F.
- Combine the sugar, cornstarch, salt and orange peel.
- Add the orange juice and butter, and heat at medium, stirring often. Boil for one minute or until mixture thickens. Pour over sweet potatoes in a casserole dish.
- Bake, covered, for one hour, stirring occasionally.

Cheryl Thompson and Mike Socha

"I would rather sit on a pumpkin and have it all to myself, than be crowded on a velvet cushion."

-Henry David Thoreau, author

RATATOUILLE

May be served either hot or cold.

Ingredients:

3 lg. onions, finely chopped
1/4 cup olive oil
3 lg. green peppers, seeded and diced
6 zucchini, unpeeled, diced
1 med. eggplant, peeled and diced
6 lg. tomatoes, peeled, seeded and diced
1 cup chopped parsley
3 garlic cloves, minced
Salt and pepper to taste
Parmesan cheese for sprinkling

Steps:
- Sauté the onions in the olive oil until golden.
- Add the green peppers and cook for three minutes.
- Add the zucchini and cook at medium heat for five minutes.
- Add the eggplant and cook for five more minutes.
- Add the tomatoes, cover the skillet, and simmer for 1 1/2 hours.
- Add the parsley, garlic, salt and pepper. Cook for 20 more minutes.
- Sprinkle with Parmesan cheese before serving.

Mimi McConnell

SAVORY GREEN BEANS

Ingredients:

2 Tbs. butter
1/2 cup onion, minced
1 garlic clove, minced
2 Tbs. parsley, chopped
1/8 tsp. dried rosemary
1 1/4 tsp. dried basil
One 9-oz pkg. frozen green beans

Steps:
- Melt the butter in a saucepan. Add the onion and garlic and sauté for five minutes.
- Add the parsley, rosemary, and basil; simmer, covered for five more minutes.
- Cook the beans according to the package directions. Drain and turn into a serving dish.
- Top beans with the savory butter mixture before serving.
- Serves 4

Mimi McConnell

VEGETABLE PIE

This recipe is quick and easy, with just a few ingredients. If you're not a vegetarian, you might serve this with a few slices of baked ham on the side (delicious)!

Ingredients:

2 pkgs. frozen chopped broccoli
One 4-oz can chopped mushrooms, drained
1 med. onion, chopped
2 Tbs. butter
1 egg
1 prepared pie shell, slightly baked
4 lg. slices Cheddar or 5 lg. slices Swiss cheese
One 9-oz. can yams (save a little syrup to use while mashing)

Steps:
- Cook the broccoli according to package directions
- Sauté the mushrooms and onion in butter, and add to the drained, hot broccoli.
- Beat the egg and add to the vegetables.
- Preheat the oven to 425°F.
- Place in a slightly baked pie shell and top with the sliced cheese.
- Heat and mash the yams, then top the pie with them. Dot the yams with butter. (You may wish to top the whole thing with a lattice crust or just to bake it with the yams as a topping.)
- Bake until heated through.
- Serves 6-8

Nancy Bourdeau

GREEN BEANS WITH PARMESAN AND SCALLIONS

Ingredients:

1 lb. green beans, trimmed and cut diagonally in 1 1/2-inch pieces
1 tsp. margarine
2 Tbs. Parmesan cheese, grated
1/4 tsp. dried basil, crushed
Salt and pepper, to taste
2 scallions, including the white part and about two inches of green, thinly sliced

Steps:
- Steam the green beans until they are tender-crisp (about eight to 12 minutes).
- Transfer the green beans to a large bowl and add the margarine, cheese, basil, salt, pepper and scallions. Toss gently.
- Serves 4

Pat Maguire

CAULIFLOWER-AND-BROCCOLI CASSEROLE

Ingredients:

1 can cream-of-chicken or cream-of-mushroom soup
4 oz. sharp Cheddar cheese, shredded
1/3 cup mayonnaise
1 tsp. curry powder
1 bunch broccoli, chopped into florets
1 bunch cauliflower, chopped into florets
1/4 cup breadcrumbs, buttered

Steps:

- Preheat the oven to 350°F.
- Combine the soup, cheese, mayonnaise and curry powder.
- Pour over the broccoli and cauliflower florets.
- Pour the whole mixture into a casserole dish.
- Sprinkle the breadcrumbs over top and bake for 30 minutes.
- Serves 10

Pat Maguire

STEWED TOMATOES

This recipe is good as both a side vegetable or as a sauce over white fish, chicken, veal or vegetables. Even mix it with pasta for a tasty supper. This recipe freezes well for up to three months.

Ingredients:

8 lg. tomatoes
1 Tbs. olive oil
1/2 cup onions, finely chopped
1/4 cup celery, finely chopped
1/4 cup green pepper, finely chopped
2 Tbs. fresh basil, chopped or 1 1/2 tsp. dried basil
2 Tbs. fresh or 1 Tbs. dried parsley
2 garlic cloves, minced
Salt and pepper to taste

Steps:

- Begin to skin the tomatoes by immersing them in boiling water until their skins split. Peel the skins off.
- Spray a large saucepan with cooking oil, and add the olive oil. Put in the onion, celery and pepper, and cook until tender over medium heat.
- Add the tomatoes, their juice and the remaining ingredients.
- Cover and cook for 20 minutes, stirring occasionally.
- Uncover and cook for five to 10 minutes over medium heat, until the desired thickness is reached.

Pat Bryant

FAIR ELIZABETH'S EGGPLANT

Serve hot or cold for a delicious twist on ratatouille. This recipe can be frozen, too.

Ingredients:

1 lg. eggplant, peeled and cut into 1" pieces
1 lg. onion, diced
1 lg. green pepper, diced
2 garlic cloves
1/2 lb. fresh mushrooms
1/3 cup oil
One 6-oz can tomato paste
1/4 cup water
2 Tbs. wine vinegar
1 Tbs. sesame seeds
2 tsp. lemon juice
1 cup green olives, chopped
Salt and pepper

Steps:

- Sauté all vegetables including the garlic and mushrooms in oil for 10 minutes.
- Add the remaining ingredients and cook covered for 10 minutes, stirring occasionally.

Cathy Shadovitz

VEGETARIAN CHILI WITH POTATOES

Ingredients:

1 Tbs. olive oil
1 med. onion, quartered and thinly sliced
1 lg. can diced tomatoes, undrained
1 garlic clove, pressed
2 tsp. chili powder
1/2 tsp. dried oregano
1 1/2 lbs. unpeeled Yukon gold potatoes, sliced into 1/4-inch slices
1 lg. can black beans, rinsed and drained
1/2 cup water
Salt and pepper, to taste
Cumin powder, to taste
1/2 cup extra-sharp Cheddar cheese

Steps:

- Heat the olive oil in a large nonstick pot and add the onion. Sauté until the onion is softened and starting to turn brown.
- Add the undrained tomatoes, garlic, chili powder, oregano and cumin. Mix well.
- Add the potatoes, beans, salt and pepper, and turn with a large spoon.
- Cover the pot and bring it to a simmer, stirring until the potatoes are tender. If necessary, add more water and keep the mixture juicy.
- Sprinkle the cheese over the top and remove the pot from the heat. Let stand for one minute or until cheese melts.

Sally Kacprowicz

COLCANNON

This dish has both Scottish and Irish roots. Traditionally a Halloween dish, the Irish make theirs with cabbage. A ring is put into the colcannon before cooking, and when it is found, it means the finder will also find love and happiness.

Ingredients:

4 potatoes (about 1 lb.), peeled and chopped
1/4 cup hot milk
2 Tbs. butter
Salt and pepper
4 cups kale, chopped
1 onion, chopped
Cheddar cheese, to taste

Steps:
- Cook the potatoes in salted water until almost mushy. Remove from the water (reserve the cooking water). Mash the cooled potatoes with the hot milk, half of the butter, salt and pepper.
- Boil the kale and onion in the reserved water and cook until tender. Drain.
- Preheat the oven to 350°F.
- Add the cooked kale and onion to the mashed potatoes with a little Cheddar cheese and the rest of the butter.
- Put in a buttered baking dish and sprinkle some more cheese on top.
- Bake until very hot and slightly brown, about 30 minutes.
- Serves 6

Marj Griffes

Chronology of Cape Cod Canal

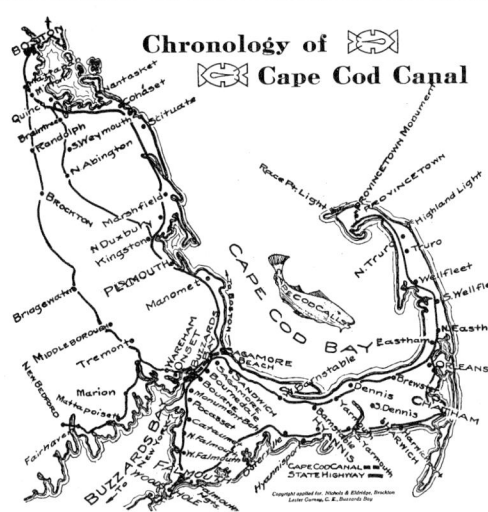

1602—Cape discovered by Bartholomew Gosnold.
1620—Arrival of the Pilgrims.
1627—Miles Standish trading at Manomett with the Dutch from New Amsterdam. Boats within three miles of each other. Small canal talked of.
1697—General Court of Massachusetts appoints a committee to view place for passage from Barnstable Bay to Manomett Bay.
1717—Capt. Cyprian Southack describes free water connection across the Cape Colony of Mass.
1776—Gen. Washington ordered Thomas Machin to survey route which would "give greater security to navigation and against the enemy." Also James Bowdoin and William Sever appointed a committee to investigate subject.
1791—John Hills and James Winthrop make survey.
1812—Isthmus used by small boats to avoid enemy.
1818—Israel Thorndike and Thomas H. Perkins employed Laommi Baldwin to make survey.
1824—United States ordered survey.
1828—Government Board reports on canal 36 feet wide and 8 feet deep to cost $669,522.
1860—Renewed interest by State and Government.
1880—Charter granted to Cape Cod Canal Co. H. M. Whitney and others interested.
1882—Gen. G. K. Warren, U. S. A. Engrs., reports to Government on canal and cost of approaches.
1883—Cape Cod Ship Canal Co. made contract with F. A. Lockwood. Excavated over 1,000,000 yds. and failed. C. M. Thompson, Engineer.
1890—Property assigned to Col. Thos. L. Livermore.
1898—DeWitt C. Flanagan, of N. Y., interested.
1899—June 1—Charter to the Boston, Cape Cod & N. Y. Canal Co., under which and its amendments present company acting.
1904—August Belmont and others interested
1907—May 8—Approved by the Commissioners.
1909—June 22—Work officially begun at Bourndale.

Cape Cod Canal Officially Opened July 29, 1914.

Published by the Cape Cod Camera Craft Co., Buzzards Bay, Mass.

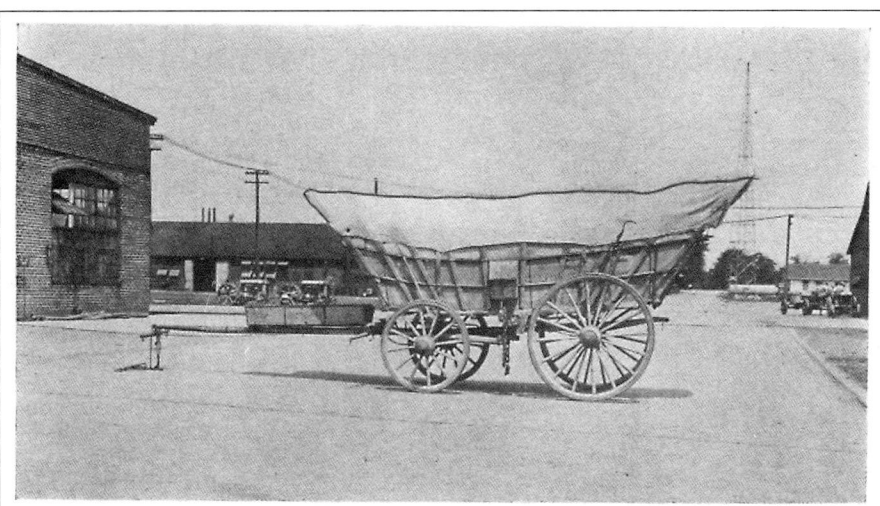

Courtesy of Mr. Henry Ford
Another famous Cape Cod product—the "Prairie Schooner." Many such were built for the GoldRush to California in 1849 by I. N. Keith at what is now Keith Car and Mfg. Co., Sagamore.

Another famous Cape Cod product—the "Prairie Schooner". Many of these were built for the Gold Rush to California in 1849 by the Keith Car and Mfg. Co. in Sagamore.

301

15.

White Cup Cake
1 Coffee cup of Cream, 1 cup of Butter 2 cups of Sugar, 4 cups of Flour, 5 eggs, Nutmeg, Cinnamon, 1 teaspoon full of Pearlash; baked in little pans

Miss Leslie.

Cup Cake.
5 cups of Flour, 2 cups of Butter 2½ cups of Sugar 1 cup of Milk 5 eggs, teaspoonfull of Saleratus. 1 Nutmeg

Martha L. Cox.

Cupc Cake.
1 cup of Butter, 2 cups of Sugar 1 cup of Sour Milk 4 cups of Flour 4 eggs scant teaspoonfull of soda or saleratus Nutmeg

Nurse Crooker's.

Page from nineteenth century hand-written book of recipes.

A

All-Bran Bread 34
Almond Bars, Holiday Chocolate 118
Almond Butter Crunch 139, 140
Almond Delight Dip 203
Almond Spritz Cookies 106
Almond-Bark Cookies 222
America's Linguine with White Clam Sauce 228
Antipasto Squares, Ginny's 11

APPETIZERS & SNACKS

Bacon and Water-Chestnut Roll-Ups 13
Baked Brie 15
Bleu-Cheese Spread 14
Crab Appetizers 205
Creamy Shrimp in Pastry Cups 12
Curried Scallop Cakes 19
Festive Roasted-Pepper Dip 18
Garden Salsa 13
Gary's Hot Clam Dip 14
Ginny's Antipasto Squares 11
Ham Crescent Snacks 205
Hot Crab Dip 11
Hot Seafood-Cheese Hors d'oeuvres............ 20
Hummus 16
Mini Quiches 204
Pineapple-Cheese Ball 18
Pistachio-Stuffed Mushrooms 16
"Puppy Chow" (Cheerios Party Mix) 20
Rum Raisin Cheddar Spread........................203
Salmon Dip 17
Spinach and Artichoke Dip 12
Summer Dip 15
Tortilla Roll-Ups 19
Turkey-Pecan Meatballs 17
Twist Sticks 205

APPLES

Apple & Lemon Relish 164
Apple Cake, Dutch..88
App;e Cake, Reggie's Knobbly........................90
Apple-Craisin Pastry Baskets with Rum Cream
....46
Apple Crisp 224
Apple Crumb Cake.. 94
Apple Jelly 154
Apple Muffins, Cinnamon-Topped 55
Apple Muffins, Low-Fat 53
Apple-Rosemary Tea Bread 39
Apple-Stuffed Acorn Squash 290
Baked Apples 135
Bavarian Apple Torte 101
Cran-Apple Pie 67

Swedish Apple Pie 97
Waldorf Salad..206
Apricot and Ginger Marmalade 157
Apricot-Pear Jam 153
Armenian Rice and Noodle Pilaf 192

ARTICHOKES

Spinach and Artichoke Dip.............................12
Artichoke Pasta Salad, Sun-dried Tomato and ..
....284

ASPARAGUS

Asparagus with Lemon-Tarragon Butter 293

B

Bacon and Water-Chestnut Roll-Ups.................. 13
Baked Apples 135
Baked Bluefish.. 233
Baked Brie 15
Baked Creamy Cod, Spinach and Egg Noodles 231
Baked Fish Mozzarella 230
Baked French Toast 47
Baked Noodle-and-Cheese Casserole................ 198
Baked Scallops 247

BANANA

Banana Bread 33
Banana Bread, Mother's 29
Banana Crumb Muffins 56
Bangladesh Kebabs 182
Barley, Beef and (Soup) 264
Bavarian Apple Torte 101
Bean Salad, Four...275

BARS, see cookies

Bark 140
Crusty Caramel "Creed" Bars 120
Hershey's Ultimate Chocolate Brownies with ..
Frosting 121
Hershey-Bar Squares 112
Holiday Chocolate-Almond Bars 118
Icebox Finger Cookies 110
Lemon Squares 120
Pumpkin Bars with Cream-Cheese Icing 119
Pumpkin-Cranberry Spice Bars 61
Treasure-Chest Bars 116

BEEF

Bangladesh Kebabs 182
Beef and Barley Soup 264
Beef and Cabbage Rolls 211
Burgundy Pot Roast 175
Chicken-and-Beef Stock 270
Five-Hour Beef Stew 176
Hamburg Stew 173
Hungarian Stuffed Peppers 176

303

Italian Meatballs and Sauce 181
Italian Pot Roast 177
Lobster-Stuffed Tenderloin of Beef 182
Meatloaf With Brown Sugar-and-Tomato Glaze
....183
Moussaka 174
Oriental-Marinated Steak Strips 179
Oven Pot Roast 175
Quick Meatballs 211
Skewered Baby Beef And Mushrooms 186
Steak Diane 178
Swedish Meatballs 178
Beef and Barley Soup 264
Beef and Cabbage Rolls 211
Beer Marinade 181
Bird Nests in Syrup (Folitses) 124

BISCOTTI
Coconut, Almond Biscotti...............................109
Pistachio and Cranberry Biscotti 73
Black Dog's Ginger Cookies 107
Black-Bottom Cupcakes 85
Black-Eyed Susans 117
Bleu-Cheese Spread 14
Bleu-Cheese Walnut Dip 204

BLUEBERRIES
Blueberry Cake, Grandma Leighton's..............84
Blueberry Conserve 160
Blueberry Cream-Cheese Pie 217
Blueberry Crumble 129
Blueberry Pancakes with Hot Blueberry Syrup 41
Blueberry-Peach Jam 151
Blueberry Streusel Coffee Cake 94
Jordan Marsh Blueberry Muffins 52
Borscht, Lazy Mama's.......................................256
Braided Buttermilk Bread 35
Braided Christmas Bread, Swiss 38
Brazilian Pork Loin in Geny's Style 184
Bread Pudding 128
Bread-and-Butter Pickles 162

BREADS
All-Bran Bread 34
Apple-Rosemary Tea Bread 39
Banana Bread 33
Braided Buttermilk Bread 35
Cottage Teahouse White Bread 38
Dinner Rolls 40
Eggnog Tea Bread 31
Favorite Cornbread 32
Foolproof Challah Bread 36
Garlic Bubble Loaf 31
Grandma's Oatmeal Bread 36
Irish Breakfast Soda Bread 30

Mother's Banana Bread 29
Oatmeal Scones 29
Pumpkin 'N' Spice Tea Bread 34
Pumpkin-Cranberry Bread..............................62
Refrigerator Dinner Rolls 33
Twist Sticks...205
Yogurt Corn Bread 30
Zucchini Bread...32
Zup fe (Swiss Braided Christmas Bread) 38
Breakfast Pie, Country 48
Breakfast Pizza 49

BROCCOLI
Broccoli Chicken 212
Broccoli-Sausage Pasta 192
Cauliflower-and-Broccoli Casserole 298
Cream of Broccoli Soup 260
Creamed Broccoli with Crunch-and-Crumbs
Topping 288
Vegetable Pie 297
Brownies, Coffee-Glazed 122

BRUNCH
Apple-Craisin Pastry Baskets with Rum Cream
....46
Baked French Toast 47
Blueberry Pancakes with Hot Blueberry Syrup
....41
Breakfast Pizza 49
Country Breakfast Pie 48
Finnish "Pannukakku" 45
Fruit-Topped Oven Pancake 44
Hangtown-Fry Omelet 43
Orange-Vanilla French Toast 51
Oven French Toast 43
Picante-Omelet Pie 46
Quiche Lorraine 50
Spinach Pie For a Crowd 42
Swedish Pancakes 44
Toad-In-The-Hole 50
Burgundy Pot Roast 175
Butter-Pecan Pie 218
Buttermilk Fried-Fish Fillets 214

C
Cabbage Rolls, Beef and..................................211
Caesar's Fish 215

CAKES
Apple Crumb Cake 94
Black-Bottom Cupcakes 85
Blueberry Streusel Coffee Cake 94
Cheesecake, Cranberry Swirl 76
Cheesecake, Pumpkin 83

304

Chocolate Butter Icing 91
Cocoa Fudge Frosting 93
Cream-Cheese Cupcakes 84
Dutch Apple Cake 88
Fluffy "Poor Man's Frosting" 91
Fresh-Ginger Cake 86
Grandma Leighton's Blueberry Cake 84
Mocha Cake 90
Mocha Frosting 91
One-Step Yogurt Pound Cake with Lemon
  Glaze 88
Pumpkin Cheesecake 83
Red-Beet Chocolate Cake 89
Reggie's Knobby Apple Cake 90
Reine de Saba (Queen of Sheba) Cake with
  Chocolate Butter Icing 92
Sour-Cream Coffee Cake 93
Sweet-Potato Pound Cake with
  Orange Glaze 86
Triple Fudge Cake 221
Ugly-Duckling Cake with Frosting 221
Calzone, Stuffed 184

CANDY, see confections
Candy Trifles 223
Cape Cod Cranberry Velvet Pie 63
Cape Codder 23
Cape-Cod Chews 74

CARROTS
Carrot Salad 207
Carrot with Fennel Soup 255
Carrot, Sweet Potato and Ginger Soup 266
Cheesy Carrot Casserole 287

CASSEROLES
Cauliflower-and-Broccoli Casserole 298
Cheesy Carrot Casserole 287
Chicken Casserole 171
Creamy Squash 'n' Tomato Casserole Au Gratin
 289
Lobster Casserole With Lemon-Herb Topping
 244
Lobster or Langastino Casserole 243
Oriental Chicken Casserole 172
Spiced Sweet-Potato Casserole 294
Summer-Squash Casserole 292

CAULIFLOWER
Cauliflower Cheese Soup 262
Cauliflower-and-Broccoli Casserole 298

CHEESE
Baked Brie 15
Baked Fish Mozzarella 230
Bleu-Cheese Spread 14

Bleu-Cheese Walnut Dip 204
Cauliflower Cheese Soup 262
Cheese Ale Soup 255
Cheesy Carrot Casserole 287
Cheesy Spaghetti 197
Chicken Cheese Rolls 171
Hot Seafood-Cheese Hors d'oeuvres.............. 20
Pineapple-Cheese Ball 18
Rum Raisin Cheddar Spread.........................203
Challah Bread, Foolproof....................................36
Cheerios Party Mix, "Puppy Chow" 20
Cheesecake, Cranberry Swirl 76
Cheesecake, Pumpkin 83
Cherry Cobbler, Easy 220
Cherry-Nut Cookies 108

CHICKEN
Broccoli Chicken 212
Chicken and Beef Stock..................................270
Chicken and Mushroom Crepes 180
Chicken and Vegetable Stew 257
Chicken Casserole 171
Chicken Cheese Rolls 171
Chicken Ruby 172
Chicken Salad Deluxe 276
Chicken Spinach Bake 212
Cranberry Salsa Chicken 65
Four-Cheese Chicken Fettucine 200
Garlic Chicken 212
Honey-glazed Broilers 170
Honey-Mustard Chicken 213
Italian Chicken 213
Italian Chicken-Lentil Soup 270
Mexican Chicken 173
Orange Mandarin Chicken 169
Oriental Chicken Casserole 172
Parmesan Chicken 170
Simple Chicken-Noodle Soup 259
Tarragon Chicken 169

CHOCOLATE
Bark 140
Chocolate Bites 223
Chocolate Butter Icing 91
Chocolate Cake, Red-Beet...............................89
Chocolate Cranberry Mousse Pie 67
Chocolate Crescents, Creamy 142
Chocolate Dessert Crepes 135
Chocolate Sprinkle Cookies 108
Chocolate-Sundae Pie, Frozen 96
Chocolate-Coated Pecan Pralines 142
Chocolate-Marshmallow Mousse 224
Chocolate-Mousse Pie with Chocolate Leaves 99
German-Chocolate Pie 219

305

Grand Marnier Chocolate Mousse 136
Heath-Bar Chocolate Trifle 134
Hersey-Bar Squares 112
Hershey's Ultimate Chocolate Brownies with ..
   Frosting 121
Holiday Chocolate-Almond Bars 118

CHOWDER, see Soups, Stews and Chowders
Christmas-Jewel White Fudge 145
Church Windows 141

CHUTNEYS
   Cranberry-Coriander Chutney, Spice-Rubbed
      Roast Pork Loin with 185
   Cranberry, Ginger and Lemon Chutney 166
   Orange Chutney 165
   Pineapple Chutney 166
Cider, Rosy Cranberry 25
Cinnamon-Topped Apple Muffins 55
Citrus Sponge Pudding 130

CLAMS
   America's Linguine with White Clam Sauce 228
   Clam Fritters 227
   Clam Soufflé 228
   Gary's Hot Clam Dip.......................................14
   New England Clam Chowder 263
   Sea-Clam Pie 227
Cobbler, Easy Cherry 220
Cocoa Fudge Frosting 93

COCONUT
   Coconut & Almond Macaroons 116
   Coconut-Almond Biscotti 109
   Coconut-Cranberry Chews 75
Coffee Liqueur 23
Coffee-Almond Tortoni 134
Coffee-Glazed Brownies 122
Colcannon 300
Cold Cucumber Soup 261
Cold Lemon Soufflé 130

CONFECTIONS
   Almond Butter Crunch 139, 140
   Bark 140
   Candy Trifles 223
   Chocolate Bites 223
   Chocolate-Coated Pecan Pralines 142
   Christmas-Jewel White Fudge 145
   Church Windows 141
   Creamy Chocolate Crescents 142
   Crispy Easter Nests 133
   Dan's Million-Dollar Fudge 143
   Divinity Fudge 146
   Peanut-Butter Bars 144
   Peanut-Butter Flakes 143

Penuche Fudge 146
Quick Peanut-Butter Fudge 144
Tempt-Me Truffles 145
White Cranberry-Walnut Fudge 141

CONSERVES
Blueberry Conserve 160
Cranberry Conserve 159
Cranberry-Pineapple Conserve 161
Plum Conserve 160
Strawberry Conserve 161
Cookie-Crust Ice-Cream Pie 218

COOKIES
Almond Spritz Cookies 106
Almond-Bark Cookies 222
Bird Nests in Syrup (Folitses) 124
Black Dog's Ginger Cookies........................... 107
Black-Eyed Susans 117
Cape Cod Chews 74
Cherry-Nut Cookies 108
Chocolate Sprinkle Cookies 108
Coconut & Almond Macaroons 116
Coconut-Almond Biscotti 109
Coffee-Glazed Brownies 122
Cranberry-Oatmeal Cookies 110
Crusty Caramel "Creed" Bars 120
Fruit-Filled Horns 115
Great-Great Grandma Emma's Sugar Cookies
  105
Hershey's Ultimate Chocolate Brownies with ..
   Frosting 121
Hershey-Bar Squares 112
Holiday Chocolate-Almond Bars 118
Icebox Finger Cookies 110
Jam Jewels 112
Lemon Squares 120
Oatmeal-Cranberry-Pecan Cookies 80
Orange Coconut Balls 222
Orange-Cranberry-Ginger Oat Bars 78
Peanut-Butter-Candy Cookies 222
Pistachio and Cranberry Biscotti 73
Pumpkin Bars with Cream-Cheese Icing 119
Pumpkin-Cranberry Spice Bars 61
Raisin-Oatmeal Cookies 105
Russian Kisses (Rum Balls) 115
Sandwich "Star" Cookies 113
Shortbread Cookies with Lavender Icing 111
Snickerdoodles 114
Swedish Farmer Cookies 106
Treasure-Chest Bars 116

CORN
   Low-Fat Corn Chowder 258

Corn Bread, Favorite 32
Corn Bread, Yogurt 30
Corn Pudding 292
Corn Relish 164
Cottage Teahouse White Bread 38
Country Breakfast Pie 48

CRAB
Crab Appetizers 205
Crab-Rangoon Wreath 242
Hot Crab Dip 11
Hot Seafood-Cheese Hors d'Oeuves 20
Paddock's Palenta Crab Cakes 241
Seafood Pasta Salad 208
Cran-Apple Pie 67

CRANBERRIES
Cape Cod Cranberry Velvet Pie 63
Cape-Cod Chews 74
Cape Codder 23
Chicken Ruby 172
Chocolate Cranberry Mousse Pie 67
Coconut-Cranberry Chews 75
Cran-Apple Pie 67
Cranberry-Blueberry Pie 68
Cranberry Coffee Cake 71
Cranberry Conserve 159
Cranberry Crumb Cake 72
Cranberry, Ginger and Lemon Chutney 166
Cranberry Jam 152
Cranberry Jezebel Sauce 65
Cranberry-Glazed Pork Roast 66
Cranberry Marmalade 156
Cranberry Muffins 69
Cranberry-Oatmeal Cookies 110
Cranberry-Orange Mini Scones 70
Cranberry-Orange Muffins 54
Cranberry-Pineapple Conserve 161
Cranberry-Raisin Pie 69
Cranberry-Raspberry Compote 75
Cranberry-Rhubarb Bread 74
Cranberry Salsa Chicken 65
Cranberry Scoop (non-alcoholic) 24
Cranberry Spinach Salad 276
Cranberry Squares 77
Cranberry-Swirl Cheesecake 76
Cranberry Turtle Bars 78
Cranberry-Walnut Fudge, White 141
Eleanor Bates' Cranberry Torte 62
Fresh-Cranberry Sauce 64
My Mother's Cranberry Pie 68
Oatmeal-Cranberry-Pecan Cookies 80
Orange-Cranberry-Ginger Oat Bars 78
Pistachio and Cranberry Biscotti 73

Pumpkin-Cranberry Bread 62
Pumpkin-Cranberry Spice Bars with
    Cream-Cheese Frosting 61
Roseann's Cranberry Nut Pie 66
Rosy Cranberry Cider 25
Traditional Ten-Minute Cranberry Sauce 64
Cream of Broccoli Soup 260
Cream Puffs 133
Cream-Cheese Cupcakes 84
Cream-Cheese Pecan Tarts 100
Creamed Broccoli with Crunch-and-Crumbs
    Topping 288
Creamy Chocolate Crescents 142
Creamy Rice Pudding 129
Creamy Shrimp in Pastry Cups 12
Creamy Squash 'n' Tomato Casserole Au Gratin ..
   289
Crepes, Chicken and Mushroom 180
Crepes, Chocolate Dessert 135
Crispy Bacon-Wrapped Oysters 216
Crispy Easter Nests 133
Crumble, Blueberry 129
Crunchy Pecan Squash 290
Crusty Caramel "Creed" Bars 120

CUCUMBERS
Cold Cucumber Soup 261

CUPCAKES
Black-Bottom Cupcakes 85
Cream-Cheese Cupcakes.....................................84

CURRY
Curried Butternut-Squash Soup.......................262
Curried Scallop Cakes 19

D
Dan's Million-Dollar Fudge 143

DESSERTS
Apple Crisp 224
Baked Apples 135
Blueberry Crumble 129
Bread Pudding 128
Chocolate Dessert Crepes 135
Chocolate-Marshmallow Mousse 224
Citrus Sponge Pudding 130
Coffee-Almond Tortoni 134
Cold Lemon Souffle 130
Cream Puffs 133
Creamy Rice Pudding 129
Crispy Easter Nests 133
Easy Cherry Cobbler 220
Fudge-Batter Pudding 132
Grand Marnier Chocolate Mousse 136

307

Grapenut Pudding 127
Heath-Bar Chocolate Trifle 134
Kahlua Mousse 132
Lemon Sponge Pudding 128
Orange Dessert 220
Quick-and-Easy Corn-Flake Pudding 127
Rhubarb and Strawberry Compote 131
Strawberry Trifle 224
Swedish Cream 131
Deviled Shrimp 240
Dinner Rolls.. 40

DIPS
Almond Delight Dip 203
Bleu-Cheese Walnut Dip................................204
Festive Roasted-Pepper Dip 18
Gary's Hot Clam Dip 14
Hot Crab Dip 11
Hummus 16
Salmon Dip 17
Shrimp Dip 203
Spinach and Artichoke Dip 12
Summer Dip 15
"Dirty" Rice 198
Divinity Fudge 146

DRESSING, see sauces

DRINKS & CORDIALS
Cape Codder 23
Coffee Liqueur 23
Cranberry Scoop (non-alcoholic) 24
Hazelnut Liqueur..24
Orange Liqueur 25
Raspberry Syrup 26
Rosy Cranberry Cider (non-alcoholic) 25
Sparkling Fruit Smoothie 26
Dutch Apple Cake 88

E
Earl's Striped Bass with Garlic-Mustard Sauce 236
Easy Cherry Cobbler 220
Easy Fish Stew 264
Easy, Cheesy Seafood Supper 234
Eggnog Tea Bread 31

EGGPLANT
Fair Elizabeth's Eggplant 299
Moussaka 174
Ratatouille 296
Eisenhower Strawberry Pie 100
Elaine's Stuffed Bay Scallops 248
Eleanor Bates' Cranberry Torte 62

F
Fair Elizabeth's Eggplant 299
Fall-Fruit Jam 151
Favorite Cornbread 32
Fettucine, Four-Cheese Chicken 200
Festive Roasted-Pepper Dip 18
Finnish "Pannukakku" 45

FISH
Baked Bluefish 233
Baked Creamy Cod, Spinach and Egg Noodles 231
Baked Fish Mozzarella 230
Buttermilk Fried-Fish Fillets........................214
Caesar's Fish..215
Earl's Striped Bass with Garlic-Mustard Sauce 236
Easy Fish Stew 264
Easy, Cheesy Seafood Supper 234
Fish Chowder 266
Friendly Fish Stew 268
Italian Cioppino 232
Legal Sea Food's Fish Cakes 230
Lemon-Crumb Topped Fish Bake 232
Lemon Dill Fish..215
Maple- and Mustard-Glazed Salmon 237
Perry's Fish Chowder....................................252
Salmon with Sizzle 236
Salmon, Onions 'n Soy 238
Sea Captain's Dinner: Cod with Salt Pork ..234
Seafood Gumbo Stew 267
Seafood-Stuffed Sole-Fillet Roll-ups 235
Tuna Steak, Grilled 217
Five-Hour Beef Stew 176
Fluffy "Poor Man's Frosting" 91
Folitses (Bird Nests in Syrup) 124
Foolproof Challah Bread 36
Four-Bean Salad 274
Four-Cheese Chicken Fettucine 200

FRENCH TOAST
French Toast, Baked..47
French Toast, Orange-Vanilla 51
French Toast, Oven 43
Fresh-Cranberry Sauce 64
Fresh-Ginger Cake 86
Fried Green Tomatoes 210
Friendly Fish Stew 268
Fritters, Clam 227

FROSTING
Chocolate Butter Icing 91
Chocolate Butter Icing , Reine de Saba (Queen of Sheba) Cake with 92

308

Cocoa Fudge Frosting 93
Fluffy "Poor Man's Frosting" 91
Frosting, Ugly-Duckling Cake with 221
Mocha Frosting 91
Frozen Chocolate-Sundae Pie 96
Fruit Salad with Yogurt Dressing 278
Fruit-Filled Horns 115
Fruit-Topped Oven Pancake 44
Fudge-Batter Pudding 132

FUDGE
Fudge, Christmas-Jewel White 145
Fudge, Dan's Million-Dollar 143
Fudge, Divity 146
Fudge, Penuche 146
Fudge, Quick Peanut Butter 144
Fudge, White Cranberry-Walnut 141

G
Garden Salsa 13
Garlic Bubble Loaf 31
Garlic Chicken 212
Garlic Soup 272
Gary's Hot Clam Dip 14
Gazpacho 272
German-Chocolate Pie 219
Ginger Lemon Scones 57
Ginny's Antipasto Squares 11
Grand Marnier Chocolate Mousse 136
Grandma Leighton's Blueberry Cake 84
Grandma's Oatmeal Bread 36
Grape Jelly 155
Grapenut Pudding 127
Great-Great Grandma Emma's Sugar Cookies 105
Greek Orzo Salad 280
Greek Spaghetti with Tomatoes and Garlic 196

GREEN BEANS
Green Bean and Hazelnut Salad with
  Herb-Mustard Dressing 278
Green Beans with Parmesan and Scallions ..297
Savory Green Beans 296
Grilled Tuna Steak 217

H

HAM
Ham Crescent Snacks 205
Onion, Ham and Cheese Chowder 258
Hangtown-Fry Omelet 43
Hazelnut Liqueur 24
Heath-Bar Chocolate Trifle 134
Hershey's Ultimate Chocolate Brownies with
  Frosting 121
Hershey-Bar Squares 112

Holiday Chocolate-Almond Bars 118
Honey-glazed Broilers 170
Honey-Mustard Chicken 213
Hot Crab Dip 11
Hot Seafood-Cheese Hors d'oeuvres 20
Hummus 16
Hungarian Stuffed Peppers 176

I
Ice-Cream Salad 206
Icebox Finger Cookies 110
ICING, see frosting
Irish Breakfast Soda Bread 30
Italian Chicken 213
Italian Chicken-Lentil Soup 270
Italian Cioppino 232
Italian Meatballs and Sauce 181
Italian Mushrooms 287
Italian Pot Roast 177

J
Jalapeno Jelly 155
Jam Jewels 112

JAMS
Apricot-Pear Jam 153
Blueberry-Peach Jam 151
Cranberry Jam 152
Fall-Fruit Jam 151
No-Cook Freezer Peach or Raspberry Jam ..153
Peach Jam 151
Pear-Pineapple-Lemon Jam 150
Strawberry Jam 150
Strawberry-Rhubarb Jam 152

JELLIES
Apple Jelly 154
Grape Jelly 155
Jalapeno Jelly 155
Jordan Marsh Blueberry Muffins 52

K
Kahlua Mousse 132

KALE
Portuguese Kale Soup 260
Karin's Seared Scallops 249
Kebabs, Bangladesh 182

L
Lasagna, Vegetable 194
Layered Salad 275
Lazy Mama's Borscht 256

309

LEEKS
Potato Leek Soup 265
Legal Seafood's Fish Cakes 230

LEMON
Lemon-Butter Sauce for Seafood 241
Lemon-Crumb Topped Fish Bake 232
Lemon Dill Fish 215
Lemon Sponge Pudding 128
Lemon Squares 120
Lemon-Tarragon Butter, Asparagus with 293
Light Shrimp Alfredo 238
Light Tomato-Basil Soup 259
Linguine, America's with White Clam Sauce 228
Linguine and Mussels 229
Linguine with Spinach Pesto and Feta 191

LIQUEURS, see drinks & cordials

LOBSTER
Lobster Cacciatore 246
Lobster Cakes 245
Lobster Casserole With Lemon-Herb Topping
....244
Lobster or Langastino Casserole 243
Lobster Stock 243
Lobster-and-Scallop Bundle with Chardonnay
Cream Sauce 244
Lobster-Stuffed Tenderloin Of Beef 182
Low-Fat Apple Muffins 53
Low-Fat Corn Chowder 258

M
Mandarin Salad with Orange-Juice Dressing ..206
Maple- and Mustard-Glazed Salmon 237
Maple-Glazed Onions 291
Marinade, Beer 181
Marinated Grilled Shrimp 216

MARMALADES
Apricot and Ginger Marmalade 157
Cranberry Marmalade 156
Pineapple-Orange Marmalade 158
Spiced Orange Marmalade 158
Spring Marmalade 156
Marvelous Mushrooms 209

MEATBALLS
Meatballs and Sauce, Italian 181
Meatballs, Turkey-Pecan 17
Meatballs, Quick 211
Meatballs, Swedish 178
Meatloaf With Brown Sugar-and-Tomato Glaze
....183
Mexican Chicken 173
Mini Quiches 204

Mocha Cake 90
Mocha Frosting 91
Mom's French Dressing 280
Mother's Banana Bread 29

MOUSSE
Mousse, Chocolate-Marshmallow 224
Mousse, Grand Marnier Chocolate 136
Mousse, Kahlua 132
Moussaka 174
Muffaletta Olive Salad 279

MUFFINS
Banana Crumb Muffins 56
Cinnamon-Topped Apple Muffins 55
Cranberry Muffins 69
Cranberry-Orange Mini Scones 70
Cranberry-Orange Muffins 54
Jordan Marsh Blueberry Muffins 52
Low-Fat Apple Muffins 53
Oatmeal-Raisin Muffins 56
Orange-Ginger Muffins 54
Pumpkin Muffins 52
Sour-Cream Maple-Pecan Muffins 58
Zucchini-Oatmeal Muffins 53

MUSHROOMS
Italian Mushrooms 287
Marvelous Mushrooms 209
Mushrooms, Skewered Baby Beef and 186
Pistachio-Stuffed Mushrooms 16
Vegetable Pie 297
Mussels, Linguine and 229
Mustard Sauce 288
My Mother's Cranberry Pie 68

N
New England Clam Chowder 263
No-Bake Pineapple-Lemon Pie 217
No-Cook Freezer Peach or Raspberry Jam 153

NOODLES
Armenian Rice and Noodle Pilaf 192
Noodle-and-Cheese Casserole, Baked 198
Noodle Salad, Oriental 279
Noodles with Hot 'n Spicy Peanut Sauce,
Oriental 199

O

OATMEAL
Oatmeal Bread, Grandma's 36
Oatmeal Cookies, Raisin- 105
Oatmeal-Cranberry-Pecan Cookies 80
Oatmeal Muffins, Zucchini 53

Oatmeal-Raisin Muffins 56
Oatmeal Scones 29
Omelet, Hangtown Fry 43
Omelet, Picante Pie 46

One-Step Yogurt Pound Cake with Lemon Glaze
....88

ONIONS
Maple-Glazed Onions 291
Onion, Ham and Cheese Chowder 258
Onion Pie 291

ORANGES
Mandarin Salad with Orange-Juice Dressing ..206
Orange Chutney 165
Orange Coconut Balls 222
Orange-Cranberry-Ginger Oat Bars 78
Orange Dessert 220
Orange-Ginger Muffins 54
Orange-Glazed Sweet Potatoes 295
Orange Liqueur 25
Orange Mandarin Chicken 169
Orange Marmalade, Spiced.........................158
Orange, Pineapple Marmalade 158
Orange-Vanilla French Toast 51
Oriental Chicken Casserole 172
Oriental Noodle Salad 279
Oriental Noodles with Hot 'n Spicy Peanut Sauce
....199
Oriental-Marinated Steak Strips 179
Orzo, Wild Rice, and Pignola Pilaf 190
Out-of-Sight Cole Slaw 280
Oven French Toast 43
Oven Pot Roast 175
Oven-Fried Pork Chops 214

OYSTERS
Crispy Bacon-Wrapped Oysters 216
Hangtown-Fry Omelet 43
Oyster Stir-Fry 251
Ron's World-Famous Oyster Soup 250
Scalloped Oysters 251

P
Paddock's Palenta Crab Cakes............................241

PANCAKES
Pancakes, Blueberry with Hot Blueberry Syrup
....41
Pancake, Oven Fruit-Topped 44
Pancake, Swedish 44
Pancakes, Zucchini 48
"Pannukakku", Finnish 45
Parmesan Chicken 170

Parsnip Soup 256
Party Potatoes 294

PASTA
America's Linguine with White Clam Sauce 228
Armenian Rice and Noodle Pilaf 192
Baked Creamy Cod, Spinach and Egg Noodles
....231
Baked Noodle-and-Cheese Casserole 198
Broccoli-Sausage Pasta 192
Cheesy Spaghetti 197
Forest Pasta Salad with Herb Dressing 277
Four-Cheese Chicken Fettucine 200
Greek Orzo Salad...280
Greek Spaghetti with Tomatoes and Garlic 196
Linguine and Mussels 229
Linguine with Spinach Pesto and Feta 191
Oriental Noodles with Hot 'n Spicy Peanut
Sauce 199
Orzo, Wild Rice, and Pignola Pilaf 190
Pasta Primavera Salad 281
Pasta Salad 208
Penne Rita 193
Rigatoni with Vegetables 189
Seafood Pasta Salad 208
Spaghetti Caesar Salad 283
Spaghetti-Cheese Bake 196
Stuffed Shells Florentine 190
Tortellini Soup 261
Vegetable Lasagna 194

PEACH
Peach-Blueberry Cream Pie 98
Peach, Bluberry Jam 151
Peach Jam 151
Peach Jam, No Cook Freezer.......................153
Peach Kuchen...102

PEANUT BUTTER
Peanut-Butter Bars 144
Peanut-Butter-Candy Cookies..................... 222
Peanut-Butter Flakes 143
Peanut Butter Fudge, Quick 144
Peanut-Butter Pie 219

PEAR
Pear, Apricot- Jam 153
Pear-Pineapple-Lemon Jam 150
Pecan Tarts, Cream Cheese 100
Penne Rita..193
Penuche Fudge 146

PEPPER
Pepper, Roasted Festive Dip 18
Peppers, Hungarian Stuffed 176
Pepper Relish, "Sweet"..................................163

311

Picante-Omelet Pie 46
PICKLES & RELISHES
   Apple & Lemon Relish 164
   Bread-and-Butter Pickles 162
   Corn Relish 164
   Ripe-Tomato Relish 162
   "Sweet" Pepper Relish..................................... 163
   Yellow-Squash Pickles 165
   Zucchini Relish 163
PIES
   Bavarian Apple Torte 101
   Blueberry Cream-Cheese Pie 217
   Butter-Pecan Pie 218
   Cape Cod Cranberry Velvet Pie 63
   Cookie-Crust Ice-Cream Pie 218
   German-Chocolate Pie 219
   Chocolate Cranberry Mousse Pie 67
   Chocolate-Mousse Pie with Chocolate Leaves 99
   Cookie Crust Ice-Cream Pie 218
   Cran-Apple Pie 67
   Cranberry-Blueberry Pie 68
   Cranberry-Raisin Pie 69
   Cream-Cheese Pecan Tarts 100
   Eisenhower Strawberry Pie 100
   Frozen Chocolate-Sundae Pie 96
   German-Chocolate Pie 219
   My Mother's Cranberry Pie 68
   No-Bake Pineapple-Lemon Pie 217
   Peach-Blueberry Cream Pie 98
   Peanut-Butter Pie 219
   Pie, Picante-Omelet...46
   Pie, Sea Clam 227
   Pie, Spinach for a Crowd.................................42
   Pie, Vegetable 297
   Plum or Peach Kuchen 102
   Roseann's Cranberry Nut Pie 66
   Strawberry-Mallow Pie 218
   Swedish Apple Pie 97
   Swedish Torte 96
PILAF
   Armenian Rice and Noodle Pilaf 192
   Orzo, Wild Rice, and Pignola Pilaf 190
PINEAPPLE
   Pear-Pineapple-Lemon Jam 150
   Pineapple Chutney 166
   Pineapple-Cheese Ball 18
   Pineapple-Lemon Pie, No Bake 217
   Pineapple-Orange Marmalade 158
   Pineapple, Pear Jam 150
   Swedish Torte 96
Pistachio and Cranberry Biscotti 73

Pistachio-Stuffed Mushrooms 16
Pizza, Breakfast...49
Plum Conserve 160
Plum or Peach Kuchen 102
Polenta Crab Cakes (The Paddock's) 241
PORK
   Brazilian Pork Loin in Geny's Style 184
   Cranberry-Glazed Pork Roast 66
   Oven-Fried Pork Chops 214
   Pork Stir Fry 214
   Spice-Rubbed Roast Pork Loin with Cranberry-
      Coriander Chutney 185
Portuguese Kale Soup 260
Potato Leek Soup 265
POTATOES
   Colcannon 300
   Onion, Ham and Cheese Chowder 258
   Orange-Glazed Sweet Potatoes 295
   Party Potatoes 294
   Potato Leek Soup 265
   Quick Potato-Cheese Bake 209
   Spiced Sweet-Potato Casserole 294
   Spicy Potatoes 209
   Stuffed Baked Sweet Potatoes 210
   Vegetarian Chili with Potatoes 299
POT ROAST
   Pot Roast, Burgundy 175
   Pot Roast, Italian 177
   Pot Roast, Oven 175
Pralines, Chocolate-Coated 142
PUDDING
   Bread Pudding 128
   Citrus Sponge Pudding 130
   Corn Pudding 292
   Creamy Rice Pudding 129
   Fudge-Batter Pudding 132
   Grapenut Pudding..127
   Lemon Sponge Pudding 128
   Quick-and-Easy Corn-Flake Pudding 127
PUMPKIN
   Pumpkin 'N' Spice Tea Bread 34
   Pumpkin Muffins 52
   Pumpkin Bars with Cream-Cheese Icing 119
   Pumpkin Cheesecake 83
   Pumpkin-Cranberry Bread 62
   Pumpkin-Cranberry Spice Bars with Cream- ....
      Cheese Frosting 61
"Puppy Chow" (Cheerios Party Mix) 20

Q

Quiche Lorraine 50

Quiches, Mini 204
QUICK & EASY
   Almond Delight Dip 203
   Almond-Bark Cookies 222
   Apple Crisp 224
   Beef and Cabbage Rolls 211
   Bleu-Cheese Walnut Dip 204
   Blueberry Cream-Cheese Pie 217
   Broccoli Chicken 212
   Butter-Pecan Pie 218
   Buttermilk Fried-Fish Fillets 214
   Caesar's Fish 215
   Candy Trifles 223
   Carrot Salad 207
   Chicken Spinach Bake 212
   Chocolate Bites 223
   Chocolate-Marshmallow Mousse 224
   Cookie-Crust Ice-Cream Pie 218
   Crab Appetizers 205
   Crispy Bacon-Wrapped Oysters 216
   Easy Cherry Cobbler 220
   Fried Green Tomatoes 210
   Garlic Chicken 212
   German-Chocolate Pie...................... 219
   Grilled Tuna Steak 217
   Ham Crescent Snacks 205
   Honey-Mustard Chicken 213
   Ice-Cream Salad 206
   Italian Chicken 213
   Lemon Dill Fish 215
   Mandarin Salad with Orange-Juice Dressing
      206
   Marinated Grilled Shrimp 216
   Marvelous Mushrooms 209
   Mini Quiches 204
   No-Bake Pineapple-Lemon Pie 217
   Orange Coconut Balls 222
   Orange Dessert 220
   Oven-Fried Pork Chops 214
   Pasta Salad 208
   Peanut-Butter Pie 219
   Peanut-Butter-Candy Cookies 222
   Pork Stir Fry 214
   Quick Meatballs 211
   Quick Potato-Cheese Bake 209
   Rum-Raisin Cheddar Spread 203
   Shrimp and Rice Salad 208
   Shrimp Dip 203
   Shrimp Marinara 216
   Spicy Potatoes 209
   Spinach Salad 207
   Stir-Fried Zucchini 210

Strawberry Trifle 224
Strawberry-Mallow Pie 218
Stuffed Baked Sweet Potatoes 210
Super Spinach Salad 207
Tortilla Rollups 204
Triple Fudge Cake 221
Twist Sticks 205
Ugly-Duckling Cake with Frosting 221
Waldorf Salad 206
Quick Peanut-Butter Fudge 144
Quick Tortilla Rollups 204
Quick-and-Easy Corn-Flake Pudding 127

R
Raisin-Oatmeal Cookies 105
Rum-Raisin Cheddar Spread 203
Raspberry Jam, No-Cook Freezer 153
Raspberry Syrup 26
Ratatouille 296
Red-Beet Chocolate Cake 89
Refrigerator Dinner Rolls 33
Reggie's Knobby Apple Cake 90
Reine de Saba (Queen of Sheba) Cake with
   Chocolate Butter Icing 92
RELISH, see pickles & relish
Rhubarb and Strawberry Compote 131
RICE
   Armenian Rice and Noodle Pilaf 192
   "Dirty" Rice 198
   Orzo, Wild Rice, and Pignola Pilaf 190
   Rice Salad 281
   Shrimp and Rice Salad 208
   Wild Rice with Mushrooms and Almonds .. 194
Rigatoni with Vegetables 189
Ripe-Tomato Relish 162
Roasted Summer Squash 293
ROLLS, see bread
Ron's World-Famous Oyster Soup 250
Roseann's Cranberry Nut Pie 66
Rosy Cranberry Cider (non-alcoholic) 25
Rum-Raisin Cheddar Spread 203
Russian Kisses (Rum Balls) 115

S
SALADS
   Carrot Salad 207
   Chicken Salad Deluxe 276
   Cranberry Spinach Salad 276
   Forest Pasta Salad with Herb Dressing 277
   Four-Bean Salad 275
   Fruit Salad with Yogurt Dressing 278

313

Greek Orzo Salad 280
Green Bean and Hazelnut Salad with Herb-
    Mustard Dressing 278
Ice-Cream Salad 206
Layered Salad 275
Mandarin Salad with Orange-Juice Dressing
    206
Mom's French Dressing 280
Muffaletta Olive Salad 279
Oriental Noodle Salad 279
Out-of-Sight Cole Slaw 280
Pasta Primavera Salad 281
Pasta Salad 208
Quick Tortilla Roll-ups 204
Rice Salad 281
Sea-Foam Salad 282
Seafood Pasta Salad 208
Shrimp and Rice Salad 208
Spaghetti Caesar Salad 283
Spinach Salad 207
Strawberry Cashew Salad with Poppy-Seed
    Dressing 282
Sun-dried Tomato and Artichoke Pasta Salad
    284
    Super Spinach Salad 207
    Waldorf Salad 206
Salmon Dip 17
Salmon with Sizzle 236
Salmon, Onions 'N Soy 238
Salsa, Garden 13
Sandwich "Star" Cookies 113
Sausage, Broccoli Pasta 192

SAUCES
Lemon-Butter Sauce for Seafood 241
Mom's French Dressing 280
Mustard Sauce 288
Savory Green Beans 296
Scalloped Oysters 251

SCALLOPS
Baked Scallops 247
Curried Scallop Cakes 19
Elaine's Stuffed Bay Scallops 248
Karin's Seared Scallops 249
Scallop and Corn Chowder 269
Scallop Bundle with Chardonnay Cream Sauce,
    Lobster and 244
Scallop Casserole 247

SCONES
Scones, Ginger-Lemon 57
Scones, Mini Cranberry-Orange 70
Sea-Foam Salad 282

SEAFOOD, also see specific varieties
America's Linguine with White Clam Sauce .. 228
Buttermilk Fried-Fish Fillets 214
Caesar's Fish 215
Crispy Bacon-Wrapped Oysters 216
Curried Scallop Cakes 19
Grilled Tuna Steak 217
Hot Seafood-Cheese Hors d'Oeuvres 20
Lemon Dill Fish 215
Sea Captain's Dinner: Cod with Salt Pork .. 234
Sea-Clam Pie 227
Seafood Gumbo Stew 267
Seafood Pasta Salad 208
Seafood-Stuffed Sole-Fillet Roll-ups 235
Shortbread Cookies with Lavender Icing 111

SHRIMP
Creamy Shrimp in Pastry Cups 12
Deviled Shrimp 240
Light Shrimp Alfredo 238
Marinated Grilled Shrimp 216
Shrimp and Rice Salad 208
Shrimp Marinara 216
Shrimp Sautéed in the Shell 239
Shrimp Scampi 240
Shrimp Dip 203
Simple Chicken-Noodle Soup 259
Skewered Baby Beef And Mushrooms 186
Smoothie, Sparkling Fruit 26
Snickerdoodles 114
Soda Bread, Irish Breakfast 30

SOUPS, STEWS & CHOWDERS
Beef and Barley Soup 264
Carrot with Fennel Soup 255
Carrot, Sweet Potato and Ginger Soup 266
Cauliflower Cheese Soup 262
Cheese Ale Soup 255
Chicken and Vegetable Stew 257
Chicken-and-Beef Stock 270
Cold Cucumber Soup 261
Cream of Broccoli Soup 260
Curried Butternut-Squash Soup 262
Easy Fish Stew 264
Fish Chowder 266
Five-Hour Beef Stew 176
Friendly Fish Stew 268
Garlic Soup 272
Gazpacho 272
Hamburg Stew 173
Italian Chicken-Lentil Soup 270
Lazy Mama's Borscht 256
Light Tomato-Basil Soup 259

Lobster Stock 243
Low-Fat Corn Chowder 258
New England Clam Chowder 263
Onion, Ham and Cheese Chowder 258
Parsnip Soup 256
Perry Fish Chowder..252
Portuguese Kale Soup 260
Potato Leek Soup 265
Scallop and Corn Chowder 269
Seafood Gumbo Stew 267
Simple Chicken-Noodle Soup 259
Tortellini Soup 261
Souffle, Clam 228
Souffle, Cold Lemon 130
Sour-Cream Coffee Cake 93
Sour-Cream Maple-Pecan Muffins 58
Spaghetti Caesar Salad 283
Spaghetti-Cheese Bake 196
Spaghetti, Cheesy 197
Sparkling Fruit Smoothie 26
Spice-Rubbed Roast Pork Loin with Cranberry- ....
   Coriander Chutney 185
Spiced Orange Marmalade 158
Spiced Sweet-Potato Casserole 294
Spicy Potatoes 209

SPINACH
Baked Creamy Cod, Spinach and Egg Noodles
  231
Chicken Spinach Bake 212
Cranberry Spinach Salad 276
Spinach and Artichoke Dip 12
Spinach Pesto and Feta, Linguine with 191
Spinach Pie For a Crowd 42
Spinach Salad 207
Stuffed Calzone 184
Stuffed Shells Florentine 190
Super Spinach Salad 207
Spinach and Artichoke Dip 12
Spring Marmalade 156

SQUASH
Apple-Stuffed Acorn Squash 290
Creamy Squash 'n' Tomato Casserole Au Gratin
  289
Crunchy Pecan Squash 290
Curried Butternut-Squash Soup 262
Roasted Summer Squash 293
Stir-Fried Zucchini 210
Summer-Squash Casserole 292
Yellow Squash Pickles..................................165
Steak Diane 178
Steak Strips, Oriental-Marinated 179
Stewed Tomatoes 298

STEWS, see soups, stews & chowders
Stir-Fried Zucchini 210
STRAWBERRIES
Strawberry Cashew Salad with Poppy-Seed
   Dressing 282
Strawberry Conserve 161
Strawberry Jam 150
Strawberry-Mallow Pie 218
Strawberry Pie, Eisenhower 100
Strawberry-Rhubarb Jam 152
Strawberry Trifle 224
Swedish Torte 96
Stuffed Baked Sweet Potatoes 210
Stuffed Calzone 184
Stuffed Shells Florentine 190
Summer Dip 15
Summer-Squash Casserole 292
Sun-dried Tomato and Artichoke Pasta Salad ..284
Super Spinach Salad 207
Swedish Apple Pie 97
Swedish Cream 131
Swedish Farmer Cookies 106
Swedish Meatballs 178
Swedish Pancakes 44
Swedish Torte 96
"Sweet" Pepper Relish 163
SWEET POTATOES
Orange-Glazed Sweet Potatoes 295
Spiced Sweet Potato Casserole 294
Stuffed Baked Sweet Potatoes 210
Sweet-Potato Pound Cake with Orange Glaze
  86
Syrup, Raspberry 26

T
Tarragon Chicken 169
Tarts, Cream-Cheese Pecan 100
TEA BREADS
Tea Bread, Apple-Rosemary 39
Tea Bread, Eggnog 31
Tea Bread, Pumpkin 'n Spice...........................34
Teahouse, Cottage White Bread 38
Tempt-Me Truffles 145
The Paddock's Polenta Crab Cakes 241
Toad-In-The-Hole 50
TOMATOES
Fried Green Tomatoes 210
Gazpacho 272
Light Tomato-Basil Soup 259
Ripe-Tomato Relish 162
Stewed Tomatoes 298

315

Torte, Bavarian Apple 101
Torte, Cranberry Eleanor Bates' 62
Torte, Swedish..96
Tortellini Soup 261
Tortilla Roll-Ups, Quick 19
Tortilla Rollups 204
Tortoni, Coffee-Almond 134
Traditional Ten-Minute Cranberry Sauce 64
Treasure-Chest Bars 116
Trifle, Heath-Bar Chocolate..............................134
Trifle, Strawberry 224
Triple Fudge Cake 221
Truffles, Tempt-Me...145
Turkey-Pecan Meatballs 17
Twist Sticks 205

U

Ugly-Duckling Cake with Frosting 221

V

VEGETABLES
Apple-Stuffed Acorn Squash 290
Cauliflower-and-Broccoli Casserole 298
Cheesy Carrot Casserole 287
Colcannon 300
Creamed Broccoli with Crunch-and-Crumbs ..
  Topping 288
Creamy Squash 'n' Tomato Casserole Au Gratin
 289
Crunchy Pecan Squash 290
Fair Elizabeth's Eggplant 299
Italian Mushrooms 287
Maple-Glazed Onions 291
Onion Pie 291
Orange-Glazed Sweet Potatoes 295
Party Potatoes 294
Ratatouille 296
Rigatoni with Vegetables 189
Roasted Summer Squash 293
Savory Green Beans 296
Spiced Sweet-Potato Casserole 294
Stewed Tomatoes 298
Summer-Squash Casserole 292
Vegetable Pie 297
Vegetarian Chili with Potatoes 299

W

Waldorf Salad 206
Water Chestnut Roll-ups, Bacon and 13
White Cranberry-Walnut Fudge 141
Wild Rice with Mushrooms and Almonds 194

Y

Yellow-Squash Pickles 165
Yogurt Corn Bread 30
Yogurt Pound Cake with Lemon Glaze, One-Step
 88

Z

ZUCCHINI
Ratatouille 296
Zucchini Bread 32
Zucchini Pancakes 48
Zucchini-Oatmeal Muffins 53
Zucchini Relish 163
Zucchini, Stir-Fried 210
Zup fe (Swiss Braided Christmas Bread) 38

316

The Hoosier Cabinet modernized the kitchen in the early 1900s.

R. L. BURGESS

❦ DEALER IN ❦

Groceries, Paints, Boots and Shoes

Also Dry Goods
and Small Wares

MAIN STREET

BUZZARDS BAY,   MASS.

Telephone 19-4

317

Highland Light, North Truro

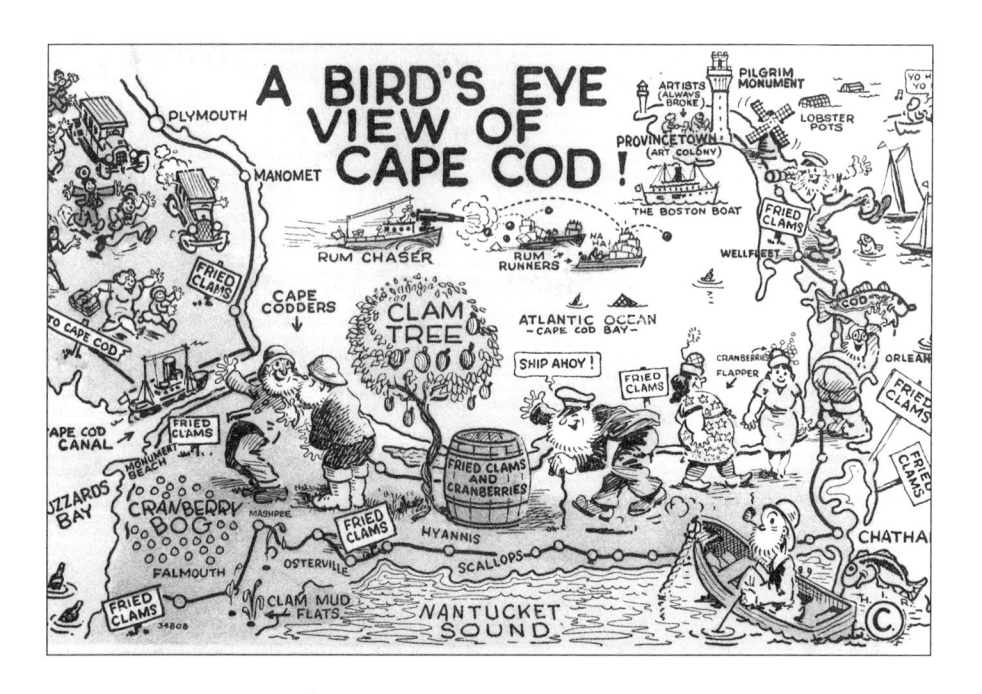

318

A Cape Cod cook book! You who stray
Far from the old sand-bordered Bay,
The cranberry bogs, the tossing pines,
The wind-swept beaches' frothing lines,
You city dwellers who, like me,
Were children, playing by the sea,
Whose fathers manned the vanished ships-
Hark! Do I hear you smack your lips?

A Cape Cod cook book! My, oh my!
I know that twinkle in your eye,
And why you're pricking up your ears,
You've turned the clock back thirty years.
I know that smile of yours; it tells
Of chowder, luscious as it smells;
And when you laugh aloud, you dream
Of berry dumpling, bathed in cream.

A Cape Cod cook book! Why, I'll bet
The doughnut crock could tempt you yet!
Those Cape Cod doughnuts! Yes, you'll take
A few of those, and then some cake-
The frosted kinds-and-let me see-
Some pie, of course, and-Mercy me!
You can't go on; it wouldn't do!
One takes on weight at forty-two.

A Cape Cod cook book! Here they are!
A breath from every cookie jar,
A whiff from ovens spicy sweet,
Two hundred secrets-good to eat!
Thanksgiving, clambake, picnic grove,
Each lends a taste, a treasure trove;
And here they are for you to buy-
What's that? You've bought one? So have I.

Joseph C. Lincoln,
Cape Cod author and playwright
August 1911

Notes